Documents of Upheaval

BY TRUMAN NELSON

The Surveyor
The Sin of the Prophet
The Passion by the Brook
The Torture of Mothers

Documents of Upheaval

Selections from WILLIAM LLOYD GARRISON'S

The Liberator, 1831–1865

Edited by

TRUMAN NELSON

American Century Series

HILL AND WANG · NEW YORK

Manufactured in the United States of America by
The Colonial Press Inc., Clinton, Massachusetts

4   5   6   7   8   9   10

Prefatory Note

Except where a change in order clarified a subject, the selections were arranged chronologically in an attempt to fix, in Garrison's own words and editorial responses, the contour of the Abolitionist struggle. It must be emphasized that all the selections were shortened, for if printed in their entirety this book would have been an enormous one. The conventional points of ellipsis (. . .) have been used to indicate every omission of text, large and small.

I wish to acknowledge with gratitude the assistance of Dorothy Potter, David Propper, and Ann Berry, the librarians at the Essex Institute of Salem, Massachusetts, whose scholarly zeal and support have been crucial, and of Mr. Peter Lenz and Professor Edward Clark, for reading the manuscript and offering many valuable suggestions. Above all, my gratitude goes to the Louis M. Rabinowitz Foundation for making it possible for me to read and ponder the thirty-five-year file of *The Liberator*.

T.N.

Salem, 1965

CONTENTS

Introduction

On New Year's Day, 1831, without a dollar in reserve or a single subscriber, William Lloyd Garrison published *The Liberator* in Boston. It was a weekly periodical of four pages, four columns wide, measuring fourteen by nine and one quarter inches, with a plain black letterhead. Its purpose was to advocate the immediate freedom of the slaves and to elevate the condition of the free Negroes. It persisted for thirty-five years with some alterations in format, but without swerving in the least from its monumental commitment. It ended when slavery ended.

Recent American historians, for the most part, have been brusque and cruel to the Abolitionists, charging them with organizing a sentimental crusade for the slaves while ignoring the misery of the free Negroes around them in the North, with thoughtless extremism, with fostering a hatred for the white South which made post-Civil War reconciliation impossible, with an inability to predict, or even understand, the problems which the slaves would have to face after their freedom came. The worst charge leveled against them was that they were single-minded fanatics with no sense of the complexities, ambiguities, and perilous depths that accompany profound social change. If any of these historians had read the thirty-five volumes of *The Liberator*, they would have discovered that the Abolitionists were variously quickened, dismayed, and then regenerated with every revolutionary impulse their society could generate.

All the great questions of the day found utterance in the pages of *The Liberator*: Transcendentalism, the citizen's relation to the state, the right of resistance, the higher-law thesis, the pleas and reasons for freedom, the problem of individual versus collective action, violence versus nonviolence, women's rights. The genesis of the utopian-communist movement, which, in the 1840's, brought to life some sixty or seventy colonies based on communal living is recorded more clearly in *The Liberator* than in any other source. Not only does it contain all the great humanitarian voices of the epoch, but it publishes, with great skill and fairness of selection, the ideas, rhetoric, and prejudices of all those opposed to human advance.

In my opinion, *The Liberator* is the most complete and accurate historical document of a time that was the high point of American ferment and culture, the age of Emerson, Thoreau, Whitman, Melville, of Daniel Webster, John C. Calhoun, John Quincy Adams, John

Brown, Jefferson Davis, Abraham Lincoln, and other great men. Garrison himself, as the editor of *The Liberator,* became the transmitter of the consciousness of his time.

Garrison's background was complex. He was a poor boy, born in Newburyport, Massachusetts, in 1805. Forced to leave school at the age of ten, Garrison had little formal education. He became an apprentice printer in 1818 and served out the required seven years' term. He then became editor and publisher of the Newburyport *Free Press.* This was unsuccessful and he later became the editor of a temperance paper, the Boston *National Philanthropist.* There was, of course, no wire service and so the newspaper editor had to obtain and select his material from "exchanges." These were newspapers sent to him from all over the country in return for what he sent them. While reading through the weekly exchanges at his editorial desk, Garrison was very much impressed by a newspaper published in Baltimore with the resounding title of *Genius of Universal Emancipation.* It was edited by a Quaker named Benjamin Lundy and it was the only periodical in the country devoted to the antislavery movement.

Lundy's position on slavery was that gradual, though total, abolition of slavery in the United States would take place if slaveholders had the assurance that the free blacks would have somewhere to go, far, far away. Lundy shouldered a knapsack and plodded through nineteen states, to Mexico, Haiti, and Canada, looking for a place where the despised black man could lay down his head with dignity and hope. The *Genius of Universal Emancipation* faithfully and sensitively recorded the rigors and sacrifices of these uncertain journeys. At other times, because the paper was published in a slave state and one of the principal shipping areas for slave transport to the Deep South, he gave agonizing eyewitness reports of slave families being torn asunder at auction sales, of Negro maidens handled and pawed over at the block, of coffles of slaves chained together on their tortuous way to the rice swamps.

Garrison could not help being moved at Lundy's display of moral grandeur. He wrote warmly about Lundy in the *National Philanthropist,* and later, when he became editor of an anti-Jackson paper, the *Journal of the Times* of Bennington, Vermont, praised him in the issue of December 12, 1828, in vibrantly Emersonian prose:

Every inch of him is alive with power. . . . Yet he makes no public appeals and goes forward in the quietude and resoluteness of his spirit, husbanding his little resources from town to town and from State to State. . . . Rivers and mountains vanish in his path; midnight finds him wending his solitary way over an unfrequented road; the sun is anticipated in his rising. Never was moral sublimity of character better illustrated.

After reading this in the winter of 1828, the sublime character took his staff in hand and walked from Baltimore to Bennington to ask Garrison to become coeditor of the *Genius* and carry on at the desk while he went on the road for subscribers. Garrison agreed enthusiastically; he had been hired by the *Journal of the Times* only for the duration of the Adams–Jackson election campaign, and he was very anxious to learn and write about slavery in a slave state.

However, between the time he decided to quit the *Journal of the Times* and his arrival in Baltimore, his convictions had undergone a profound and revolutionary change. He now believed that the gradual abolition of slavery was persisting in sin. He felt now that immediate, unconditional emancipation, without expatriation, was the right of every slave, and could not be withheld by his master an hour without sin. He confessed his change of heart to Lundy upon arrival. Lundy must have felt that his new viewpoint was disastrous. The *Genius* was supported for the most part by Southern Quakers who wept over the plight of the poor slave but felt strongly that sudden emancipation would be, by far, the greater evil. They pitied the masters almost as much as the slave, did not blame them for not wanting their throats cut by freed and revenge-maddened bondsmen, and assigned the real guilt of the institution to its long-dead originators. The problem was going to be overcome, someday.

When Garrison came in with his terrible blast and denied the slaveowners the moral right to keep a single slave in bondage a single hour, the Quakers deserted Lundy in droves. When Lundy had first heard Garrison's new position he tried to solve the dilemma with true Quaker liberalism: "Well," said Lundy, "thee may put thy initials to thy articles, and I will put my initials to mine, and each will bear his own burden."

But Garrison's intransigence was very much Lundy's burden. When it became clear that Garrison was really attacking Lundy's refined form of colonization, and in his own paper, for every new subscriber Lundy signed on, a dozen canceled out. The subscription list dwindled. But Garrison, fraternizing with the educated Negroes in Baltimore, was told by them that he was right and that all attempts to remove the black people from the soil they had nourished with their blood and sweat were deeply resented.

There is another charge brought against the Abolitionists: that they never went south and did not know of the actual conditions of the slave. Garrison, in Baltimore, *was* in the South, walking the streets of this slave-exporting city. Every day he stood by, sickened and silent, while men and women were sold at the market like so much meat. He concealed for two days a slave who had been whipped with a cowskin from neck to buttock and counted thirty-seven bleeding gashes on his back. And this for failing to load a wagon fast enough. He could often hear from the upper rooms of decorous houses the sound of whips against naked flesh and shrieks of anguish. This was an almost daily occurrence. He became well known in the city and met hostility and threats wherever he went. Finally, and as an inmate, not a visitor, he saw the inside of the jail, where black fugitives and slaves en route to new masters were confined.

In the *Genius* of November 20, 1829, he wrote that a vessel owned by a Newburyport man, Francis Todd, was being used to transport seventy-five slaves. For this he was convicted for libel and served time in the prison. This material is covered in "The First Demonstration," the first selection of the book, and no more need be said about it here.

When, after forty-nine days of confinement, Garrison was released from the Baltimore jail, he went on a lecture tour. He wanted first to raise money to help Lundy reinstitute the *Genius* and second to strike a blow for instant abolition with three lectures on slavery. He ran into great opposition on his tour and found sympathetic listeners only among the free Negroes who were everywhere opposed to colonization schemes. He was so confident that he was right that he felt that he could communicate to people of influence what he had learned about slavery in the marts of Baltimore and, if they were the great and good men he felt them to be, they would take this task of advocating immediate abolition off his hands and he could "return to the printing business."

Boston seemed the ideal city for this transference of responsibility. The great Lyman Beecher was there solving all the moral problems of the Universe; those who objected to his orthodoxy listened to William Ellery Channing's pleas to reduce human suffering. Great voluntary associations, Bible, tract and missionary societies, had memberships of thousands. They were regarded with reverence and awe by church members who felt that they would be irresistible in redeeming all the moral sluggards around them. Garrison went to the heads of all these organizations with his revelations: not one of them showed any sympathy with his ideas. None would take the torch from his uncertain grasp.

Garrison was dumbfounded at the indifference shown by Lyman Beecher to the antislavery crusade. Beecher was Garrison's chosen preacher and it was he who had indoctrinated him with the notion that it was the duty of every sinner to repent instantly and give his soul to Christ. This was the source of Garrison's *immediatism*. He could not understand how Lyman Beecher or any other Christian minister could advocate *gradualism* for the eradication of slavery, the sum of all villainies; it was as if they told the drunkard, the thief, the wife-beater, that they must refrain from these crimes gradually and aim at some indefinite, far-off reformation. He seemed, at this point, not to realize the revolutionary potential in his immediatism. Nor did he realize that the preachers and social leaders in Boston that he was so vociferously beseeching to enter the struggle on his advanced plane looked upon him as a tiresome fanatic, an interloper invading their territory without benefit of ordination. In his autobiography Henry Clark Wright speaks of a ministerial gathering where the topic of what to do with Garrison and his Boston following came up.

Hubbard Winslow, of Bowdoin Street Church, was opposed [to granting the church for abolition meetings and lectures], and said the abolitionists were utterly beneath any notice; that Garrison was a low-lived, ignorant, insignificant mechanic; that he was connected with no church, and responsible to nobody; that the abolitionists, as a body, were among the poorest, obscurest and most ignorant of the people. . . . This was the view taken by all present, except Mr. Crosby and myself.

Garrison, in presenting the moral guardians of the Boston community this do-it-now solution to a problem which they felt they really did not have to solve, only aroused their hatred. In his social obtuseness, he could not understand why, instead of hailing his revelation as noble and prudent and giving it cordial support, they received him with indignation and contempt. It he had suggested, rather than immediate freedom for a suffering people, that they should be liquidated by an induced plague of yellow fever or smallpox, he could not have been regarded with more hostility and indignation. He realized, in the late months of 1830, that he, and he alone, had to begin the struggle for immediate emancipation. He explained his mission on the first page of the first number of *The Liberator*.

During my recent tour for the purpose of exciting the minds of the people by a series of discourses on the subject of slavery, every place that I visited gave fresh evidence of the fact, that a greater revolution in public sentiment was to be effected in the free states—*and particularly in New England*—than at the South. I found contempt more bitter, opposition more active, detraction more relentless, prejudice more stubborn, and apathy more frozen, than among slave owners themselves. Of course, there were individual exceptions to the contrary. This state of things afflicted, but did not dishearten me. I determined, at every hazard, to lift up the standard of emancipation in the eyes of the nation, *within sight of Bunker Hill and in the birth place of liberty* . . .

 . . . I *will be* as harsh as truth, and as uncompromising as justice. On this subject I do not wish to think, or speak, or write, with moderation. No! no! Tell a man whose house is on fire to give a moderate alarm; tell him to moderately rescue his wife from the hands of the ravisher; tell the

mother to gradually extricate her babe from the fire into which it has
fallen;—but urge me not to use moderation in a cause like the present. I
am in earnest—I will not equivocate—I will not excuse—I will not retreat
a single inch—AND I WILL BE HEARD. The apathy of the people is enough
to make every statue leap from its pedestal, and to hasten the resurrection
of the dead. . . .

After using Bunker Hill as a revolutionary symbol on the first
page, Garrison put a poem of pacifist sentiments on the second, because he was, first of all, a pacifist at heart, and, secondly, he knew
the belligerence of his portrayal of the slaveholder could be taken as
a direct incitement to violence against him.

> Not by the sword shall your deliverance be;
>   Not by the shedding of your masters' blood;
> Not by rebellion, or foul treachery.
>   Upswinging suddenly, like swelling flood:
>   Revenge and rapine ne'er did bring forth good.
> God's *time is best!*—nor will it long delay:
>   Even now your barren cause begins to bud,
> And glorious shall the fruit be!—Watch and pray,
> For, lo! the kindling dawn, that ushers in the day!
>   G——

In the thirty-five years of its existence *The Liberator* published
every possible incitement to wrath against the slaveholder along with
pious injunctions for everyone to become nonresistants and to return
good for evil. Wendell Phillips, who was not a pacifist, said Garrison really did this to keep out of jail. Garrison's daily protestations
of nonviolence, of dependence upon the weapons of the spirit only,
gave him license to be revolutionary in a legal way, without invoking
the treason laws in the Constitution: "Treason against the United
States shall consist only in levying war against them. . . ." He constantly renounced violence as an instrument of social change: "I
have said that slavery and insurrection, like cause and effect, are
inseparable. That no insurrection has taken place since Nat Turner
is attributable to the fact that the slaves are acquainted with the
peaceful and loving sentiments of the Abolitionists."

He did all this without curbing the "incendiary" character of *The
Liberator*. In its seventeenth number the plain heading was replaced
by a cut of a slave auction being held in Washington, D.C., with a
flag labeled "Liberty" floating over the Capitol. In the foreground
stands a sorrowing family of slaves about to be divided and sold,
along with a sign saying "horses and cattle also sold." In the dust,
underfoot, a copy of the Indian Treaties can be seen. When *The
Liberator* was sent to Southern post offices, illiterate slaves picking
up the mail could see that someone, somewhere, was thinking of their
plight. Senator Thomas Hart Benton of Missouri, in his *Thirty*

Years' View, complained: "For what purpose could such a picture be intended unless to inflame the passions of slaves?"

Garrison was already well known in Boston among the free Negroes for a speech he had made at the Park Street Church on July 4, 1829. The speech was published in the *National Philanthropist and Investigator,* July 22, 1829. It contained Garrison's basic position toward the Negro. He felt there was only *one* race, the human race, and that differences between men were merely complexional, and the hatred and deprivation the black man had to undergo was simply because he was black. In this speech he said:

Suppose that—by some miracle—the slaves should suddenly become white. Would you shut your eyes upon their sufferings, and calmly talk of Constitutional limitations? No, your voice would peal in the ears of the taskmasters like deep thunder; you would carry the Constitution by force, if it could not be taken by treaty; patriotic assemblies would congregate at the corners of every street; the old Cradle of Liberty would rock to a deeper tone than ever echoed therein at British aggression; the pulpit would acquire new and unusual eloquence from our holy religion. The argument, that these white slaves are degraded, would not then obtain. You would say that it is enough that they are white, and in bondage, and they ought immediately to be set free. You would multiply your schools of instruction, and your temples of worship and rely on them for security. . . .

Wendell Phillips, who understood Garrison the best of all his associates, said the antislavery cause owed its ultimate success to Garrison's forgetting that he was white, to the fact that he looked upon the great questions posed by the state and by the church as a Negro looked on them. Most people who read *The Liberator* without personal knowledge of its editor thought Garrison was black. This was one of the reasons it infuriated the South so much, and why he was directly accused of having fomented the Nat Turner Insurrection of 1831. (See pages 28–38.) Garrison was having hard sledding with *The Liberator,* barely keeping it alive. He knew he had to develop some organizational support for it and decided to form a society to promote immediate emancipation. In August, 1831, a Virginia slave named Nat Turner led an insurrection against his white neighbors and slaveholders in which fifty-seven whites were killed. Instead of being discouraged by this bloody incident, which filled most of the North with horror, Garrison began to organize his antislavery society. Because he was not afraid of extremism and a revolutionary morality he knew that the best time for raising a controversial question could be at its most critical phase. Everybody told him not to talk about freeing the slaves in the backwash of a bloody uprising but he knew that a time of upheaval is the most fruitful one in which to confront the masses with the problem they are required to solve. *The Liberator* was giving voice to proposals which, if understood and followed to the letter, would have prevented this insurrection and later saved a cruel civil war from decimating the country. Nat Turner and Garrison never met, but they were locked into the same synthesis. If there had been no Nat Turner, there would have been no Garrison.

The organization and operation of the New England, and then the American, Anti-Slavery Society is another story, but the destinies of these societies and that of Garrison and *The Liberator* were inextricable. The voice in *The Liberator* is Garrison's. The task of the American Anti-Slavery Society was the one he chose. The man that emerged from this struggle was the sum total of all its elements. His personal life cannot be separated from it. He made some of his most daring moves at the time of greatest desperation. He was married in 1834 at a time when the paper was about to collapse. He had fallen in love with Helen Benson, the daughter of a former president of the New England Anti-Slavery Society. He had to change his life of eating, sleeping, and working in the dingy garret where the paper was printed and accept some kind of domestic conventionality. He had no money then, or later, but his wife kept a good home for him and raised five children who cherished her virtues. She was never known to have criticized her husband in any way, or to act other than with unquestioning love toward him at all times. The need created by his marriage forced Garrison to try to obtain some substantial support for the paper. Only one fourth of its subscribers were white; the people of color who supported it were themselves poor, but somehow the money came in, in dribs and drabs, and the paper was able to exist until the next crisis.

Something should be said here, in a general way, of Garrison's character and achievement. Garrison thought he could end human slavery by moral suasion, by a peaceful appeal to the hearts of the slaveholders. He demanded that all who called themselves Christians act like Christ. He wanted to convert them, to make them *say* they were sinning against their brothers. He imitated Jesus in stirring up strife, in evoking reaction and hostility and then putting it down with affirmations of all-encompassing love. The Abolitionist revolution brought forth both an Old Testament prophet and a New Testament prophet, John Brown and William Lloyd Garrison.

He really could not understand why people complained about his harshness of language. Compared to some of the orthodox preachers, condemning everyone in the congregation to eternal damnation for some doctrinal fault, some variation of belief for which they would be burned in lakes of fire, pinched by red-hot tongs, and this for eternity, he was quite mild. The rub was that he was talking about a real sin, a clear and present sin, a sin as tangible as sweaty chains and bloody backs, a sin, moreover, that could be redeemed quite easily, a sin with money value on it that a little hard cash could expiate. So his ministry and his prophecy was one of embarrassing reality in the real world of pain and wrong.

The most persistent and logical protests against his harsh language came from the Unitarians, the fixed liberals of their day. Their clergymen realized uneasily that the sense of sin Garrison was evoking was not the Calvinist doctrine and dogmatism that humanism must resist, but a true sin coming with consistent cruelty from one human toward another and having nothing to do with intellect, education, and surface gentility. He made the Unitarians face what their theology virtually denied; that educated, ethically cultivated people can act with cruelty every day, and what is more, can allow it to become institutionalized.

The true, sad splendor of Garrison's vision of man was that he felt that every revolutionary program he offered had an excellent chance of being adopted by the millions; by everyone who called himself a Christian. He asked no more of anyone than that they accept the moral system of the prophet Jesus. He was always unhappy and often ill when he had to attack society. He often invited mass hostility against himself. He invented the moral mob of the passive resistants. He constantly initiated acts, demonstrations, nonviolent, direct "actions from principle." Many people who followed his urging and direction were imprisoned, beaten, alienated, and exiled from their communities. This took a terrible toll of him. He began to develop a way to disassociate his followers from his extreme and vulnerable positions. He would say this or that form of co-operation with the government or slavery was "sin for *me*," and so save them from associative guilt. Phillips, who well understood the skill with which Garrison let himself bear the brunt of counterattack, said:

Saints do not march in regiments and martyrs do not travel in battalions; they come along once in an age. You cannot create an anti-slavery sentiment so durable, so unrelenting, so vigilant that the government cannot outwit and undermine it. Consequently the only way you can save the slave is to arrange political circumstances so that there will be no such government in existence.

Certainly, someone or something *arranged* the United States government as it was between 1776 and 1862 "out of existence." Perhaps Garrison did do it. Lincoln said of the Emancipation, which completely altered the major compromise of the Constitution (that of slavery), "The logic and moral power of Garrison and the Antislavery people of the country and the army have done it all."

Garrison today is denied both logic and moral power. His exaggerations, his highly poetic language, his inability to adjust to political expediencies have created a current judgment that he stated the obvious at the top of his voice too many years and too repetitively to be taken seriously as a major prophet. But this fearsome energy, this keeping up of the demoniac clang of dissent, is in itself a form of genius. Men as uncomfortable as Garrison can be dealt with in only two ways: you must disprove the logic of their arguments or you must suppress them.

Many excellent, talented, intellectual people were devoted followers of Garrison. He inspired them, day in, day out. His raging realities, his open wound, his flowing blood, came from a single source, his hatred of racism. His catechism was simple: Negroes were enslaved, hated, feared, and dehumanized, "because they were black." And how he bled! This creativity, pouring out of his anguish over what was happening to somebody else, was proof to his followers that the fullest renewal, the sweetest redemption, the most resurgent euphoria, comes out of the revolutionary experience, whether it is one on the humble scale of defending some remote incident of chaos and change, or participating in a great revolutionary event. Phillips said of this: "My friends, if we never free a slave, we have at least freed ourselves in the effort to emancipate our fellow man."

Slowly Garrison became aware that his policy of moral suasion was not going to work; that the change he wanted to see could only come through a complete overturn of the present state, church, and society. In a letter of August 3, 1840, to his English friend Joseph Pease, he writes,

. . . there is not any instance recorded, either in sacred or profane history, in which the oppressors and enslavers of mankind, except in individual cases, have been induced, by mere moral suasion, to surrender their despotic power, and let the oppressed go free; but, in nearly every instance, from the time that Pharaoh and his hosts were drowned in the Red Sea, down to the present day, they have persisted in their evil course until some sudden destruction came upon them, or they were compelled to surrender their ill-gotten power in some other manner.

However, Garrison was still a pacifist to the core and the society he represented went along with him in this. He felt only one aspect of moral suasion would work, the persuasion of terror. His problem now was to work on the white South's deadly fear of a slave upheaval, to keep threatening it by predicting it, without ever having to go through with it. It reduced him to the absurdity of really saying, Love God and man in His image or He will kill you! It was the daily confrontation of this ambiguity that made him one of the most seminal of American thinkers and *The Liberator* the most fascinating document of its time. The push and pull between moral suasion and crude denunciation, between advocacy of violence and nonviolence, forced him to seek more grandiose solutions. The last phase of his struggle was agonizing, bitterly Sophoclean in its intensity and moral grandeur. His every appearance was an explosive demonstration against the existing church and state. He hammered incessantly on the visible contradiction that everything condemned in the white Christian morality—adultery, neglect of the Bible and Christ's teachings, and of the Sabbath, kidnapping, rape, theft, seizing the private property that is the fruit of man's daily toil—was not only permitted, but encouraged between master and slave and in one half of the United States of America. His method now was mainly organizational, to hold together, with *The Liberator* and constant regular meetings and ceremonies, his small, extremist group, his revolutionary congregation, and have it act as a saving remnant in a sinful nation.

All this became the build-up for his final tactic, revolutionary separatism. In 1844 he proclaimed in the name of the American Anti-Slavery Society that conscientious Americans could no longer give their allegiance to a slaveholding and racist government and a higher allegiance to God, and fidelity to human freedom, "Requires that the existing national compact should be instantly dissolved."

Most of the Society went along with him. It now consisted largely of women and free Negroes whose involuntary separation from "the Union" already existed. Three regular and continuing members of the American Anti-Slavery Society protested against this move on the grounds "That the abjuration of the Constitution of the United States and the dissolution of the Union, do not seem to us to tend in the slightest degree towards a peaceful abolition of slavery; but, rather, to its abolition by force on the part of the free States, thus released from their connexion from the South, or by means of a servile insurrection, countenanced and sustained by the North."

Whether they knew it or not, they said what Garrison wanted them to say. They warned the South of the wrath to come, of Harper's Ferry and Gettysburg. The first phase of its fulfillment erupted in the Kansas Wars of 1856 in which the North and South faced one another behind the sights of loaded guns, and in the Frémont presidential campaign of 1856, and in the emergence of Captain John Brown, who created a new revolutionary presence by showing at Pottawatomie that there was one white man willing to kill another of his race solely for being a partisan of chattel slavery.

Out of this ferment and upheaval came distorted, suppressed news of slaves rising in countless frustrated acts of rebellion. How could the Garrisonian pacifists now continue to tell black people not to take up arms after they, the Garrisonians, had dismally failed in their attempt to equalize the struggle by disarming the whites?

The stress of this dilemma broke through to the base of their organization. To condone violence and arms went against the primary doctrine of the society. Men who had followed Garrison for twenty-five years as the purest man they knew found him vacillating and pettifogging on principles which he would have let the organization go smash rather than modify by a hair's breadth. The controversy pierced deeper and created more dissension than any other. Yet somehow he was able to overcome it. He opened his platform to Abolitionists of a new school, Theodore Parker, Henry Ward Beecher, George Cheever, and T. W. Higginson, who talked openly of insurrections and cleaving the heads of tyrants. Garrison knew he could never deny the Negro what he wanted, come what may. Charles Lenox Remond, a great Negro Abolitionist and Garrisonian, found a way of rising above these inconsistencies: "I believe this movement is the only possible way to effect the peaceful emancipation of slaves. I admit my hopes are not strong that the slave will be emancipated by such means. I believe American Slavery will go down in blood."

And so it did. Immediate and unconditional emancipation did come, and in the context of the revolutionary separatism which was Garrison's main contribution to the struggle. When the war came, he supported it, as he had supported John Brown. Condoning any violence whatsoever disturbed him to the depths of his being but when John Brown went to the gallows in Virginia he felt that John Brown, dying, lived and that he, living, died. In a great Homeric defeat, he allowed the moral core of his pacifist movement to disintegrate, because it was, in a sense, befouled by this inevitable violence and blood. Yet he still felt enough of the Old Testament in him to know the Lamb Must Be Slain, and in his own early prophecies he had cried out that this guilty, racist nation should be rent asunder by a judgment of God.

No man in history was ever presented with a greater illusion of triumph than Garrison. On the last day of January, 1865, the Thirteenth Amendment, abolishing slavery forever, passed the House. He was again mobbed in the streets of Boston: this time the people touched him with love and pride. The press congratulated him on the transformation of public sentiment over the years in respect to slavery, property, and his long-rejected doctrine of immediate and unconditional emancipation. Lincoln wrote him. Secretary of War

Edward Stanton wrote him. His advice and approval was sought in the highest councils of state.

He was invited to come to Fort Sumter for a great jubilee and a raising of the Stars and Stripes. He went to Charleston, South Carolina, and stood over the grave of John C. Calhoun, his mighty antagonist, who had called slavery a positive good, saying, "Down to a deeper grave than this, slavery has gone and for it there is no resurrection." Standing later in front of St. Michael's Church, he heard a regimental band marching down the street playing "John Brown's Body" and he burst into uncontrollable tears.

The great climax of his day in Charleston came when he was carried triumphantly on the shoulders of liberated slaves to a platform in Zion's Church, surrounded by thousands of black men who knew, at last, what he was trying to do, and that he had done it. He told them,

For many a year I have been an outlaw in the South for your sakes, and a large price was set on my head, simply because I endeavored to remember those in bonds as bound with them. I have faithfully tried, in the face of the fiercest opposition, and under the most depressing circumstances, to make your cause my cause, my wife and children your wives and children, subjected to the same outrage and degradation; myself on the same auction block, to be sold to the highest bidder. . . .

This triumph, in its deepest sense, could only be ashes in his mouth. He knew, from talking to the ruling powers of the North that they were aware that if leniency and concessions were made to the leaders of the rebellion there would be another military build-up of the Confederacy, and another explosion of pain and death. "There seems to be one feeling," he wrote in 1865, "that sound policy demanded that fullest justice be meted out to the colored population of the South, whose terrible wrongs had brought this tempest of fire and blood on our land, and upon whose loyalty and valor the chief reliance must be placed in holding the South hereafter to the performance of her constitutional duties."

And how was this to be done? Not with moral suasion, he knew. By the sword must their deliverance be—and in the hands of the Negroes themselves. A long period of violence, both for and against the Negro was beginning and might not ever end. He was still a man of love and peace and the Anti-Slavery Society he had shaped was a pacifist society. He could not begin again the task of transforming a people to redeem itself by love alone, creating a nation of saints. The cause had to merge, to dissolve itself into the revolutionary demands, however harsh and brutal, of the whole people.

A sad, internecine struggle broke out over the question of the dissolution of the Anti-Slavery Society. Some of his best friends left him, feeling that it had to be carried on. But he was sick, old, and tired, and he wanted at last to join the whole people of the country. He wanted to finally achieve, as he had always confidently tried, union with the nonslaveholding millions. "Let us not assume to be better than other people when we are not any better. When they are reiterating all that we say, and are disposed to do all that we wish to be done, what more can we ask? . . . Let us work with the millions and not exclusively as the American Anti-Slavery Society."

The beauty and the triumph of William Lloyd Garrison was that he *had* always worked with the millions, with society as it was, even though he was wrong, even though his program of conversion and bloodless redemption did not work. He tried to develop the goodness, the tenderness of man, and have it overcome the badness around him. He could not stay in a sect or a church in which people swear every Sunday to uphold the rule of Christ on earth and then hate and degrade their brothers every other day of the week. He could not give loyalty to a country which promised freedom and equality as an absolute and dealt out slavery and exceptionalism, and worshiped property as a god. He did not go away and construct little models of a new form of society which tried to screen out all human ugliness, error, and cruelty. He took man as he was, with all his sin and darkness on him, and tried to ignite in him, by the abrasive power of statement, conviction, and sacrifice, a flood of

CLEANSING LIGHT.

Documents of Upheaval

The First Demonstration

The most significant lines Garrison set, with his own hand, in the first issue of The Liberator, *January, 1831, were not those oft-quoted ones about being "as harsh as truth" (eloquence was dirt-cheap in those days) but his account on page two of his trial, sentence, and punishment in Baltimore for libel against one Todd of Newburyport, in the City Court session for February, 1830.*

Garrison's account is taken verbatim from the Baltimore Gazette. *He was indicted in that city for gross libel—for comments he had made in the* Genius of Universal Emancipation—*found guilty, and fined fifty dollars and costs, the whole amount coming to over a hundred dollars. This Garrison refused to pay and went cheerfully to Baltimore jail. The* Gazette *reported, "that as Mr. Todd had no vindictive feelings to gratify, the suit would be withdrawn, if a proper apology, and recantation of the calumny were put upon record. This offer Mr. Garrison not only refused, but while in confinement, published a pamphlet containing, with* his *report of the trial, a republication of the libel, and a number of gross insinuations against the Chief Judge of the Court."*

Garrison refused to apologize for telling the "truth" and explained later that he took this stand to show that he "disregarded sectional feelings," to prove prejudice against the blacks in New England was only a little less than in the South, and to see if "the publication would ever after deter Mr. Todd from venturing into the domestic slave trade: and that it would be a rod over the backs of New England merchants generally."

*A fuller discussion of the episode does not warrant space here, as it occurred in his pre-*Liberator *days. But his brilliantly blunt republication of the "libel" itself in Boston, which opened the way for further legal action against him, convinced the Northern blacks that here was one white man committed enough to perform an* act *for their cause and ready to put himself in peril for them, every day. It also served to goad the Northern politicians who tolerated the domestic slave trade, even in Washington itself . . . through which were driven coffles of slaves, in chains and under whips. They were brutally sold there whenever a customer appeared. They were locked in filthy jails overnight while in transit, although they had committed no crime, there and throughout every other Southern state. The domestic slave trade was more agonizing and degrading to the slave who had been born in the land of the free and then been sold into terrible bondage, often by his own white father, than the foreign slave trade was to the African who had arrived there as a prisoner of war.*

So it is no wonder that, after launching his operation without a single subscriber or a penny in reserve, with borrowed type and paper obtained on the shakiest of credit, he quickly picked up 450 subscribers, of whom 400 were Negroes. The "libel" follows:

January 1, 1831

BLACK LIST

HORRIBLE NEWS—DOMESTIC AND FOREIGN

THE SHIP FRANCIS

This ship, as I mentioned in our last number,* sailed a few weeks since from this port [Baltimore—T.N.] with a cargo of slaves for the New Orleans market. I do not repeat the fact because it is a rare instance of domestic piracy, or because the case was attended with extraordinary circumstances; for the horrible traffic is briskly carried on, and the transaction was effected in the ordinary manner. I merely wish to illustrate New England humanity and morality. I am determined to cover with thick infamy all who are concerned in this nefarious business.

I have stated that the ship Francis hails from my native place, Newburyport (Massachusetts,) is commanded by a yankee captain, and owned by a townsman named

FRANCIS TODD.

Of Captain Nicholas Brown I should have expected better conduct. It is no worse to fit out piratical cruisers, or to engage in the foreign slave trade, than to pursue a similar trade along our coasts; and the men who have the wickedness to participate therein, for the purpose of heaping up wealth, should be ☞ SENTENCED TO SOLITARY CONFINEMENT FOR LIFE; ☜ *they are the enemies of their own species—highway robbers and murderers;* and their final doom will be, unless they speedily repent, *to occupy the lowest depths of perdition.* I know that our laws make a distinction in this matter. I know that the man who is allowed to freight his vessel with slaves at home, for a distant market, would be thought worthy of death if he should take a similar freight on the coast of Africa; but I know, too, that this dis-

* In *Genius of Universal Emancipation,* Nov. 13, 1829.—T.N.

tinction is absurd, and at war with the common sense of mankind, and that God and good men regard it with abhorrence.

I recollect that it was always a mystery in Newburyport how Mr. Todd contrived to make profitable voyages to New Orleans and other places, when other merchants, with as fair an opportunity to make money, and sending at the same ports at the same time, invariably made fewer successful speculations. The mystery seems to be unravelled. Any man can gather up riches, if he does not care by what means they are obtained.

The Francis carried off *seventy-five* slaves, chained in a narrow place between decks. Captain Brown originally intended to take *one hundred and fifty* of these unfortunate creatures; but another hard-hearted shipmaster underbid him in the price of passage for the remaining moiety. Captain B., we believe, is a *mason*. Where was his charity or brotherly kindness?

I respectfully request the editor of the Newburyport Herald to copy this article, or publish a statement of the facts contained herein—not for the purpose of giving information to Mr. Todd, for I shall send him a copy of this number, but in order to enlighten the public mind in that quarter—G.

David Walker and the Accursed Question

With the very first issue of the paper, Garrison was plunged into a dilemma which was to plague him all his life: what to do about the black people who wanted to defend themselves against their oppressors. He had been in Boston when David Walker wrote his pamphlet* calling on the slaves to rise up against their masters. Walker was greatly admired there among the people of color who were being profoundly affected by the tides of revolutionary liberation sweeping in from Europe. Garrison was constantly pressured to give his judgment on the Walker pamphlet. His judgment was rather ambiguous; he deplored the physical militancy of its spirit but felt it was a remarkable document in itself and completely justifiable in terms of the language whites used to each other at Fourth of July celebrations. It is interesting to contrast here the responses of Garrison and Lundy to Walker. Lundy takes the customary Quaker-pacifist position against any suggestions or appeals for violence, whether coming from the oppressed or the oppressor. This may be why Lundy never achieved a considerable following among the free blacks while Garrison's following was crucial and sustaining. Lundy's comment, appearing in the Genius of Universal Emancipation *for April, 1830, is so typical of the liberal position on Negro "violence" or "self-defense" today, I cannot resist printing it here.*

WALKER'S BOSTON PAMPHLET

I had not seen this far-famed production until within a few days. A more bold, daring, inflammatory publication, perhaps, never issued from the press, in any country. I can do no less than set the broadest seal of condemnation upon it. Such things can have no other earthly effect than to injure our cause. The writer indulges himself in the wildest strain of reckless fanaticism. He makes a great parade of technical phraseology, purporting to be religious; but religion has nothing at all to do with it. It is a labored attempt to rouse the worst passions of human nature, and inflame the minds of those to whom it is addressed.

Granting that the colored race have as much cause for complaint as this writer intimates, (and I readily grant it,) yet this is not the way to obtain redress for their wrongs. The *moral,* not the physical, power of this nation must be put in requisition. Any attempt to obtain their liberty and just rights, by force, must for a long time to come end in defeat, if not the extermina-

---

* *David Walker's Appeal to the Coloured Citizens of the World, But in Particular, and Very Expressly, to Those of the United States of America, 1829.*

4

tion of the colored people. It is to avert so direful a catastrophe, that the wise and the good are now exerting themselves, in various parts of our country. . . . A disposition to promote turbulent and violent commotion, will only tend to procrastinate the march of justice, and defer the enfranchisement of the colored race among us; of course every appearance thereof should be discountenanced by persons of every color and condition. And I am glad to find that some of the colored people have *publicly* condemned the pamphlet in question.

January 1, 1831

WALKER'S PAMPHLET

The Legislature of North Carolina has lately been sitting with closed doors, in consequence of a message from the Governor relative to the above pamphlet. The south may reasonably be alarmed at the circulation of Mr. Walker's Appeal; for a better promoter of insurrection was never sent forth to an oppressed people. In a future number, we propose to examine it, as also various editorial comments thereon—it being one of the most remarkable productions of the age. We have already publicly deprecated its spirit.

January 8, 1831

WALKER'S APPEAL. NO. 1

Believing, as we do, that men should never do evil that good may come; that a good end does not justify wicked means in the accomplishment of it; and that we ought to suffer, as did our Lord and his apostles, unresistingly—knowing that vengeance belongs to God, and he will certainly repay it where it is due;— believing all this, and that the Almighty will deliver the oppressed in a way which they know not, we deprecate the spirit and tendency of this Appeal. Nevertheless, it is not for the American people, as a nation, to denounce it as bloody or monstrous. Mr. Walker but pays them in their own coin, but follows their own creed, but adopts their own language. *We* do not preach rebellion—no, but submission and peace. Our enemies may accuse us of striving to stir up the slaves to revenge; but their accusations are false, and made only to excite the prejudices of the whites, and to destroy our influence. We say, that the possibility of a bloody insurrection at the South fills us with dismay; and we avow, too, as plainly, that if any people were ever justified in throwing off the yoke of their tyrants, the slaves are that people. It is not we, but our guilty countrymen, who put arguments into the mouths, and swords into the hands of the slaves. Every sentence that they write—every word that they speak—every resistance that they make, against foreign oppression, is a call upon their slaves to destroy them. Every Fourth of July celebration must embitter and inflame the minds of the slaves. And the late dinners, and illuminations, and orations, and shoutings, at the south, over the downfal of the French tyrant, Charles the Tenth, furnish so many reasons to the slaves why they should obtain their own rights by violence.

Some editors have affected to doubt whether the deceased Walker wrote this pamphlet.— On this point, skepticism need not stumble: the Appeal bears the strongest internal evidence of having emanated from his own mind. No white man could have written in language so natural and enthusiastic.

A Case of Inconsistency

Garrison was ethically prepared for all the consequences of his advocacy of immediate emancipation. His idea was simply to desist from the sin of slavery under moral suasion so that the oppressor and the oppressed could enter with clean hands into a new era of reconciliation and brotherhood. However, having given himself up to transmitting as directly as he could the real feeling of the black people against slavery and racism, he was obliged to print, over and over again, calls for revolutionary action from them, and some severe disagreements with his pacifism. The writer of the following communication, prefaced by Garrison's comments, is unknown.

July 9, 1831

A highly esteemed friend in New-York, during our recent visit to that city—(a keen controvertist and an indefatigable writer) —while waiting for our appearance at the hotel, sat down and enditied the following pithy communication. How will the advocates for resistance to oppression meet his argument? Will they have the effrontery to contend, that our fathers were justified in their rebellion against the mother country, for a petty tea-tax, and yet that the slaves (trodden down to the earth, as they are, by the iron heel of tyranny) have no right to regain their liberty by violence? Let us hear how they will reconcile such a gross paradox. *Let us hear,* we say.

THE NON-RESISTANCE DOCTRINE

To the Editor of the Liberator.—SIR: What are we to understand by the sentiment frequently advanced in the Liberator, teaching non-resistance? Is it, that men are to fight under *no* circumstances? Is it, that the Poles ought not to shake off the yoke of the Autocrat? that France ought to have submitted to the usurpation of Charles the Tenth? that Greece ought to have continued under the imperious Turk? that South America ought not to have revolted from Spain? that St. Domingo ought have continued enslaved to France? that *we* ought not to protect our frontiers against Indian incursions, or liberate our citizens from

7

Barbarian captivity, or exterminate the West India pirates, or resist the *Tea Act* of a British parliament, or prevent a Caesar from usurping our liberties, or repel an invading power, or prevent ourselves from being enslaved, or even defend our own property and lives against robbers and murderers? Is this the meaning? If so, few indeed will assent to the doctrine. Why, Sir, the Poles are regarded as Patriots, and have the sympathies of the whole world. And the French Revolution, and the Haytian Revolution, and the American Revolution, are they not considered glorious achievements? And would not our country be considered even criminal, to permit the Indians to butcher, and the Barbarians to enslave, and the Pirates to murder her citizens? Would not a man be considered a poltron, yea, a wretch, who should, unresistingly, permit his wife to be rifled, and his children to be manacled and beaten and enslaved? Would not the nation be adjudged deserving of subjugation, that should tamely submit thereto?

But it will be said, that all these arguments, if legitimately followed out, would go to justify the rebellion of slaves. Would they so, indeed? Is it verily so, that the fact of the lawfulness of resistance in defence of property, liberty, wife, children, and even of life itself, would render resistance lawful on the part of slaves? *If* it *is* so, the fault is not mine.

There are those who deem resistance, under *any* circumstances, unlawful; but as they are a very small minority of mankind, they are not to assume the question, and force it upon others. But, especially, should they not apply it *particularly* to the case of slaves. They should likewise call the Poles to order, and reprimand the heroes of our Revolution; yea, and the man who defends himself against the highwayman, and the ship's crew that repels the assault of the piratical cruiser, and the citizen who defends his own house against the midnight robber; not forgetting, however, that in so doing, they are only giving the views of *one party*, on a controverted question, instead of enjoining a truth universally admitted.

The conclusion of the matter, then, is this: the friends of peace are not to say to slaves, *you* ought not to resist—you *particularly*: but that *none* ought to resist—that is, *in their opinion*. But, perhaps, some of the opponents of slavery have not these peculiar views of peace and war, and they might judge resistance to be lawful. They would, of course, inculcate their views. And it would remain for those concerned, to judge between the opposing sentiments. Indeed, it *is* for them to judge *now* between warlike and pacific principles. They are not to be bound by the dictum of either party, on this, any more than on any other question. No one is to assume either side of a controverted question, for a third party. That party is to judge for itself. And as slaves are like other men, it is to be feared that, whether right or wrong, the time will ere long arrive, when *they* will judge resistance to be allowable. *Right* or *wrong,* Sir, methinks this country will yet see troublous times from her slaves. There is no prospect of the termination of slavery, except by physical force; for behold the circling system. Say the abettors of slavery—We cannot liberate our slaves, because their ignorance would render them dangerous as freemen, and we dare not give them intelligence, because this would render them dangerous as slaves. Here, then, we have it *in perpetuo.* The question then, is, *will* slaves continue to wear their chains forever, or rise in their majesty, and assert their rights? I inquire not, now, what they *ought* to do. Even if it were admitted that such resistance would be wrong, yet how can it be expected of slaves, goaded to frenzy by oppression, to be better, and exercise greater forbearance, than other men? It is *not* to be expected. And, should they rise, they should and would be ranked with all those who have fought for liberty, the world over—blameable or praiseworthy as they are.   CONSISTENCY

What Shall Be Done?

Following is Garrison's answer, at this stage of his development, to the familiar "educational program" of the liberal Abolitionists.

July 30, 1831

WHAT SHALL BE DONE?

The solemn inquiries are often anxiously made, what shall be done for the abolition of slavery, and wherein can the people of the free States act efficiently? A full and satisfactory reply to these inquiries demands a series of numbers. In the present essay, I shall sketch out only the outlines of a few feasible schemes.

First of all, I want every man and every woman to discard their criminal prejudices, their timorous fears, and their paralyzing doubts. I want them to feel that two millions of their brothers and sisters are groaning under the thraldom of slavery; that they are bound, by every conceivable motive, to assist in breaking their fetters; and that they are capable of effecting their desires, through divine assistance.—The work of reform must commence with *ourselves*. Until *we* are purified, it will be fruitless and intrusive for *us* to cleanse *others*. I say, then, that the *entire abstinence* from the products of slavery is the duty of every individual. . . .

In England, more is doing, perhaps, by females towards overthrowing slavery in the British Colonies, than by the other sex. Each member of a Free Produce Society pays annually a few shillings into the treasury thereof—with which money, tracts, illustrative of the horrors of slavery, and filled with pathetic entreaties, are circulated far and wide. . . . The ladies of this country ought not to be outdone in this benevolent and holy enterprise.

2dly. Religious professors, of all denominations, must bear unqualified testimony against slavery. They must not support, they must not palliate it. . . .

'For this thing which it cannot bear, the earth is disquieted.'
The Gospel of Peace and Mercy preached by him who steals,
buys and sells the purchase of the Messiah's blood! . . .

3dly. The formation of an American Anti-Slavery Society is
of the utmost importance; and it is now, I am happy to say,
in embryo. The objects of this Society will be, to consolidate
the moral power of the nation, so that Congress and the State
Legislatures may be inundated with petitions;—to scatter tracts,
like rain-drops, over the land, on the subject of slavery;—to
employ active and eloquent agents to plead the cause constantly,
and to form auxiliaries;—to encourage planters to cultivate their
lands by freemen, by offering large premiums;—to promote education and the mechanical arts among the free people of color,
and to recover their lost rights. The people, at large, are as-
tonishingly ignorant of the horrors of slavery. Let information
be circulated among them as prodigally as the light of heaven,
and they cannot long act and reason as they now do.

4thly. Slavery in the District of Columbia is sustained in our
national capacity: it ought, therefore, to be prostrated at a blow.

5thly. The clause in the Constitution should be erased, which
tolerates, greatly to the detriment and injustice of the free states,
a slave representation in Congress. Why should property be
represented from the impoverished south, and not from the opu-
lent north?

6thly. We want, at this moment, at least one hundred periodi-
cals over the land, expressly devoted to the cause of emancipation. . . . 'What more shall we do?' It will be seasonable
enough to answer this question, when we shall have done what
has been already suggested.

Walker's Appeal: A Confrontation

Garrison's pacifist program did not satisfy Negro admirers of Walker. Garrison then had the pamphlet reviewed by a writer now unknown to history, signing himself "V."

May 14, 1831

WALKER'S APPEAL, NO. 2

In commenting on a work like this, so pregnant with interest, so full of matter of mighty import, there is, no doubt, wherewith to extend my remarks far beyond the limits of a newspaper. I find so much, sir, worthy of attention, that I must say, before proceeding farther, that I shall be obliged to skip many points I would gladly dwell upon, and confine myself to the more prominent features of the book. In continuation of the remarks with which my last letter concluded, I will quote one of Walker's periods:

'Do they not institute laws to prohibit us from marrying among the whites? I would wish, candidly, however, before the Lord, to be understood, that I would not give a *pinch of snuff* to be married to any white person I ever saw in all the days of my life. And I do say it, that the black man, or man of color, who will leave his own color (provided he can get one who is good for anything) and marry a white woman, to be a double slave to her, just because she is *white,* ought to be treated by her as he surely will be, viz: as a NIGER!! It is not, indeed, what I care about intermarriages with the whites, which induced me to pass this subject in review; for the Lord knows that there is a day coming when they will be glad enough to get into the company of the blacks, notwithstanding we are, in this generation, levelled by them, almost on a level with the brute creation; and some of us they treat even worse than they do the brutes that perish.'

12

It is not my purpose to discuss the propriety of intermarriages between the two races here. I bring in the paragraph merely to show the spirit in which our black apostle wrote. He tells us that he would not 'give a pinch of snuff' for any white woman living, but revolts at the prohibitory law, conceiving it to be a manifesto of the supposed inferiority of his people. This is a proper view of the subject, nor does the pride manifested in his language lower him in my esteem.

Walker next, in speaking of the condition of the free blacks, affirms, that they are, one and all, the prey of white rogues, who are constantly defrauding them. As an illustration of his position he says, that when a negro dies possessed of property (a rare case,) it usually falls into the hands of some white, to the detriment of the natural heirs. Having very little acquaintance with the blacks, I am unable to say how far his assertion is true; you, Mr Garrison, probably know. Granting the fact to be as Walker states it, I do not think the case of his compeers peculiar: the weak are ever and must be, to a considerable extent, the prey of the strong; those who think, have and will always prevail over those who merely work. It seems to me that the wrongs of which Walker complains must be attributed not to the color of his people, but to their ignorance. His next complaint relates to the common opinion that the negro is a distinct genus, inferior to the human race, and nearly allied to the *simia* species. Walker, in my opinion very justly, thinks this an insupportable insult, and speaks of it with the utmost indignation. Without entering into a discussion of the opinion, first broached, I believe, by Mr Jefferson, I would only say, that I think it calculated to embitter the feelings of the blacks toward us, and it may one day be, that every drop of ink wasted in its support will cost a drop of human blood.

Walker next speaks in bitter terms of such blacks as, by giving information, &c., aid the whites to keep their brethren in subjection, and thinks that but for their hindrance the slaves would ere this have been free. Here, I think, he is mistaken: it is not treason but ignorance that rivets their chains. The law makers of some of the slave states have done wisely (in some points of view) in making it highly penal to teach a slave to read. If things are to remain as they are, it is sound policy: that is, supposing it practicable to enforce such laws. Yet I think they will only put off, not prevent the catastrophe. A few years since, being in a slave state, I chanced one morning, very early, to look through the curtains of my chamber window, which opened upon a back yard. I saw a mulatto with a newspaper in his hand, surrounded by a score of colored men, who were listening, open mouthed, to a very inflammatory article the yellow man was reading. Sometimes the reader dwelt emphatically on particular passages, and I could see his auditors stamp and clench their hands. I afterwards learned that the paper was published in New-York, and addressed to the blacks. It is but reasonable to suppose that such scenes are of common occurrence in the slave states, and it does not require the wisdom of Solomon to discern their tendency.

The following paragraph appears to me to contain the gist of Walker's argument, and to explain his motive for publishing his book:

'Remember that unless you are united, keeping your tongues within your teeth, you will be afraid to trust your secrets to each other, and thus perpetuate our miseries under the *Christians!!* Remember, also, to lay humble at the feet of our Lord and Master Jesus Christ, with prayers and fastings. Let our enemies go on with their butcheries, and at once fill up their cup. Never make an attempt to gain our freedom or *natural right,* from under our cruel oppressors and murderers, until you see your way clear—when that hour arrives and you move, be not afraid or dismayed; for be you assured that Jesus Christ the King of heaven and of earth, who is the God of justice and of armies, will surely go before you. And those enemies who have for hundreds of years stolen our *rights,* and kept us ignorant of Him and His divine worship, He will remove. Millions of whom are, this day, so ignorant and avaricious, that they cannot conceive how God can have an attribute of justice, and show mercy to us because it pleased him to make us black— which color Mr Jefferson calls unfortunate!! It is not to be understood here, that I mean for us to wait until God shall take us by the hair of our heads and drag us out of abject wretchedness and slavery, nor I do mean to convey the idea for us to wait until our enemies shall make preparations, and call us to seize those preparations, take it away from them, and put every thing before us to death, in order to gain our freedom which God has given us. For you must remember that we are men as well as they. God has been pleased to give us two eyes, two hands, two feet, and some sense in our heads as well as they. They have no more right to hold us in slavery than we have to hold them; we have just as much right, in the sight of God, to hold them and their children in slavery and wretchedness, as they have to hold us, and no more.'

Here then is a clear, undeniable exhortation to insurrection. The facts stated by Walker as incentives, are *facts,* not suppositions, and in my opinion, his inferences are just. The question is, whether such language can conscientiously be held by a white man, having a clear view of its result, to a black. 'Grant your opinions to be just,' a slave owner once said to me, 'if you talk so to the slaves, they will fall to cutting their masters' throats.' 'And in God's name,' I replied, 'why should they not cut their masters' throats?' I am, however, no preacher of reform. If the blacks can come to a sense of their wrongs, and a resolution to redress them, through their own instrumentality or that of others, I shall rejoice. They are my fellow creatures and countrymen as well as their masters. It would indeed grieve me to hear that one of my southern brethren had died by the hands of his slaves: it is still more grievous to think that he holds a score of my black brethren in degrading thraldom. Of two evils I prefer the least, and it is better that one man should lose his life than that a score should lose their liberty. Yet I do not conceive it my duty, nor have I any vocation to set myself up as a redresser of wrongs, or an occulist for the mentally blind. For those good men who think otherwise, who seek the greater good of the greater number, to their own danger and prejudice, I respect and esteem, but cannot imitate them. When, as in the present instance, my opinion is asked, it shall be freely given, but I do not think myself bound to advance it unasked.

Walker then speaks of the advertisements of slaves to be sold, runaways, &c., so constantly found in the southern papers. He speaks of husbands torn from their wives, babes from their mothers, and remarks that in the same columns the Mussulmans are reproved for their barbarity to the Greeks. I have often seen such inconsistencies as he mentions, but they are too melancholy to evoke a smile. The Greeks in the Ottoman empire pay tribute and are subject to vexatious exactions, but they are not slaves, unless taken in rebellion. Even then they recover their freedom at the end of seven years. The severities inflicted on them by their Mahometan lords are cakes and gingerbread in comparison with those practised by Christian masters on their slaves. But our slaves are black, and that, it seems, destroys their claim to sympathy. Strange that the dark pigment, which is its coloring matter, should render a negro's skin as callous as the shell of a lobster, and infect the veins of his very heart so as to render him incapable of social affections. I suppose this must be a common opinion of the slave owners, or we should hear less of the abominations of which Walker speaks. To be serious, I would advise southern editors to exclude the advertisements above mentioned and their accompanying engravings from their papers, lest some of them should find their way to Europe and prove our declaration of independence hypocritical.

> 'The man who would not fight under our Lord and Master Jesus Christ, in the glorious and heavenly cause of freedom and of God—to be delivered from the most wretched, abject and servile slavery that ever a people was afflicted with since the foundation of the world to the present day—ought to be kept, with all his children or family, in slavery, or in chains, to be butchered by his *cruel enemies.*'

Well done, David Walker! I like your spirit, for it will work out the salvation of your brethren. Verily, David Walker was a *man!* Then follows a comparison of the slavery of other lands with our own, and an examination of Mr Jefferson's opinion. Next comes much declamation and a sweeping denunciation of the whites as 'unjust, jealous, unmerciful, avaricious and bloodthirsty beings.' Surely a black has a right to think so. Thus ends the first of the four articles into which the 'Appeal' is divided.

As a specimen of Walker's style, when he betakes himself to declamation, I beg you to print the following:

'Are we men!—I ask you, O my brethren! are we MEN? Did our Creator make us to be slaves to dust and ashes like ourselves? Are they not dying worms as well as we? Have they not to make their appearance before the tribunal of Heaven, to answer for the deeds done in the body, as well as we? Have we any other Master but Jesus Christ alone? Is he not their master as well as ours?—What right then, have we to obey and call any other Master, but Himself? How we could be so *submissive* to a gang of men, whom we cannot tell whether they are *as good* as ourselves or not, I never could conceive. However this is shut up with the Lord, and we cannot precisely tell—but I declare, we judge men by their works.'

Here let us pause and reflect. What is to be the end of the American system of oppression? Will it, can it last for ever? And if it does not, how is it to be terminated—by the consent of the whites, or by the hands of the blacks? The question involves no less than the fate of all that portion of our country which lies south of the Potomac. Three ways occur to me by which the slaves may possibly be emancipated without bloodshed, viz. by colonizing them elsewhere, by gradual abolition, or by free labor becoming more profitable than that of thralls. I will, if you wish it, consider these things in another place, not here. As to the prospect of their liberation by some means or other, I consider it certain. There are now about as many colored persons within the limits of the union as there were whites at the commencement of our revolution, and it seems to me impossible that they can be prevented from discovering their wrongs. All the laws that can be made cannot wholly exclude the rudiments of learning from among them. The name of Walker alone is a terror to the south, and it is probable there are or will be more men like him. Negroes have showed their mental capacity in St Domingo, where, thirty-two years ago, they were as much or more debased than they now are in the United States. That example of bloodshed and misery is before the eyes of our slaves; that tragedy, it seems to me, will soon be enacted on an American stage, with new scenery, unless something is speedily done to prevent it. The actors are studying their parts, and there will be more such prompters as Walker. At present, they only want a manager. I fear, very much fear, that the retribution predicted in the book in question is at hand. It is a hard case for the south to be sure. The southern planter has not himself instituted the present state of affairs: it came down from his fathers. It is hard for him to give up his inheritance, and still harder to overcome the habits in which he was bred. Even the immediate emancipation of his slaves, and the restoration of their natural rights, would, perhaps, produce much evil. It will be harder for his children to see this change brought about by the red hand. But—when the slaves shall have attained even the limited degree of knowledge possessed by the free blacks, if they do not rise and strike for freedom, if they do not settle the account that has been scored for two centuries, Mr Jefferson will have been proved to be right in his opinion. When they shall no longer have the excuse of ignorance, and shall not avail themselves of their strength, they will indeed be proved to be baboons, unworthy of the name or privileges of men. It is astonishing, Mr Garrison, to hear some of the free and intelligent sons of New-England speak on this subject. A lawyer, of no mean attainments, said, a few days ago, in my presence, that the slaves in the south are well enough; that their condition is preferable to that of the poor whites here; and, in short, that they were happy. I have often heard similar opinions expressed. They are indeed contented, and so is a horse or an ox, and for the same reason. It is the happiness of a brute—not of a man. If to eat, drink and sleep, without a thought of the past or future, constitutes earthly felicity, then are slaves happy indeed, and their condition cannot be bettered. Even then they are not quite so happy as a horse, for they feel the whip more sensibly. Ask any white who expatiates on this happiness, if he would, if he could, get rid of his cares and perplexities by changing conditions with a slave. No; but the slaves are black, and that argument oversets all the rules of logic—it is unanswerable   V.

May 28, 1831

WALKER'S APPEAL, NO. 3

Walker begins the second article of his Appeal with a retrospective view of the glories of Carthage and Egypt, and promises his brethren that in due time the Lord will give them a Hannibal to lead them to victory and liberty. That some black temporal Messiah may arise, some man of mighty mind, who shall rend asunder the bonds of prejudice and captivity, is by no means unlikely. The darkest regions of the earth have produced their extraordinary men: Persia had her Nadir, the Goths their Alaric and Attila, Tartary had her Genghis Khan; why may not African America produce her champion? But that the Almighty will send a special messenger to our slaves, and strike for those who will not strike for themselves, you will allow me to doubt. I am sorry to see so much of the delusion of fanaticism mingled with so much sound sense and noble feeling.

A dreadful prediction follows, and if it be not fulfilled sooner or later, the order of things will have changed. I would that all slave owners could read it: it might teach them a salutary though unwelcome lesson.

'The whites want slaves, and want us for their slaves, but some of them will curse the day they ever saw us. As true as the sun ever shone in its meridian splendor, my color will root some of them out of the face of the earth. They shall have enough of making slaves of, and butchering, and murdering us in the manner which they have. No doubt some may say that I write with a bad spirit, and that I, being a black, wish these things to occur. Whether I write with a bad or good spirit, I say if these things do not occur in their proper time, it is because the world in which we live does not exist, and we are deceived with regard to its existence.—It is immaterial, however, to me, who believe, or who refuse—though I should like to see the whites repent, peradventure God may have mercy on them; some, however, have gone so far that their cup must be filled.'

Walker says that a great portion of the miseries of the slaves springs from their want of unity of feeling and fidelity to each other. In support of this position, he quotes an account of the mutiny of a gang of slaves against their driver. The blacks, it seems, overpowered the whites and would have slain one of them, had not a black woman assisted him to escape. He speaks of this woman in bitter terms, and says it is owing, in a great measure, to such persons, that the whites are able to keep the blacks under. Eight blacks, he says, if thoroughly roused, are a match for fifty whites. I can conceive that a band of blacks, goaded to fury, smarting with the sense of wrong, with everything before them to gain, and nothing behind to lose, would be more than a match for treble their number of men who should have no such motives to urge them on. In this sense he may be right.

The following passage has more force, more reason, and puts the condition of the free blacks in a stronger light, than any other in the book. It is written in a sincere and patriotic spirit. Let those who believe in the mental inferiority of the blacks, read it and acknowledge that *if* their theory is true, David Walker was an exception to it.

'Men of color, who are also of sense, for you particularly is my APPEAL designed. Our more ignorant brethren are not able to penetrate its value. I call upon you therefore to cast your eyes upon the wretchedness of your brethren, and to do your utmost to enlighten them —*go to work and enlighten your brethren!*—Let the Lord see you doing what you can to rescue them and yourselves from degradation. Do any of you say that you and your family are free and happy, and what have you to do with the wretched slaves and other people? So can I say, for I enjoy as much freedom as any of you, if I am not quite as well off as the best of you. Look into our freedom and happiness, and see of what kind they are composed!! They are of the very lowest kind —they are the very *dregs!*—they are the most servile and abject kind that ever a people was in possession of! If any of you wish to know how FREE you are, let one of you start and go through the southern and western States of this country, and unless you travel as a slave to a white man (a servant is a *slave* to the man whom he serves) or have your free papers, (which if you are not careful they will get from you) if they do not take you up and put you into jail, and if you cannot give good evidence of your freedom, sell you into eternal slavery, I am not a living man: or any man of color, immaterial who he is, or where he came from, if he is not *the fourth from the negro race!!* (as we are called) the white Christians of America will serve him the same; they will sink him into wretchedness and degradation forever while he lives. And yet some of you have the hardihood to say that you are free and happy! May God have mercy on your freedom and happiness!! I met a colored man in the street a short time since, with a string of boots on his shoulders; we fell into conversation, and in course of which, I said to him, what a miserable set of people we are! He asked, why?—Said I, we are so subjected under the whites, that we cannot obtain the comforts of life, but by cleaning their boots and shoes, old clothes, waiting on them, shaving them, &c. Said he (with the boots on his shoulders) "I am completely happy!!! I never want to live any better or happier than when I can get a plenty of boots and shoes to clean!!" Oh! how can those who are actuated by avarice only, but think, that our Creator made us to be an inheritance to them forever, when they see that our greatest glory is centered in such mean and low objects? Understand me, brethren, I do not mean to speak against the occupations by which we acquire enough and sometimes scarcely that, to render ourselves and family comfortable through life. I am subjected to the same inconvenience, as you all.—My objections are, to our *glorying* and being *happy* in such low employments; for if we are men, we ought to be thankful to the Lord for the past, and for the future. Be looking forward with thankful hearts to higher attainments than *wielding the razor* and *cleaning boots and shoes.* The man whose aspirations are not *above,* and even *below* these, is indeed, ignorant and wretched enough.'

He next opposes the erroneous opinions of his brethren on the subject of education, and exhorts them to get a knowledge of things rather than of words and fair penmanship. He mentions a fact that I deem remarkable, viz. Not one in thirty of the young men of color who have been to school, and who are believed by their parents to be well educated, can answer the easiest question in English Grammar, or point out the errors in an ill-constructed sentence, however simple. Is this so? And if so, what is the reason of it? According to the 'Appeal,' it is because no

white schoolmaster will communicate a particle of useful instruction to a black boy. I have attended a Sunday School where
black infants were taught by bigoted, silly women, and have
seen them taught their letters, and have heard them answer questions on the church catechism. I have seen their cent-a-week
spending money wrung from their little hands to endow a missionary, or, perhaps, to help expatriate their parents, but I never
saw one item of practical knowledge given or received. Our free
black brethren are to blame for this state of things. If they will
pay for instruction for their children, they can command it. Interest is stronger than prejudice, and white teachers may be
found in multitudes who will impart the stores of the mind for
a convincing consideration. I say to you, black men, into whose
hands these remarks shall fall, if you wish to see your children
happy, prosperous and respected, give them knowledge. There is
no able bodied laboring man so poor as cannot spare from his
earnings enough to give at least one child as much learning as is
necessary or desirable for a seaman, a mechanic, or a tradesman.
Give your children the advantages of a good school, and they
will be something better than barbers and shoe blacks. There are
enough of you to support a school, and, if you can manage to support him, I will myself engage to find a competent and willing
instructor.

The principal part of the third article of the 'Appeal' is a dis-
sertation on the advantages of religion, and as I do not deem myself a competent critic on such topics, I will, if you please, Mr
Garrison, prætermit the subject altogether. After this, Walker
institutes a comparison between the treatment of negroes at the
hands of Americans here and of Englishmen elsewhere. The result is in favor of John Bull, as might have been expected. He
says that there is no intelligent black who does not esteem an
Englishman. Should England ever get a hostile footing in one of
the southern states, what might be the consequence of such a
feeling?

The fourth and last article begins with a discourse on the miseries inflicted on the blacks by the visionary scheme of colonizing
them in Africa. Mr Clay comes in for a share of censure, for
having lent his countenance to the Colonization Society. May
the Lord forgive Walker for the aspersion he ignorantly casts on

that virtuous and eminent man. Mr Clay saw a great evil in the land, the curse of bondage, and like many other good men, caught desperately at the only means to ameliorate it that occurred to his mind.

A panegyric on the late good Bishop Allen, some further remarks on the Colonizing scheme and a criticism of the Declaration of Independence, make up the remainder of the article. In one passage he asks the reason why the blacks are so easily overawed and oppressed by the whites. I will quote his answer, for it is well worthy of note.

'They keep us miserable now, and call us their property, but some of them will have enough of us by and by —their stomachs shall run over with us; they want us for their slaves, and shall have us to their fill. We are all in the world together!!—I said above, because we cannot help ourselves, (viz. we cannot help the whites murdering our mothers and our wives) but this statement is incorrect—for we can help ourselves; for, if we lay aside abject servility, and be determined to act like men, and not brutes—the murderers among the whites would be afraid to show their cruel heads. But O, my God!—in sorrow I must say it, that my color, all over the world, have a mean, servile spirit. They yield in a moment to the whites, let them be right or wrong—the reason they are able to keep their feet on our throats. Oh! my colored brethren, all over the world, when shall we arise from this death-like apathy!—and be men!! You will notice, if ever we become men, I mean *respectable* men, such as other people are, we must exert ourselves to the full. For, remember, that it is the greatest desire and object of the greater part of the whites, to keep us ignorant, and make us work to support them and their families.—Here now, in the Southern and Western sections of this country, there are at least three colored persons for one white; why is it, that those few weak, good-for-nothing whites, are able to keep so many able men, one of whom can put to flight a dozen whites, in wretchedness and misery? It shows at once, what the blacks are; we are ignorant, abject, servile and mean—and the whites know it—they know that we are too servile to assert our rights as men —or they would not fool with us as they do. Would they fool with any other people as they do with us? No, they know too well, that they would get themselves ruined. Why do they not bring the inhabitants of Asia to be body servants to them? They know they would get their bodies rent and torn from head to foot. Why do they not get the Aborigines of this country to be slaves to them and their children, to work their farms and dig their mines? They know well that the Aborigines of this country, (or Indians) would tear them from the earth. The Indians would not rest day or night, they would be up all times of night, cutting their cruel throats. But my color, (some, not all,) are willing to stand still and be murdered by the cruel whites.'

This is the root of the matter. Were not the slaves of a mean and servile spirit (the consequence of their utter ignorance) they were slaves no longer. They are strong enough to free themselves, and if that object cannot be effected by peaceable means, in God's name let it come in any way, be the consequence what it may, rather than that this great wickedness should pollute our otherwise favored land. The tears of the innocent and the groans of the oppressed cry to Heaven for vengeance, and though I do not look for the arrival of any relief through supernatural agency, I am persuaded that a great change must take place before the lapse of another century. How any one can think and feel otherwise with regard to this subject, I can only account for by supposing that they do indeed regard the blacks as another and an inferior species. Let but an American seaman be impressed into the British navy, where, by the way, he is clad, fed, paid, and not very ill treated, and the tocsin of alarm is sounded, and the country is in a flame from Maine to Florida. But let a Georgia planter starve or scourge his slaves to death, or shoot them down for his amusement, and the most deathlike apathy prevails. How long, O, Lord, how long!

Walker's remarks on the Declaration of Independence are pointed and to the purpose, but the sum of that argument may be given in few words. The instrument has a most unhappy beginning, for its very first clause, in the mouth of a white inhabitant of any of the slave states, is a base lie, or, at best, a vile piece of national hypocrisy. This language is not stronger than the occasion justifies. How can any man who holds a slave, or assists another to hold him, say that all men are born free and equal? Any foreigner has a right to call him a fool or a hypocrite. By your leave, I will close my cogitations on this subject with a few remarks on the plan of colonizing our negroes elsewhere.

1. It is cruel.
2. It is unjust.
3. It is impracticable.
4. Were it none of these, it is impolitic.

1. No man of color who knows his own interest will consent to emigrate to a land of which he knows nothing. If advantage is taken of a negro's ignorance to entice him from a soil where he has friends and kindred, and where he may eat bread by the sweat of his brow, to one that offers only other equal advantages, it is cruel. If his situation is changed for the worse, it is doubly cruel. A sudden change of climate, of habits, is, to say the least, no advantage, and I never heard that a black received a remuneration for the trouble and hardship of settling in a new country; for a hardship it certainly is. If, as I believe, the land of promise is a miserable country, at the mercy of savages, and still worse, of greedy speculators, it is the height of cruelty to send him thither, whether willingly or unwillingly.

2. To tell a man that he shall not or cannot enjoy the rights his Maker endowed him withal, but on condition of forsaking the land of his birth, to which his dearest sympathies and affections cling, is unjust. To say to a black, 'here you cannot be respected or respectable, nor shall your children be so after you,' is downright abuse, for who can say what changes may take place? This country is their country as much as ours, and they have as much right to remain in it. They know no other land; no other language; it is their country. Suppose that the blacks should become more numerous than ourselves, and should set about colonizing us in Europe, what should we say to the plan? Should we not call it downright insult?

3. The whole number exported by the Colonization Society, from its establishment till now, would not balance the increase of a single week. When the ocean can be drained with a bucket, shall we get rid of our black population by such means—but not till then.

4. To what purpose send three millions of our fellow country-

men into exile? Are they not as capable of being useful here as an equal number of whites? If they can be happy and respectable elsewhere, it only depends on ourselves to make them so here. They will make themselves so, if suffered. Supposing we should send an equal number of poor whites to Liberia, should we not suffer in consequence? Who would carry the hod, pave the streets, &c. for us? Certainly blacks are as able to labor as whites. One tenth of the males would suffice to win ten pitched battles for their country.

I will conclude by hoping that what has fallen from my pen may induce some few of both colors to reflect on these matters.

V.

A Colored Philadelphian

Garrison's favorable handling of the Walker tract brought in even more approving and militant letters; "V." was a frequent contributor and his position was generally upheld.

August 20, 1831

. . . When we take a retrospective view of things, and hear of almost every nation fighting for its liberty, is it to be expected that the African race will continue always in the degraded state they now are? No. The time is fast approaching when the words 'Fight for liberty, or die in the attempt,' will be sounded in every African ear throughout the world; and when he will throw off his fetters, and flock to the banner which will be then floating in the air with the following words inscribed on it—'Liberty or Death'; and when they will die to a man sooner than be slaves any longer to persons (I am sorry to say) not so good as themselves, merely because their skin is something of a darker hue than their own. O Liberty! sound delightful to every African ear! And when the sound has once struck them, may they seize upon it like a drowning man would to anything that comes within his grasp, and never let go till they get that which they ought to have enjoyed ever since they have been in existence, but which has been torn from them by a set of persons who can be termed nothing but pirates. . . .   A Colored Philadelphian.

Insurrection in Virginia: Nat Turner

In June, 1831, Garrison was invited to address a Convention of the Free People of Color in Philadelphia. He told them that although his own race was calling him "a madman, a fanatic, a disturber of the peace, a promoter of rebellion," he was not going to let up, but was determined to give the slaveholders and their apologists as much uneasiness as possible. "I believe," he said, "as firmly as I do my own existence that the time is not far distant when you and the trampled slave will all be free . . . free in the spirit as well as in the letter . . . and enjoying the same rights in this country as other citizens. Every one of you shall sit under your own vine and fig tree and none shall molest you or make you afraid."

The address he gave there was not printed in The Liberator *but its revolutionary sentiments were widely circulated in a pamphlet. So it was not at all strange that when Nat Turner, only two months later, led a slave revolt in Southampton, Virginia, in which some sixty whites were killed, Garrison was blamed for it in the national press.*

The selections following, and Garrison's editorial comment on the insurrection, are taken from The Liberator *during this period.*

September 3, 1831

THE INSURRECTION

What we have long predicted,—at the peril of being stigmatized as an alarmist and declaimer,—has commenced its fulfilment. The first step of the earthquake, which is ultimately to shake down the fabric of oppression, leaving not one stone upon the other, has been made. The first drops of blood, which are but the prelude to a deluge from the gathering clouds, have fallen. The first flash of lightning, which is to ignite and consume, has been felt. The first wailings of a bereavement, which is to clothe the earth in sackcloth, have broken upon our ears.

In the first number of the Liberator, we alluded to the hour of vengeance in the following lines:

Wo if it come with storm, and blood, and fire,
 When midnight darkness veils the earth and sky!
Wo to the innocent babe—the guilty sire—

28

Mother and daughter—friends of kindred tie!
Stranger and citizen alike shall die!
Red-handed Slaughter his revenge shall feed,
And Havoc yell his ominous death-cry,
And wild Despair in vain for mercy plead—
While hell itself shall shrink and sicken at the deed!

Read the account of the insurrection in Virginia, and say whether our prophecy be not fulfilled. What was poetry—imagination—in January, is now a bloody reality. 'Wo to the innocent babe—to mother and daughter!' Is it not true? Turn again to the record of slaughter! Whole families have been cut off—not a mother, not a daughter, not a babe left. Dreadful retaliation! 'The dead bodies of white and black lying just as they were slain, unburied'—the oppressor and the oppressed equal at last in death—what a spectacle!

True, the rebellion is quelled. Those of the slaves who were not killed in combat, have been secured, and the prison is crowded with victims destined for the gallows!

'Yet laugh not in your carnival of crime
Too proudly, ye oppressors!'

You have seen, it is to be feared, but the beginning of sorrows. All the blood which has been shed will be required at your hands. At your hands alone? No—but at the hands of the people of New-England and of all the free states. The crime of oppression is national. The south is only the agent in this guilty traffic. But, remember! the same causes are at work which must inevitably produce the same effects; and when the contest shall have again begun, it must be again a war of extermination. In the present instance, no quarters have been asked or given.

But we have killed and routed them now—we can do it again and again—we are invincible! A dastardly triumph, well becoming a nation of oppressors. Detestable complacency, that can think, without emotion, of the extermination of the blacks! We have the power to kill *all*—let us, therefore, continue to apply the whip and forge new fetters!

In his fury against the revolters, who will remember their wrongs? What will it avail them, though the catalogue of their sufferings, dripping with warm blood fresh from their lacerated bodies, be held up to extenuate their conduct? It is enough that the victims were black—that circumstance makes them less precious than the dogs which have been slain in our streets! They were black—brutes, pretending to be men—legions of curses on their memories! They were black—God made them to serve us!

Ye patriotic hypocrites! ye panegyrists of Frenchmen, Greeks, and Poles! ye fustian declaimers for liberty! ye valient sticklers for equal rights among yourselves! ye haters of aristocracy! ye assailants of monarchies! ye republican nullifiers! ye treasonable disunionists! be dumb! Cast no reproach upon the conduct of the slaves, but let your lips and cheeks wear the blisters of condemnation!

Ye accuse the pacific friends of emancipation of instigating the slaves to revolt. Take back the charge as a foul slander. The slaves need no incentives at our hands. They will find them in their stripes—in their emaciated bodies—in their ceaseless toil—in their ignorant minds—in every field, in every valley, on every hill-top and mountain, wherever you and your fathers have fought for liberty—in your speeches, your conversations, your celebrations, your pamphlets, your newspapers—voices in the air, sounds from across the ocean, invitations to resistance above, below, around them! What more do they need? Surrounded by such influences, and smarting under their newly made wounds, is it wonderful that they should rise to contend—as other 'heroes' have contended—for their lost rights? It is *not* wonderful.

In all that we have written, is there aught to justify the excesses of the slaves? No. Nevertheless, they deserve no more censure than the Greeks in destroying the Turks, or the Poles in exterminating the Russians, or our fathers in slaughtering the British. Dreadful, indeed, is the standard erected by worldly patriotism!

For ourselves, we are horror-struck at the late tidings. We have exerted our utmost efforts to avert the calamity. We have warned our countrymen of the danger of persisting in their unrighteous conduct. We have preached to the slaves the pacific precepts of Jesus Christ. We have appealed to christians, philanthropists and patriots, for their assistance to accomplish the great work of national redemption through the agency of moral power—of public opinion—of individual duty. How have we been received?

We have been threatened, proscribed, vilified and imprisoned—a laughing-stock and a reproach. Do we falter, in view of these things? Let time answer. If we have been hitherto urgent, and bold, and denunciatory in our efforts,—hereafter we shall grow vehement and active with the increase of danger. We shall cry, in trumpet tones, night and day,—Wo to this guilty land, unless she speedily repents of her evil doings! The blood of millions of her sons cries aloud for redress! IMMEDIATE EMANCIPATION can alone save her from the vengeance of Heaven, and cancel the debt of ages!

September 3, 1831

☞ ☞ ☞ ☞ ☞ ☞

INSURRECTION IN VIRGINIA!

Extract of a letter from a gentleman to his friend in Baltimore, dated

RICHMOND, August 23d

'An express reached the governor this morning, informing him that an insurrection had broken out in Southampton, and that, by the last accounts, there were seventy whites massacred, and the militia retreating. Another express to Petersburg says that the blacks were continuing their destruction; that three hundred militia were retreating in a body, before six or eight hundred blacks. A shower of rain coming up as the militia were making an attack, wet the powder so much that they were compelled to retreat, being armed only with shot-guns. The negroes are armed with muskets, scythes, axes, &c. &c. Our volunteers are marching to the scene of action. A troop of cavalry left at four o'clock, P.M. The artillery, with four field pieces, start in the steam boat Norfolk, at 6 o'clock, to land at Smithfield. Southampton county lies 80 miles south of us, below Petersburg.'

════

From the Richmond Whig, of Tuesday.

Disagreeable rumors have reached this city of an insurrection of the slaves in Southampton County, with loss of life. In order to correct exaggeration, and at the same time to induce all salutary caution, we state the following particulars:

An express from the Hon. James Trezvant states that an insurrection had broken out, that several families had been murdered, and that the negroes were embodied, requiring a considerable military force to reduce them.

The names and precise numbers of the families are not mentioned. A letter to the Post Master corroborates the intelligence. Prompt and efficient measures are being taken by the Governor, to call out a sufficient force to put down the insurrection, and place lower Virginia on its guard.

Serious danger of course there is none. The deluded wretches have rushed on assured destruction.

The Fayette Artillery and the Light Dragoons will leave here this evening for Southampton; the artillery go in a steamboat, and the troop by land.

We are indebted to the kindness of our friend Lyford for the following extract of a letter from the Editors of the Norfolk Herald, containing the particulars of a most murderous insurrection among the blacks of Southampton County, Virginia.— *Gaz.*

NORFOLK, 24th Aug. 1831

I have a horrible, a heart rending tale to relate, and lest even its worst feature might be distorted by rumor and exaggeration, I have thought it proper to give you all and the worst information, that has as yet reached us through the best sources of intelligence which the nature of the case will admit.

A gentleman arrived here yesterday express from Suffolk, with intelligence from the upper part of Southampton county, stating that a band of insurgent slaves (some of them believed to be runaways from the neighboring Swamps,) had turned out on Sunday night last, and murdered several whole families, amounting to 40 or 50 individuals. Some of the families were named, and among them was that of Mrs. Catharine Whitehead, sister of our worthy townsman, Dr. N. C. Whitehead,—who, with her son and five daughters, fell a sacrifice to the savage ferocity of these demons in human shape.

The insurrection was represented as one of a most alarming character, though it is believed to have originated only in a design to plunder, and not a view to a more important object—as Mrs. Whitehead being a wealthy lady, was supposed to have had a large sum of money in her house. Unfortunately a large number of the effective male population was absent at Camp Meeting in Gates county, some miles off, a circumstance which gave a temporary security to the brigands in the perpetration of their butcheries; and the panic which they struck at the moment prevented the assembling of a force sufficient to check their career.

As soon as this intelligence was received, our authorities met, and decided on making an immediate application to Col. House, commanding at Fortress Monroe, who, at 6 o'clock this morning, embarked on board the steam boat Hampton, with three companies and a piece of artillery for Suffolk. These troops were reinforced in the Roads by detachments from the U.S. ships Warren and Natchez, the whole amounting to nearly 300 men.

To-day, another express arrived from Suffolk, confirming the disastrous news of the preceding one, and adding still more to the number of the slain.—The insurgents are believed to have from 100 to 150 mounted men, and about the same number on foot. They are armed with fowling pieces, clubs, &c. and have had a rencounter with a small number of the militia, who killed six and took eight of them prisoners. They are said to be on their way to South Quay, probably making their way for the Dismal Swamp, in which they will be able to remain for a short time in security. For my part, I have no fears of their doing much further mischief.—There is very little disaffection in the slaves generally, and they cannot muster a force sufficient to effect any object of importance. The few who have thus rushed headlong into the arena, will be shot down like crows, or captured and made examples of. The militia are collecting in all the neighboring counties, and the utmost vigilance prevails.—I subjoin a list of the victims of their savage vengeance.

[This list—which is embraced in a subsequent account—comprises 58 persons of all ages.]

Muskets, pistols, swords and ammunition have been forwarded to Suffolk to-day, by Com. Warrington, at the request of our civil authorities, and a number of our citizens have accoutred and formed themselves as a troop of cavalry, and set off to assist their fellow citizens in Southampton. I trust the next news you hear will be that all is quiet again.

In haste, yours.

=====

Extract of another letter to the same gentleman, dated at Norfolk, 5 o'clock, P.M.

'It is now 5 o'clock,—Thompson's Stage has just arrived—the above statement is confirmed; and in addition states that 300 negroes well mounted and armed, and headed by one or two white men, is the amount of the insurgent force.'

=====

BELFIELD, (Greensville Co.) Aug. 24

'In the greatest haste I write you a few lines.—I can merely say that we are all in arms and in great excitement on account of the insurrection, which broke out on Sunday night last—between 80 and a hundred of the whites have already been butchered—their heads severed from their bodies. The intention of the negroes was to reach the Dismal Swamp. I think, however, that we have them so hemmed in as to render it impossible for them to do so. On Monday night I reached Belfield (head quarters of the troops) and was given the command of a small body, and a piece of Artillery which I stationed so as to command the bridge. I was up the whole night visiting each one of my sentinels every ten minutes.—At Jerusalem, the blacks made three desperate attempts to cross the bridge, but were repulsed with some loss. No whites have been lost in any of the skirmishes which have taken place. Those fellows commence by murdering a family, taking their arms and horses, and pushing on to the next house with all possible speed, where they massacre every white, even to the infant in the cradle.

'They continue in this manner until they are interrupted, when they disperse and skulk about the woods, until another favorable opportunity occurs of collecting together and repeating their horrible massacres. Between 25 and 30 familes have already been entirely destroyed. Three familes were yesterday murdered, one consisting of ten persons.—Something will be effected to-day, as very active officers and well armed men are at the heels of these villains. Yesterday a very spirited resistance was made by a party, sent out to reconnoitre and discover the position of these fellows, consisting of four against twenty blacks; the whites repulsed them, killed three or four, and took several prisoners.—Many of the blacks are well mounted; their leader was shot in the attempt made to force the bridge at Jerusalem.

'We do not yet know their strength, but think they are now effectually hemmed in and must all perish within a few days. Dr. Scoot left Belfield yesterday with a strong party of horse, and the determination of pursuing them until every man of them was taken or destroyed.'

=====

MURFREESBOROUGH, N.C. Aug. 25

'You have no doubt heard something of the horrid conduct of the blacks in Southampton this week, and the deep interest that all must feel, and the very extravagant stories that have been circulated. I have been induced to think a brief statement of the case necessary to be made public.

'It is not known that any mischief has been done in North Carolina; and although strong suspicions are entertained that there existed an understanding among the blacks, yet no evidence has been found to confirm them.

'On Monday morning last, about 3 o'clock, the massacre commenced at Mr John Traver's—the exact order in which they proceeded is not stated, and probably not known. Unfortunately for us, it was at the time of our County Court, and the principal part of the citizens of this place was there, (at Winton,) about 12 miles off, so that it was late in the day before we were apprised of it generally. The few men who were in town immediately collected, and about 6 P.M. Capt. Camp, of the Governor's Guards, arrived, and instantly made the proper arrangements for the protection of the town.

'In the mean time, the Colonel was not idle, and so soon as a sufficient number was organized, a party, composed of horse and foot, say a company of each, was ordered to the scene of action, where they arrived on Tuesday evening. The massacre of the whites was over, and the white people had commenced the destruction of the negroes, which was continued after our men got there, from time to time as they could fall in with them, all day yesterday.

'We have heard nothing from them to-day. From the best information, nearly thirty negroes have been killed, and the jail at Jerusalem is full to overflowing. We suppose them entirely suppressed, if they are not all killed and taken. The great force in arms, from Virginia, rendered any further aid from us unnecessary. Our people describe the situation of the country there, in the most gloomy colors. The dead bodies of white and black lay just as they were slain, unburied. However, preparation for their interment was making. I annex a list of the dead whites, but it is supposed there are more dead, of whom no account has been received. I do not pretend to vouch for the correctness of their statement, but it is such as we have received.

Respectfully yours,

JOHN WHEELER'

List of white persons ascertained to be killed—Joseph Travers, wife and 3 children; Luther Francis; William Reese and mother; Mrs Eliza Turkner and 2 others; Henry Bryant, wife, child and mother; Mrs C. Whitehead, 3 daughters, 2 sons, and 1 grandson; Trajan Doyle; Mrs Williams and child, (wife of John Williams); Nat. Francis's 2 children and overseer; Thomas Barrow, (who bravely fought between 20 and 30 negroes till his wife escaped); Mrs Waller, 8 children, and a young lady; two daughters of Francis Felts; B. Jones's daughter; Mr and Mrs Williams and two others; Jacob C. Williams, wife and 3 children; Taswell Worrell's wife and child; Rebecca Vaughan, 2 sons and niece; James Story and wife. Total 59.

Passengers by the Fayetteville stage say that by the latest accounts 120 negroes had been killed.

Attack and Repulse

Any ordinary man would have been crushed by the Southern wrath and blame that was heaped on Garrison for the Nat Turner Rebellion. Instead of running for cover, Garrison kept the discussion hot by replying to the press attacks on him in such a righteous vein that people thought more than ever that his protestations of pacifism were some form of revolutionary duplicity. The national press and Southern legislatures exhausted every form of invective and threat upon him. The National Intelligencer *called* The Liberator *an "incendiary publication, a diabolical paper, intended by its author to lead to precisely such results as the Southampton Tragedy," called Garrison, "the instigator of human butchery . . . a deluded fanatic or mercenary miscreant, a cut throat," and said that to publish such a paper was "a crime as great as that of poisoning the waters of life to a whole community."*

Garrison rose above it, replied with the courage and effrontery of a maligned prophet, and boldly went on a speaking tour through New England to see how the public would receive him. His reception was very encouraging and he drew crowds much larger than before the insurrection. He then had the genius to use this excitement and curiosity aroused over his presence and personality to hold the first organizational meeting of the New England Anti-Slavery Society on January 1, 1832. This was the first organized group in the United States to press for the immediate emancipation of the slaves without compensation to the slave-owners.

October 22, 1831

RALEIGH, (N.C.) Oct. 13

A number of the 'Liberator,' a paper printed in Boston, came to the Post Office in this place last week, containing the most illiberal and cold-blooded allusions to the late supposed insurrection amongst our slaves. The paper found its way into the hands of the Attorney General, who submitted an indictment to the Grand Jury (who were then in session) against William Lloyd Garrison and Isaac Knapp, the editors and publishers of the paper, for its 'circulation and publication' in this county, in contravention to the act of the last General Assembly. The Grand Jury, we learn, found a 'True Bill.' So, we suppose, the accused will be demanded by the Governor of this State; but whether they will be surrendered or not by the Executive of Massachusetts, is a matter about which we are not prepared to hazard a conjecture. The act makes the offence Felony—whipping and imprisonment for the first offence, and death, without benefit of clergy, for the second.

October 29, 1831

INFORMATION WANTED. The Hon. Robert Y. Hayne, of Columbia, S. C., (through the medium of a letter,) wishes to know of the Mayor of Boston who sent a number of the Liberator to him, a few weeks ago? The Mayor of Boston (through the medium of a deputy) wishes to know of Mr Garrison whether he sent the aforesaid number to the aforesaid individual? Mr Garrison (through the medium of his paper) wishes to know of the Hon. Robert Y. Hayne, of Columbia, S. C. and the Mayor of Boston, what authority they have to put such questions?

A Bid for a Freeman of Massachusetts

Like most men undergoing political persecution, Garrison had to en-
dure much scorn and disbelief when he stated this or that threat against
his person coming from the South. In the pages of The Liberator *at the*
end of the year 1831, he mentions that the Legislature of Georgia has
put a price on his head. However, he did not print the actual document
until August, 1833, having copied his first version from a Southern paper.
The following selections show, first, the actual bill drawn against him
(printed in 1833) and, second, his response when he first heard of it in
December, 1831.

August 3, 1833

A BID FOR A FREEMAN OF MASSACHUSETTS

The copy of the following resolutions passed by the State of
Georgia, was sent to us . . . But as the act has never appeared
entire in the Liberator, and as many persons in this quarter of
the country are known to be sceptical as to its having an existence, and as others are known to suppose that it was merely
offered and rejected, or at worst was adopted by one branch only
of the Legislature of Georgia,—we have thought it proper to give
the piece a more conspicuous type and place . . .

IN SENATE, November 30, 1831
Resolved by the Senate and House of Representatives
of the State of Georgia, in General Assembly met, That
the sum of FIVE THOUSAND DOLLARS, be, and the
same is hereby appropriated, to be paid to any person or
persons who shall arrest, bring to trial and prosecute to
conviction under the laws of this State; the editor or publisher of a certain paper called the Liberator, published in
the town of Boston, and State of Massachusetts; or who
shall arrest, bring to trial and prosecute to conviction
under the laws of this State, any other person or persons,
who shall utter, publish or circulate within the limits of
this State, said paper called the Liberator, or any other
paper, circular, pamphlet, letter or address of a seditious
character. . . .

And resolved further, That his Excellency the Governor cause the foregoing resolutions, to be published in the public journals of this State, and such other papers as he may think proper, and pay for the publication thereof, out of the contingent fund.

Read and agreed to

THOMAS STOCKS, President . . .

In the House of Representatives

Concurred in, Dec. 24, 1831 . . .

Approved, Dec. 26, 1831

WILSON LUMPKIN, Governor

December 7, 1831

A BRIBE TO KIDNAPPERS!

. . . Scarcely has a proposition of so monstrous a nature ever been submitted to any public body in any country. Yet, we presume, so indifferent or servile are nineteen-twentieths of the newspapers that it will elicit scarcely a single editorial rebuke. Of one thing we are sure: all southern threats and rewards will be insufficient to deter us from pursuing the work of emancipation. As citizens of the United States, we know our rights and dare maintain them. We have committed no crime, but are expending our health, comfort and means for the salvation of our country, and for the interest and security of the infatuated slaveholders, as well as for the relief of the poor slaves. We are not the enemies of the south, because we tell her the truth.

We Are All Guilty

Garrison began the second year of The Liberator *with a high-spirited apostrophe to the revolutions breaking out all over the world, calling for them to be continuous until every government on earth "be elective and republican." He then raised a very troublesome constitutional question which he was to develop later with great power and intensity.*

January 7, 1832

THE LIBERATOR AND SLAVERY
Introductory Remarks

The past has been a year more than ordinarily eventful to this country and the world. Henceforth there is to be no peace on the earth—no cessation of revolutionary movements—no exhausted imbecility—until unjust rule be at an end; until personal thraldom be broken; until thrones be scattered in ashes to the winds; until hereditary titles and distinctions be effaced; until knowledge be diffused as freely as sun-light, and be as readily inhaled by all classes of the people as the vital atmosphere; until landed monopolies be distributed in equitable shares; until all labor be voluntary, receive its just remuneration, be protected in its own earnings, be a crown of honor and not a mark of servitude; until every government be elective and republican; until the right to worship God, according to the dictates of every man's conscience, be secured; until, in short, freedom of thought and speech and writing—freedom of choice—freedom of action—be not only the inalienable right but the positive exercise of every rational creature. The Spirit of Liberty is no longer young and feeble—it is no longer to make an abortive struggle, and then be passive for years: it is abroad with power—thundering at castle-gates and prison-doors: from revolutionizing neighborhoods, it is going on to revolutionize nations: instead of agitating a kingdom, as formerly, it is now shaking the world. When it once fairly gets the mastery over its enemy Oppression, will not its retaliation be terrible? Wo to those who dress in purple and fine linen, and fare sumptuously every day, having defrauded the laborer of his

hire and oppressed the poor! Wo to those who entrench themselves behind hereditary privileges and conduct, and declare that
for the crimes which they commit, their ancestors must be responsible! Wo to that policy or system which has no other
foundation than injustice, tyranny and wrong! which consults
expediency and not right! which expects to satisfy the hungry
with a crumb of knowledge—to content the benighted wanderer
with a few scattered rays of light—to comfort the naked with
half a blanket, or a whole suit of rags! which mocks the remonstrances of prudence, repels the suggestions of wisdom, forgets all
the lessons of history, discredits the uniform results of experience, defies the moral and physical power of its victims! Wo,
wo, for all that is oppressive—for all that lives by usurpation—
for those who hearken not to the voice of nature—for the persecutors of their fellow men, wherever they may be found! There
will be no discrimination with God or man, in favor of any class
of despots: they who tread, with iron heels, upon the necks of
their slaves in this country, will not be thought less blameworthy
than the tyrants of Europe. Despotism in a republic is as sure of
punishment, as in a monarchy.

Happy will it be for us, as a people, if, treasuring up these
truths in our memories, we check the retributive thunders of
justice 'in mid volley,' by a timely repentance. We are a nation
of blind, unrelenting, haughty, cruel, heaven-daring oppressors.
The chains which we rivet upon the bodies of two millions of our
fellow-countrymen, are as galling and heavy as were ever forged
for human limbs. Shall those chains be broken by physical or
moral power? Infatuated as we may be, we are conscious that,
at some period or other, in some way or other, our slaves must
be free. Gigantic as may be our strength, we are too intelligent
to believe that it will enable us always to oppress with impunity.
Secure as we may feel, we tremble for posterity—for our children, and our children's children. . . .

Guilt of New-England

. . . So long as we continue one body—a union—a nation—
the compact involves us in the guilt and danger of slavery. If the
slaves, goaded to desperation by their cruel masters, should rise
en masse to obtain redress, do the citizens of New-England reflect, that they are constitutionally bound to assist the southern

taskmasters in subduing or exterminating the blacks and are liable to be drafted at a moment's warning? Perhaps we imagine, that there is little danger of a general insurrection among the slaves—(the recent events at the south to the contrary, notwithstanding)—but does this circumstance remove the responsibility from our shoulders? No matter what is the *probability* in this case. The question is, whether we are not solemnly pledged to put down a black rebellion in the south? At the present moment, indeed, appearances seem to indicate a double rebellion in that section of the Union; a rebellion against the Government by the whites, and a rebellion against the whites by the blacks; so that the 'tug of war' may be nearer than the people of the free states imagine. What protects the south from instant destruction? OUR PHYSICAL FORCE. Break the chain which binds her to the Union, and the scenes of St. Domingo would be witnessed throughout her borders. She may affect to laugh at this prophecy; but she knows that her security lies in northern bayonets. Nay, she has repeatedly taunted the free states with being pledged to protect her: tyrannise long and cruelly as she may, they are bound to give her life, and, if necessary, to slaughter her slaves. How, then, do we make the inquiry, with affected astonishment, 'what have we to do with the guilt of slavery?' Is this a novel view of the subject? Must we now begin to inquire, for the first time, what are our duties and responsibilities as American citizens?

Perhaps we internally resolve never to march against the blacks—never to bear arms south of the Potomac. But such a decision would be full of treachery to the people of the south. Let us give them fair warning when we intend to leave them to their fate; and let us not practise studied cruelty and deceit. Hear the language of a Representative from Massachusetts [Mr. Dwight] in the Congressional session of 1827:

'In an internal commotion in Georgia, where should its white population seek a shelter? Not, certainly, in the little fort of Savannah. In such an event, [and he hoped the day was far distant,] they would not look to the forts erected for maritime defence, but to the *stout hearts* and *sympathetic feelings* of their *northern brethren;* and he did not hazard too much in saying, that in such a case the north will *pour out its blood like water* to assist the south!'

Are these indeed our sentiments? Can we cover ourselves with laurels in a war of oppression? What! ready to pour out our blood like water, in order that a large portion of our fellow countrymen may be kept in servile bondage!

It is awful to reflect, that it is solely by the authority of the free states that slavery is tolerated in our land. The south is only our agent. We form a powerful combination which cannot be resisted, and give her a broad license to kidnap, plunder and oppress; promising our united aid, in case she is in personal danger! Yet we complacently wipe our mouths, and say, 'We commit no evil—the south is the victim to be sacrificed.' This is certainly an improvement upon the Holy Alliance. We are guilty —all guilty—horribly guilty. . . .

Incendiary Slaveholders

A most unusual debate broke out in the Virginia legislature in January, 1832, on the slavery question, brought on by a resolution that

> the children of all female slaves, who may be born in this state, on or after the 4th day of July, 1840, shall become the property of the Commonwealth, the males at the age of twenty one years, and females at the age of eighteen, if detained by their owners within the limits of Virginia, until they shall respectively arrive at the ages aforesaid, to be hired out until the net sum arising therefrom, shall be sufficient to defray the expense of their removal, beyond the limits of the United States, and that said committee have leave to report by bill or otherwise.

It was also stated directly that the discussion came out of "the melancholy occurrences growing out of the tragical massacre in Southampton." Garrison treated the occasion with great glee and irony, publishing at length many of the speeches. William H. Broadnax, of the county of Dinwiddie, was Chairman of the Committee to examine the matter. He was for some form of liberation, as was a Mr. Moore, another delegate. As Garrison predicted, it came to nothing, but it was a near miss and a discussion of the peculiar institution in such realistic terms never took place again. The discussion was technically terminated by a resolution that it was "inexpedient, for the present, to make any legislative enactments for the abolition of slavery," but this tragic postponement was effected by a mere 7 votes, 65 being for postponement, 58 opposed.

January 14, 1832

INCENDIARY SLAVEHOLDERS!

It seems that some of the slaveholders are imitating the example of the 'incendiary' Liberator, and actually discoursing about the gradual emancipation of their slaves. Strange that they wish to disturb so *embarrassing* a question! Strange that they are so resolutely determined to create an *excitement!* Strange that they pursue a course of conduct so well calculated to make their slaves *uneasy!* Certainly they ought to be indicted forthwith, and a reward of five thousand dollars offered for each of their heads. Cruel, cruel men! seriously talking of breaking the fetters of their *happy* and *loving* slaves, and casting them

45

upon the cold charities of the world. What infatuation! This must never be: if this emancipation should take place, our throats would be cut, our houses pillaged and burnt, and the land given over to desolation! Indeed, the mischief that would result from such a step is inconceivable! Why then take it? The slaves don't wish to be free; they feel more contented and are far better off than the laboring classes of Great Britain and France; they will not leave their indulgent drivers and gentle masters unless driven away by force!

Irony aside. So excessive is the terror of the people of the south in view of the inevitable results of their oppression, that they begin to feel the necessity of checking the growth of the slave system. While we rejoice to see them in some measure brought to a sane state of mind, we are free to acknowledge that we cannot place the least reliance upon any measure they may propose for the mitigation of the evil. They will never voluntarily emancipate their slaves, unless at the same time they can drive them from the country. As for gradual abolition, it is a delusion which first blinds and then destroys. . . .

VIRGINIA LEGISLATURE

Extracts from the recent speech of Mr. Moore, in the House of Delegates of Virginia, on the subject of Slavery.

. . . A third consequence of slavery is, that it detracts from the ability of a country to defend itself against foreign aggression. Every slave occupies the place of a freeman, and if we regard them merely as neutrals, they impair the force of the State in full proportion to their numbers. But we cannot rationally regard them as neutrals, for the desire of freedom is so deeply implanted in the human breast, that no time or treatment can entirely eradicate it, and they will always be disposed to avail themselves of a favorable opportunity of asserting their natural rights. It will consequently be necessary to employ a certain proportion of the efficient force of the whites to keep them in subjection. What that proportion will be, I will not undertake exactly to determine; but it may be safely assumed, that, wherever the slaves are as numerous as the whites, it will require one half of the effective force of the whites to keep them quiet; and such is the fact as to the whole of Eastern Virginia. . . . I think it can hardly be contended, that I have estimated the force necessary for keeping the slaves in subjection too high, when it is recollected that they are intimately acquainted with all the secret passes, strong holds, and fastnesses of the country, and being restrained by no moral or patriotic considerations, will ever be ready to act as guides to an invading foe, and to flock to his standard whenever he may be disposed to attempt them to it, by holding out the strongest temptation which can ever be presented to the human mind—namely; the possession of liberty. . . .

I lay it down as a maxim not to be disputed, that our slaves, like all the rest of the human race, are now, and will ever continue to be, actuated by the desire of liberty—and it is equally certain, that whenever the proportion of slaves in this State, to our white population, shall have become so great as to inspire them with the hope of being able to throw off the yoke, that then an effort will be made by them to effect that object.—What the proportion between the slaves and the freeman must be which will embolden the former to make such an attempt, it is not material for me to inquire, for if it be admitted, that any disproportion however great, will have that effect, it is susceptible of the clearest demonstration, that it must be made within a period so short, that many of us may expect to witness it. And I need not go into an enquiry whether or not such an attempt can, at any time, or under any circumstances, be attended with success; for it is certain, that whenever it is made, it will be the beginning of a servile war; and from what we know of human nature generally, and from what we hear of the spirit manifested by both parties in the late Southampton rebellion, it is very evident that such a war must be one of extermination, happen when it will. . . .

=====

February 4, 1832

[From the Richmond (Va.) Enquirer]

Our oldest readers will do us justice to say, that we had forborne to touch the subject of colored population, for 27 years. We felt that none is more delicate and none more beset with difficulties. But at length the outbreaking in Southampton

spread horror throughout the Commonwealth. We saw the flood-
gates of discussion for the first time raised, in consequence of
this unparalleled event.—We saw meetings of the citizens held.
Memorials were addressed to the Legislature.—The Press, too,
broke the silence of fifty years. And we have seen the whole
subject referred to a committee of the House of Delegates for
their best consideration. And what is *more remarkable* in the
History of our Legislature, we now see the whole subject ripped
up and discussed with open doors, and in the presence of a
crowded gallery and lobby—Even the press itself hesitating to
publish the Debates of the body. All these things were indeed
new in our history. And nothing else could have prompted
them, but the bloody massacre in the month of August.

═══

The large slaveholder will at last be left alone to combat for
slavery, against united Virginia. The small slaveholder, the
yeomanry, the mechanic, the merchant, the youth of the country,
will ultimately combine to remove it. These classes will not
consent to live in perpetual jeopardy—they will not consent that
their wives and children shall live exposed to a fate too terrible
for description. Are not thousands of the poorer and middling
classes year after year removing off? And would this be the
case if they could live at home—if slaves did not eat the bread
which otherwise they would earn . . . ? Are not the small free-
holders, the yeomanry, in whose patriotism and strong arm every
country finds its safety, daily diminishing from this cause, and
is not lower Virginia, like Jamaica, becoming a country of large
plantations, peopled with slaves?—*Ibid.* [Richmond *Whig*—T.N.]

═══

Slavery in Virginia.—The debates in the House of Delegates
of Virginia upon this subject, have been terminated by the
adoption of a preamble and resolution reported by the select
committee, to whom the memorials had been referred, with amend-
ments. The resolution as finally adopted, declares that it is inexpedient to make any legislative enactments at present, for the
abolition of Slavery; but the preamble assigns the reason for
this declaration, by stating, that the removal of the free people
of color, and of those who may become free, will absorb all the

present means of the State; and that a further action for the removal of the Slaves should await a more definite developement of public opinion. Some of the warmest friends of abolition voted in favor of the acceptance of the report.

The following remarks were made by Mr. Broadnax, in a late debate in the Legislature of Virginia:

'He knew, that in this vicinity there existed feelings which placed him in a most delicate situation—feelings of doubt, and a want of decision as to what ought to be done. The confidence of the people was gone; and when that was lost, something must be done. *When men were found to lock their doors at night, and open them in the morning to receive their servants to light their fires, with pistols in their hands, surely some measures to restore confidence and security were necessary.* Under such circumstances, life became a burthen; and it were better to seek a home in some distant realm, and leave the graves of their fathers, than endure so precarious a condition. . . . Let me ask, said Mr. B., is there one man in Virginia, who does not lament that there ever was a slave in the State? . . .

The Virginia Hotspur

After this episode, the slavery argument reverted to the familiar pattern of mutual denunciations between the Abolitionists and the slaveholders. Garrison received tons of these letters of abuse and threat and often replied to them with a gusto and power that revealed the enormous enjoyment he got from receiving them.

March 31, 1832

To Wm. Lloyd Garrison:

There has been accidentally thrown in my way a paper headed *'The Liberator.'* The beautiful cuts with which it is decorated, attracted my attention, and induced me to peruse its contents. Your paper, Sir, is a lame and impotent production, designed obviously for the most base and infamous purpose; and can have no other ultimate effect than to render the negroes dissatisfied with their condition, and thereby make it necessary to hold them in stricter subjection. . . .

There is another small matter between us, Master Garrison. You don't seem to like the law of your State, which prohibits the unholy alliance between white and black. Suppose you were to take a fancy to a brute; would you not make the same objections to the law against Sodomy? Answer me *that*, Master Garrison. The white man or woman who would consent to marry a negro, deserves to be hung with a knotty grape vine, without benefit of Clergy. *'Fleas* are not *Lobsters*—d—m their souls.' Negroes and white men are essentially distinct in their nature. It is a most *odious* and *odorous* comparison. The dark complexion, peculiar features, woolly hair and small skulls of the negroes, are not their only characteristics. Their blood is not of the temperature of ours by two degrees; and their mental capacities are an hundred degrees below that of their white 'brethren,' as you are pleased to call us. It is idle to take the intelligence of a few individuals, as a criterion by which to judge of their intellect as a people. Such instances only serve to unite these two links in the chain of creation, which extends from the honorable, free-born, high-born, high-bred Virginian, down to the meanest reptile in existence, such as your ignoble self. The progeny of a Yankee and Negro would indeed be a nondescript in natural history; uniting the selfishness, duplicity, canting hypocrisy and vicious propensities of the one, to the recklessness, obstinacy and folly of the other: in short, just such a monster as yourself. Publish this without mutilation or alteration. I dare you. Answer me without equivocation or evasion. I defy you. And if your infamous and villanous paper should ever again pollute my sight, *I'll* publish you from Dan to Beersheba, until you cry 'hold, enough.' HOTSPUR

. . . The logic of this writer dishonors his understanding: but a man-stealer may as well attempt to fly, as to reason coherently on the subject of slavery. . . .

I have never expressed any opinion of the propriety or impropriety of intermarriage with persons of color. I neither advocate nor oppose an honorable amalgamation. It is not my province, nor that of any body of men, to regulate human affection or prescribe objects of attachment. I call for the repeal of the marriage law of this State, because it not only discredits the good sense of the Commonwealth, but is a direct invasion of an inalienable right, and one of the links of that chain which binds millions of our race in servitude. But the impudence of the Virginia 'hotspur' is exceeded only by his indecency. *He* scouts a *lawful* connexion between whites and blacks, who is doubtless holding an illicit and constant commerce with his female slaves! Ay, even the 'honorable, free-born, high-bred Virginian' is nightly mingling his *pure* blood with other blood, between the temperature of which are 'two degrees'! and he often contrives to live by selling a certain number of his own children annually!! I might tell some tales, with regard to this intercourse, even of the first men in Virginia; but their recital would be too disgusting for the public eye.

A Bold Advocate of Slavery

Since the Virginia legislature decided abolition was "inexpedient," the only alternative was the immediate suppression of any further talk about it; the free blacks must be driven off and the revolutionary impulse among the slaves stamped out with a finality which would permit no future Nat Turners. Garrison published a letter from Benjamin Watkins Leigh, signed "Appomattox," one of the ablest politicians in Virginia. This letter helped establish the system of suppression that worked until the John Brown Raid in 1859.

April 7, 1832

TO THE PEOPLE OF VIRGINIA

[From the Richmond (Va.) Enquirer]

. . . I do say if . . . such an insurrection shall break out, it will be owing, not to the hallucinations or imposture of another Nat Turner, nor to the seditious practices of negro preachers, nor to the machinations of the organized convention of free blacks in Philadelphia, nor to the dissemination of the incendiary writings of The Liberator, or the African Sentinel, or the Genius of Universal Emancipation—but to measures proposed, and to speeches delivered, in our own Legislature, published and disseminated by our own public journals. . . .

. . . I am convinced that no plan for the abolition of slavery, and the deportation of the slaves, is possible. . . . It might be possible to remove and colonize the whites; the adoption of any of these schemes for abolition, may, in effect, expel us from our country: but it is morally, politically, physically, impossible to remove and colonize the black population en masse. *Necessity,* it has been argued, imperiously dictates abolition and deportation. On the contrary, we lie under an *invincible necessity* to keep them here, and hold them in subjection; a necessity imposed upon us by Providence. . . .

Now, I too think, *something must be done;* and I shall give my fellow-citizens, without reserve, my deliberate opinion what it behooves them to do.

1. I earnestly recommend them to provide (quietly and silently,

but, at the same time, promptly and sufficiently) arms and ammunition for the defence of themselves, and their families and neighbors; to concert their plans of action among themselves, in anticipation of any insurrectionary spirit that may manifest itself among the slaves; to hold themselves in constant readiness to meet and suppress servile rebellion, at a minute's warning; to arrange voluntary bodies of minute men, in short, appointing convenient places of rendezvous for them; meantime, to maintain the strictest discipline; to stifle the slightest breath of sedition, to exercise the closest vigilance, to infuse the utmost activity, the highest order and prudence into their ordinary police, of which it is susceptible. Let no man shun the patrole duty. Let there be no inhumanity towards the blacks, whatever cause of excitement may arise—for our own credit, none—but no neglect, no imprudent indulgence. If we exercise due caution, no want of discretion in others will endanger our peace; if we neglect or remit a proper care for ourselves, we need not *now* expect that others will exercise any care for us, and our wives and children must bear the consequences of our supineness and folly.

. . . Let us pay no regard to the claim which may be asserted for the independence, of the press: if, in the exercise of their independence, they choose to print, we, in the exercise of our independence, may choose to suppress, to the utmost of our power, what we deem inflammatory, dangerous, mischievous. Every man has a perfect right to withdraw his subscription from any newspaper, and to discourage the circulation of it; and if he thinks the opinions it maintains likely to produce evil, he is bound in duty to his country, to exercise that right. . . . The claim to such independence of the press, as not only gives it freedom to publish, but a right to free unrestrained circulation among those whom the circulation may injure, is, in truth, a claim to absolute dominion; which I shall never acknowledge in any man or set of men whatever. I want no sedition laws—I would have none—there is a check, a sufficient check, in the influence of public opinion, if timely, promptly and vigorously exerted; and, in my deliberate judgment, prudence, justice, necessity, require the people of the whole slaveholding country to unite in the exercise of that check, upon the present occasion. . . .

APPOMATTOX

Woman and the Cause

Garrison's insistence that women become full partners in the crusade added the element of sex to The Liberator. *There were many descriptions in it describing the sexual molesting of black women by white men, which must have made unusual reading in that day. His feminist position made him many powerful enemies who claimed that he intended to undermine society by throwing white women into sexual contact with Negro men and that he was a libertine at heart. However, these accusations never deterred him in any way.*

July 14, 1832

FEMALE ANTI-SLAVERY SOCIETY

Two capital errors have extensively prevailed, greatly to the detriment of the cause of abolition. The first is, a proneness on the part of the advocates of immediate and universal emancipation to overlook or depreciate the influence of women in the promotion of this cause; and the other is, a similar disposition on the part of the females in our land to undervalue their own power, or through a misconception of duty, to excuse themselves from engaging in the enterprise. These errors, we repeat, are capital, and should no longer be suffered to prevail. The cause of bleeding humanity is always, legitimately, the cause of WOMAN. Without her powerful assistance, its progress must be slow, difficult, imperfect.

A million females in this country, are recognized and held as property—liable to be sold or used for the gratification of the lust or avarice or convenience of unprincipled speculators— without the least protection for their chastity—cruelly scourged for the most trifling offences—and subjected to unseemly and merciless tasks, to severe privations, and to brutish ignorance! Have these no claims upon the sympathies—prayers—charities —exertions of our white countrywomen? . . .

The Great Crisis

Many people in the North were disturbed about the national purse and sword being used to put down Nat Turner's Insurrection. They were opposed to slavery, "in the abstract," and the national commitment placed them directly in support of it. The Southern politicians reminded them that the Constitution was a "sacred" compact and Southern property had to be protected under it. Garrison here continues his earlier argument by a strong attack on the Constitution and lays out one of his most important lines of assault.

December 29, 1832

THE GREAT CRISIS!

. . . There is much declamation about the sacredness of the compact which was formed between the free and slave states, on the adoption of the Constitution. A sacred compact, forsooth! We pronounce it the most bloody and heaven-daring arrangement ever made by men for the continuance and protection of a system of the most atrocious villany ever exhibited on earth. Yes —we recognize the compact, but with feelings of shame and indignation; and it will be held in everlasting infamy by the friends of justice and humanity throughout the world. It was a compact formed at the sacrifice of the bodies and souls of millions of our race, for the sake of achieving a political object— an unblushing and monstrous coalition to do evil that good might come. Such a compact was, in the nature of things and according to the law of God, null and void from the beginning. No body of men ever had the right to guarantee the holding of human beings in bondage. Who or what were the framers of our government, that they should dare confirm and authorise such high-handed villany—such a flagrant robbery of the inalienable rights of man—such a glaring violation of all the precepts and injunctions of the gospel—such a savage war upon a sixth part of our whole population?—They were men like ourselves—as fallible, as sinful, as weak, as ourselves. By the infamous bargain which they made between themselves, they virtually dethroned the Most High God, and trampled beneath their feet their own solemn and heaven-attested Declaration, that all men are created equal, and endowed by their Creator with certain inalienable rights—among which are life, liberty, and the pursuit of happiness. They had no lawful power to bind themselves, or their posterity, for one hour—for one moment—by such an unholy alliance. It was not valid then—it is not valid now. Still they persisted in maintaining it. A sacred compact! a sacred compact! What, then, is wicked and ignominious?

This, then, is the relation in which we of New-England stand to the holders of the slaves at the south, and this is virtually our language toward them—'Go on, most worthy associates, from day to day, from month to month, from year to year, from generation to generation, plundering two millions of human beings of their liberty and the fruits of their toil . . . we do not wish nor mean to interfere, for the rescue of your victims, even by expostulation or warning—we like your company too well to offend you by denouncing your conduct—'although we know that by every principle of law which does not utterly disgrace us by assimilating us to pirates, that they have as good and as true a right to the equal protection of the law as we have; and although we ourselves stand prepared to die, rather than submit even to a fragment of the intolerable load of oppression to which we are subjecting them—yet, never mind—let that be—they have grown old in suffering and we iniquity—and we have nothing to do now but to speak *peace, peace,* to one another in our sins. . . . Go on, from bad to worse—add link to link to the chains upon the bodies of your victims—add constantly to the intolerable burdens under which they groan—and if, goaded to desperation by your cruelties, they should rise to assert their rights and redress their wrongs, fear nothing—we are pledged, by a sacred compact, to shoot them like dogs and rescue you from their vengeance. . . . We pledge you our physical strength, by the sacredness of the national compact—a compact by which we have enabled you already to plunder, persecute and destroy two millions of slaves, who now lie beneath the sod; and by which we now give you the same piratical license to prey upon a much larger number of victims and all their posterity. Go on —and by this sacred instrument, the Constitution of the United

States, *dripping as it is with human blood,* we solemnly pledge you our lives, our fortunes, and our sacred honor, that we will stand by you to the last.'

People of New-England, and of the free States! is it true that slavery is no concern of yours? Have you no right even to protest against it, or to seek its removal? Are you not the main pillars of its support? How long do you mean to be answerable to God and the world, for spilling the blood of the poor innocents? Be not afraid to look the monster SLAVERY boldly in the face. He is your implacable foe—the vampyre who is sucking your life-blood—the ravager of a large portion of your country, and the enemy of God and man. Never hope to be a united, or happy, or prosperous people while he exists. He has an appetite like the grave—a spirit as malignant as that of the bottomless pit—and an influence as dreadful as the corruption of death. Awake to your danger! the struggle is a mighty one—it cannot be avoided—it should not be, if it could.

It is said if you agitate this question, you will divide the Union. Believe it not; but should disunion follow, the fault will not be yours. You must perform your duty, faithfully, fearlessly and promptly, and leave the consequences to God: that duty clearly is, to cease from giving countenance and protection to southern kidnappers. Let them separate, if they can muster courage enough—and the liberation of their slaves is certain. Be assured that slavery will very speedily destroy this Union *if it be let alone;* but even if the Union can be preserved by treading upon the necks, spilling the blood, and destroying the souls of millions of your race, we say it is not worth a price like this, and that it is in the highest degree criminal for you to continue the present compact. Let the pillars thereof fall—let the superstructure crumble into dust—if it must be upheld by robbery and oppression.

In Praise of Gradualism

The American Colonization Society was a gradualist emancipatory organization which proposed to purchase slaves and ship them, along with free Negroes, back to Africa.

The Liberator, *January 14, 1832, reprinted the following brief history of the Society from the* New-England Magazine:

> The American Colonization Society was founded in 1816, by the Rev. Robert Finley, of New-Jersey, and its first meeting was held in Washington. No active measures resulted from its organization till, in the year 1818, two clergymen sailed to Africa in quest of information on which the future operations of the board might be based. In 1820, the society's agent and two agents for the government of the United States followed them, with eighty more emigrants. The first location of the colony was so ill chosen that twenty-seven of this party, including the three agents, fell victims to the climate within a few weeks of their arrival. However, the friends of the society were not discouraged, and another exportation of free blacks took place the following year. The climate proving absolutely incompatible with human life, the settlers were removed to Sierra Leone, where they remained for a short time by the suffrance of the British colonial authorities. Here the same mortality prevailed. Two of the new agents perished among the others. After much difficulty, the natives were persuaded to cede a tract of land about and including Cape Montserado, which became the permanent site of the colony, and received the name of Liberia. The emigrants had here to contend with the enmity of the natives, who attacked them repeatedly, and had well nigh extirpated them in 1822. Since that time, about a hundred emigrants have been sent to Liberia annually.

After the Turner revolt the Society noticeably increased its agents and activities. This activity, Garrison thought, would create prejudice in the North against the free Negro, so that if the slave won his freedom by some local or general revolutionary action, he would be so unwanted in the North that he would have no alternative but to eliminate the entire master class in the region where the revolt took place—the tactic Nat Turner had attempted. The white South, playing cleverly on the North's utter horror of supporting paupers in their villages, saw to it that there was a general and legal degradation and dehumanization of the Negro. The Colonization Society spread this doctrine and the managers of the Colonization Society of Connecticut said, in 1828: "In every part of the United States there is a broad and impassable line of demarkation between every man who has ONE DROP *of African blood in his veins, and every other class in the community. . . . The African in this country belongs by birth to the very lowest station in society, and from that station he can never rise, be his talents, his enterprise, his* VIRTUES *what they may . . . they are, and in this country, always must be a depressed and abject race"* (Lib., *May 4, 1833).*

Garrison came into head-on collision with this and took great pains to point out that the process of gradualism only deepened the planned degradation of the black man, free and slave. He allowed Joshua Danforth, the Society's leading agent, to express the gradualist view in his own words. Danforth, in a meeting in Salem, Massachusetts, once pointed his finger at Garrison and said he had been offered several thousand dollars to kidnap him and take him South. The Garrisonians interpreted this as an attempt to spur some adventurer to claim this reward.

May 4, 1833

JOSHUA N. DANFORTH'S LETTER
TO COL. STONE

BOSTON, March 28, 1833

To WILLIAM L. STONE, Esq.
Chairman of the Executive Committee of the
  New-York City Colonization Society

. . . Reformation has in no instance been accomplished by an instantaneous stroke. It is not the way of Providence. It cannot, therefore, be the way by which human means are to operate. No sudden irruption of human benevolence can achieve these moral triumphs. Not redemption itself burst upon the world in this manner. The deliverence was *gradual.* I should rather say it *is* gradual, for the work is still going on, and the world is now *looking forward* to grander results.

In perfect harmony, as I conceive, with providential arrangements and achievements like these, is the scheme of the AFRICAN COLONIZATION, which owes its conception and prosecution to the existence of a mighty evil in the bosom of our own country. The reasons for action in some form were numerous and urgent. The safety of the whites—the ignorance and degradation of the free blacks—the comfort of the slaves—State policy—considerations of patriotism—the peace of the country—the prospects of the African race generally—the horrors of the slave trade—the uncancelled obligations of the Christian community—all urged the formation of *some* plan, which should at least open a view through the vista of hope, if it did not conduct us into it. At this juncture, the *American Colonization Society* was formed, very properly, at the central city of the Republic. . . .

In the midst of all these successful endeavors, there appears a young man within the last two years, of the name of Garrison, whose pen is so venomous, that the laws enacted for the peace of the community and the protection of private character, have in one instance actually confined him in jail, as they would a Lunatic. This man, who according to his own account has only since 1830 turned against the Colonization cause, in favor of which he delivered his sentiments in public twelve years after the Society was formed; this man, who is considered such a disturber of the tranquillity of Southern Society, that $10,000 reward have been offered me for his person, and the most touching appeals as well as official demands made to us in this region, that he should be publicly discountenanced, and even given up to justice; who is in fact this moment in danger of being surrendered to the civil authorities of some one of the Southern States; this man, in connection with a few like-minded spirits, has been engaged in forming what they call 'The New-England Anti-Slavery Society,' one object of which is, 'to effect the abolition of slavery in the United States.' If you have ever seen the incendiary publication, the Liberator, you may form some idea of the nature of the harangues of the agents of this Society, which are very severe against the South, and the Colonization Society. . . . I have taken special pains to ascertain public sentiment at the South regarding our Society.

All the friends and advocates of emancipation there, regard it as the only hope of the south, and they say, if we will let them alone, they will try to work their way out of the slave system. 'Nothing is more dreaded,' says a Virginian, in a letter to me, 'by the great mass of persons opposed on principle to slavery in this region, than such inflammatory publications, (alluding to Garrison's,) *as they throw increased obstacles in the way of emancipation,* and if they could have all the influence that seems to be aimed at, they would bring on a struggle that must result in the extermination of the blacks.' . . .

. . . The people of the South must, however, know that they do not speak the voice of New-England. If they did, we must soon look for a separation of the States. I have conversed freely with the Governor of this Commonwealth, and other leading men, on this subject, and they express a decided disapprobation of Garrison's course. For a while he tried the effect of his Liberator upon the Governor by sending it to him. His Excellency, however, did not think it worth the postage and ordered it stopped. Garrison is now preparing to go to England, doubtless to repeat *viva voce* the defamation of the South and the Colonization Society, which has been already sent over in print, and re-echoed in this country as authentic British opinions.

I have already adverted to the Colonization system, as wisely designed by Providence, gradually, like all great remedies, to meet with a calm and subduing energy, the great evil which affects our country. How is it thus adapted? 1. By engaging the South itself in the work of renovation. Look at those States which warmly advocate the system—for example, Virginia, Maryland and Kentucky. The first two have acted officially in the premises. The latter is coming on, and her voice will soon be heard. 2. By inviting and urging thought, discussion, plans, contributions for the benefit of the colored people. All this is done openly, but constitutionally, with kindness to slave owners, but with a steady adherence to the great principles of universal liberty. Vested rights are not boldly invaded, while the standard of moral duty is raised high to the view of those most deeply concerned. 3. The creation of a new republic in Africa out of the ruins of the colored race in this country, free, elevated and independent, enacting their own laws, and administering justice among themselves, will constitute a more substantial argument and motive for their universal emancipation, than volumes of wild declamation against slavery, and of fierce denunciation of slaveholders, unaccompanied by a single practical movement for the benefit of whites or blacks. 4. The removal of the free colored population from the presence of the slaves, to an enlightened and industrious community, removes from the latter the sources of temptation to idleness, insubordination and insurrection, saves them the distress of a more rigorous bondage, consequent on rebellion, and furnishes the former with employment and a means of elevation.

5. The Colonization Society appeals to the will of the masters, instead of appealing to the passions of the slave, and seeks to turn it to the policy of universal emancipation. 6. It invites the co-operation of the friends of freedom throughout the Union, and throughout Europe. It has agents in the Northern States and in England. This looks little like stifling the voice of Liberty. 7. It has adopted vigorous measures against the foreign slave trade, the success of which must lead to the extinction of the domestic slave trade. 8. It has already enlisted many influential individuals in the southern and Western States; who are on principle opposed to slavery, but who, in common with others, are as yet restrained by State legislation from emancipating their slaves, except on condition of removal. 9. It takes away from those who are disposed to emancipate their slaves the necessity of retaining them, when the slaves are willing to emigrate to Africa. 10. By its undeviating regard to the Constitution of the Union, and the laws of the States, it secures a confidence which has been strengthened with every revolving year, and will ultimately be of immense benefit to its policy, while a more abrupt and violent mode of operation would quickly extinguish every hope of relieving the slave population. 11. By aiming at a united action of all the States—giving the South and West the lead, it avoids sectional jealousies, and preserves fraternal feeling throughout the Union. The exclusive separate action of a portion of the States would be difficult and dangerous. Hence those Northern enthusiasts, who are now essaying to take the work in their own hands, find, according to their own confession, a tremendous force of public opinion against them. This they expect to overcome, and ride upon the storm of Northern indignation, as it sweeps over the prostrate slaveholders of the South. 12. By engaging the prayers of all Christians for our deliverance from slavery, for the triumph of liberty, and of that Christianity, which 'proclaims liberty to the captive and the opening of the prison to them that are bound,' it has put a moral lever under the foundations of this execrable system, which at no distant time must effect its overthrow.

. . . To pull down is easy. The Ephesian incendiary with a single torch laid the beautiful temple in ruins. A knave may wrap a whole city in a conflagration. But can he rebuild it, or repair the loss? Fortunately for our society, the materials of which it is composed, are such that the hottest fire proves to be like the 'gold seven times purified.'

I am, very truly,

Your obedient servant,

J. N. DANFORTH

Gen. Agent Am. Col. Society

The Prudence Crandall Case

The more the property-owning class in the North thought of the South, slavery, and Nat Turner, the more they realized that the South was actually "containing" the horrors of the institution for them, keeping the "shiftless, ignorant, pauperized" Negro from the North's homogenous villages.

The most effective exposé of the basic inhumanity of the Colonizationists came with Garrison's manipulation of the Prudence Crandall case. She was a young graduate of the Friends' Boarding School of Providence, Rhode Island, who opened a school for young ladies in Canterbury, Connecticut, in 1831. In January, 1833, she wrote to Garrison saying that she had been given The Liberator *to read by a Negro hired girl and now wanted to devote her life to "benefit people of color." She wanted his opinion, and if favorable, his aid in enlisting twenty or thirty Negro girls to attend her school. Garrison warmly encouraged her, after they had met and talked, and placed a notice in* The Liberator.

Her town of Canterbury was thrown into a frenzy of opposition, led by Andrew T. Judson, whose new house was located across the street from the Negro school. He was then, or was shortly to become, a leading Colonizationist. Town meetings were held to suppress the school and Garrison's followers rallied to help Miss Crandall.

George W. Benson, the writer of the letter following, was Garrison's brother-in-law and close associate for many years.

March 9, 1833

INFAMOUS CONDUCT

One of the most disgraceful exhibitions of human pride and prejudice, on record, is given in the following letter from as devoted a friend to the cause of emancipation as lives in our land. We trust Miss Crandall will be sustained triumphantly in her excellent purposes, and that the inhabitants of Canterbury will not utterly disgrace themselves by any fresh acts of outrage and persecution. We cannot enlarge on this subject, to-day. If neither self-respect, nor the claims of honor, will deter them from assailing a worthy and heroic lady, we shall see what virtue there is in the press to bring them to their senses. . . .

PROVIDENCE, 3d mo. 5th, 1833

DEAR FRIEND—My heart had been cheered by the delightful intelligence that a high school for young colored misses was to be established in Canterbury, (Ct.) some weeks previous to the official notice published in the Liberator of the 2d inst. On the morning of that day, I was informed by a friend, that much excitement prevailed on that subject in the above mentioned town; that two or three meetings of the inhabitants had been called; that the unholy prejudices of the people were aroused to such a degree that they were fully determined, if possible, to prevent the school from going into operation. The great importance of the object induced me to leave this city for that place immediately, where I arrived at an early hour the following morning, and received a cordial welcome from the *persecuted,* but truly benevolent young lady, who has so nobly espoused the cause of suffering humanity. I found her calm and undaunted, amid the unmanly threatenings of those who should have befriended her. She informed me, that immediately after her intention transpired, several gentlemen convened in the neighborhood, and chose a committee to wait upon her, one of whom, a great advocate of the temperance cause, told her that by putting her design into execution, she would bring disgrace and ruin upon them all. She requested to know their objections, and was answered by a noted physician of that place, that if she received her expected scholars, the blacks of that town (10 or 15 in number) would begin to look up, and claim an equality with those who came to her school; and her scholars would claim an equality with the whites; and if they were all placed upon an equal footing, PROPERTY AND LIFE would be no longer safe! It was farther stated that the value of property would be greatly depreciated. The committee professed to feel a real regard for the colored people, and were perfectly willing they should be educated, provided it could be effected *in some other place!*—a sentiment, you will say, worthy of a true colonizationist.

Just before the morning meeting for worship commenced, I observed a gentleman who I knew filled the offices of County Attorney, Justice of the Peace, and also one of the Selectmen of the town, proceed to the sign-post, (situated nearly opposite the meeting-house) and affix a written communication, proclaiming that a town meeting was legally warned to be convened on Saturday next, to adopt measures for preventing the establishment of such an institution, shewing, by such an act, on the first day of the week, that the far famed Blue Laws of that State had become *obsolete,* or at least that the *prevention* of Miss Crandall's school was to be considered an *act* of *mercy,* a *labor* of *love,* which might lawfully be performed on the Sabbath. From thence I proceeded to Brooklyn, and the next morning returned to Canterbury, accompanied by one of the Vice Presidents of the New-England Anti-Slavery Society, and after some consultation, we thought it advisable that he should attend the town meeting next Saturday, and give an exposition of our views relative to the measures we proposed to adopt for the melioration of the condition of the colored population, and offer, in behalf of the friends of abolition, to give bonds to any amount to secure the town from the introduction of paupers; as some of the legal opponents of this measure have so far distorted an old law which was made to prevent any foreigners from being chargeable to the town, as to claim the power to warn and carry out of the place, all who may come from another State; and if this offer should not avail with them, then, to say on our behalf, that if they persist in enforcing such a legal process against the pupils of this school, we shall try the *constitutionality* thereof in the *Supreme Court of the United States.* And I trust that all the true friends to this cause will feel and see the necessity of taking effective measures to establish and support this school, in despite of all the opposition which may be raised by the ignorant but violent prejudices of the people, relying upon the constitution of our NOMINALLY free country, and firmly believing that our colored brethren are entitled to all the privileges that we ourselves enjoy. Let us resolve as one man, by the assistance of the Almighty, that we will not cease from our labors until we effect this blessed consummation.

Yours, &c.

GEORGE W. BENSON

Garrison persisted in recording this remarkable demonstration of the hostility of the North to the advancement of the Negro through education. Miss Crandall became frightened and entreated him to handle the prejudices of her neighbors with "all the mildness possible," advice Garrison never heeded in his life. Miss Crandall was tried and imprisoned briefly, her friends were forbidden to see her under penalty of a fine, shops would not sell her provisions, public transportation would not carry her or her pupils, her house was smeared with excrement, pelted with rotten eggs and stones almost nightly, and finally set on fire. Garrison never let up in his excoriation of the town fathers of Canterbury and they finally indicted him for libel.

May 18, 1833

More Barbarism

Georgia men-stealers have never been guilty of a more flagrant and heaven-daring transgression of the laws of humanity than is disclosed in the following document. Andrew T. Judson and his malignant associates bid fair to eclipse the infamy of Nero and Benedict Arnold!! . . .

The IMPERIAL ORDER of the Persecutors of Miss Eliza Ann Hammond, a pupil of Miss Prudence Crandall, aged 17 years . . . is here given for the inspection of all good citizens.

To the Sheriff of the County of Windham, his Deputy, or either of the Constables of the Town of Canterbury, within said County,

GREETING:—

. . . 'The Select Men of any town shall be . . . authorized . . . to warn any person not an inhabitant of this State, to depart such town, and the person so warned, shall forfeit and pay to the Treasurer of such town one dollar and sixty-seven cents per week, for every week he or she shall continue in such town, after warning given as aforesaid, and when such person who shall be convicted of the breach of this act, in refusing to depart on warning as aforesaid, hath no estate to satisfy the fine, such person *shall be whipped on the naked body not exceeding ten stripes,* unless he or she depart the town within ten days next after sentence is given and reside no more therein without leave of the Select Men' . . . the Select Men of said Canterbury did warn the said Eliza Ann Hammond, to depart the town of Canterbury . . . she the said Eliza Ann, against the provisions of said

statute did continue in said town of Canterbury . . . the said
Eliza Ann Hammond hath forfeited and become liable to pay
. . . the defendent hath never paid the same though often requested and demanded, and now to recover the said sum of $1.67
and the cost of suit, this action is brought. . . .

Signed, RUFUS ADAMS, Justice of the Peace

A writ has been served upon Miss Crandall for receiving Miss
Hammond as her pupil. . . . Shame to the Persecutors! Burning shame to the *gallant and noble Inflictors of stripes upon innocent and studious Females!* . . .

September 21, 1833

O! SHAME! SHAME!!

☞ The following paragraph is extracted from the Unionist
of last week:

> 'The laudable efforts of the Canterbury worthies to
> drive Miss Crandall from her purpose, by withholding
> from her the necessaries of life, will have the effect to
> perpetuate their own well earned fame, if not to attain
> its primary object. The latest measure which we have
> heard of their adopting, is the FILLING MISS C'S
> WELL WITH MANURE FROM THE BARNYARD,
> *and then refusing to give her water from their own
> wells.*'

November 2, 1833

ACKNOWLEDGMENT. Just before midnight, on Sabbath evening
last, in Brooklyn, Connecticut, the Deputy Sheriff of Windham
County, in behalf of those zealous patrons of colored schools,
those plain, independent republicans, those high-minded patriots,
those practical christians,

ANDREW T. JUDSON,
RUFUS ADAMS,
SOLOMON PAINE,
CAPT. RICHARD FENNER,
DOCTOR HARRIS,

presented me with five indictments for a panegyric upon their
virtuous and magnanimous actions, in relation to Miss Cran-

dall's *nigger school* in Canterbury, inserted in the Liberator of March 16, 1833. I shall readily comply with their polite and urgent invitation to appear at the Windham County Court on the second Tuesday of December, to show cause why, &c. &c. As they have generously given me *precept upon precept,* I shall give them in return *line upon line—here;* (in the Liberator,) a little, and *there,* (in the court room,) a great deal.

The Recreant American

*Early in May, 1833, Garrison was sent to England to raise money for a
School for Negro Boys and to head off the efforts of a Colonization agent
there to present his society to the English as the only solution to the race
problem in the United States. Garrison sailed after several hairbreadth
escapes from the arms of the law. ("After he left Brooklyn, Monday
noon, a sheriff came up from Canterbury with a writ . . . believe they
are going to take him for the heading put on the letter of March 12 . . .
on the ground it is libelous"—letter from Henry Benson to Isaac Knapp.)
He boarded the ship in New York two hours before the arrival there of
the injured gentlemen of Canterbury in hot pursuit.*

*In England, he attacked the peculiar institution and the hypocrisy of
his native land with a ferocity still unsurpassed. When he returned on
October 1, the newspapers of New York published inflammatory notices
of the coincidence of his arrival and a meeting to form a New York
Anti-Slavery Society. A huge mob stormed the building in which this
meeting was to be held, screaming for Garrison's blood. He was standing
there among them, unrecognized. The founders of the new society left by
the back door of the hall announced for their meeting, just as the mob
entered the front, and carried out their business successfully at another
place.*

*Garrison returned openly to Boston to face a similar paroxysm of
hatred and threats and spared no pains to inform everyone of what he
had said in England. Out of all this turbulence and disorder came the call
to assemble in Philadelphia to found the American Anti-Slavery Society,
with Arthur Tappan as its first president. The "notorious Garrison, the
recreant American" wrote its nonviolent Declaration of Sentiments, forming with his own hand the principles, method, and organizational structure
which Wendell Phillips claimed, "finally marshalled the nation for and
against the system in a conflict that came near rending the Union."*

October 12, 1833

[From the Boston Evening Transcript, Oct. 8.]

. . . The following handbill was circulated yesterday very generally throughout the city. . . . The Liberator office was surrounded last night by a dense mob, breathing threatenings which
foreboded a storm.

BOSTONIANS AWAKE!!

The true American has returned, *alias* William Lloyd Garrison, the "Negro Champion," from his disgraceful mission to the British metropolis, whither he went to obtain pecuniary aid, and the countenance of Englishmen to wrest the American citizen's property which he has fought and labored for, from out of their hands, and thereby deprive the southern section of our happy union the only means of obtaining a livelihood. He has held meetings in the city of London, and slandered the Americans to the utmost of his power, calling them a set of *infernal Rene-gadoes, Turks, Arabs,* &c, and also countenancing the outrageous conduct of Daniel O'Connell, who at one of his (Garrison's) meetings, called us "a set of *sheep-stealers, man-murderers,* and that the blackest corner in Hell's bottomless pit, *ought to be, and would be the future destination of the Americans!*" And this said Garrison stood by his side and assisted him in his infamous harangue. Americans! will you brook this conduct? I think not. He is now in your power—do not let him escape you, but go this evening, armed with plenty of *tar and feathers,* and administer him justice at his abode at No. 9, Merchants' Hall, Congress-st.   A NORTH ENDER.
Boston, Oct. 7, 1833.

October 12, 1833

TO THE PATRONS OF THE LIBERATOR AND THE FRIENDS OF ABOLITION

RESPECTED CO-WORKERS:

Once more upon my native soil do I greet you! The God of the oppressed has graciously preserved my life, and abundantly prospered my mission: to Him let us ascribe the honor, and render thanksgiving and praise. . . .

The great object of my mission,—namely, the exposure of the real character and object of the American Colonization Society, —has been accomplished, expeditiously, comprehensively, and effectually. The philanthropists of Great Britain now see clearly the deformity and foulness of that Society, and their detestation of it is equalled only by their indignation at having been so basely deceived, and so extensively defrauded, by its corrupt and pusillanimous 'representative.' . . .

I regret to say that the Bill for the abolition of slavery throughout the West India Colonies, which passed through both houses of Parliament before I left England, is a complete triumph of colonial chicanery over the philanthropy of the British people. It is not an example for us to imitate, but a precedent for us to shun. It is as base in its principles, as it is impracticable in its requirements. It pleases neither the West Indian slave proprietors nor the abolitionists of England—although the former have cause for great exultation, and the latter for great lamentation. As soon as convenient, I shall publish the Bill in the Liberator, with some of the numerous protestations which have been made against it in various parts of the kingdom. Let us, however, console ourselves with the certainty of the complete emancipation of all the slaves in the British Colonies within seven years.

The progress of the abolition cause in this country, during my absence, has outrun my anticipations. We have ceased to be insignificant in numbers—in devotion and courage we are unsurpassed—our moral strength is mighty—daily additions are made to our ranks. Ours is no longer the meagre victory of a skirmish, but the splendid triumph of a general engagement. Our banner is floating over many a citadel, in various States—much territory has been conquered, and nothing lost. The southern kidnappers and their northern allies have lost much of their courage, but none of their malignity. They hate us with a perfect hatred, and they fear us more than they affect to despise us. That great blasphemer, the colonization monster, cannot long survive: his present terrific struggles are but the throes of death.

One important measure remains to be effected—*a national organization of our strength.* A Circular, I am happy to perceive, has been laid before you, in which it is stated that a meeting will be held in Philadelphia for the purpose of forming a National Anti-Slavery Society, and a general invitation to the friends of immediate abolition is given, to assemble for that purpose. In the next Liberator, it is probable the day of the meeting will be designated. . . .   WM. LLOYD GARRISON

Boston, Oct. 11, 1833

November 9, 1833

GREAT ANTI-COLONIZATION MEETING IN EXETER HALL, LONDON

. . . GEORGE THOMPSON, Esq. in announcing Mr. GARRISON to the meeting, said—Will you permit me to say that Mr. GARRISON is the accredited Agent of the New-England Anti-Slavery Society, an infant association formed for the entire extinction of slavery throughout the United States? He is a delegate from that Society to England, for the purpose of holding communication with the leading abolitionists of our own country. It is hoped that when we have witnessed the extinction of the last figment of slavery in our own Colonies, England will not be reluctant in co-operating with the inhabitants of America in promoting the great cause of universal emancipation.

Mr. GARRISON then stood forward and was received with loud applause. He spoke as follows:

MR. CHAIRMAN—It is long since I sacrificed all my national, complexional and local prejudices upon the altar of Christian love, and, breaking down the narrow boundaries of a selfish patriotism, inscribed upon my banner this motto:—*My country is the world; my countrymen are all mankind.* (Cheers.) It is true, in a geographical sense, I am now in a foreign territory; but still it is part of my country. I am in the midst of strangers; but still surrounded by my countrymen. There must be limits to civil governments and national domains. There must be names to distinguish the natural divisions of the earth, and the dwellers therein. There must be varieties in the form, color, stature, and condition of mankind. All these may exist, not only without injury, but with the highest possible advantage. But whenever they are made the boundaries of human disinterestedness, friendship, sympathy, honor, patriotism and love, they are as execrable and destructive, as, otherwise, they are beautiful and preservative. . . .

I cherish as strong a love for the land of my nativity as any man living. I am proud of her civil, political and religious institutions—of her high advancement in science, literature and the arts—of her general prosperity and grandeur. But I have some solemn accusations to bring against her.

I accuse her of insulting the majesty of heaven with the grossest mockery that was ever exhibited to man—inasmuch as, professing to be the land of the free and the asylum of the oppressed, she falsifies every profession, and shamelessly plays the tyrant.

I accuse her, before all the nations, of giving an open, deliberate and base denial to her boasted Declaration, that 'all men are created equal; and that they are endowed by their Creator with certain inalienable rights; that among these are life, liberty, and the pursuit of happiness.'

I accuse her of disfranchising and proscribing nearly half a million free people of color, acknowledging them not as countrymen, and scarcely as rational beings, and seeking to drag them thousands of miles across the ocean on a plea of benevolence, when they ought to enjoy all the rights, privileges and immunities of American citizens.

I accuse her of suffering a large portion of her population to be lacerated, starved and plundered, without law and without justification, at the will of petty tyrants.

I accuse her of trafficking in the bodies and souls of men, in a domestic way, to an extent nearly equal to the foreign slave trade; which traffic is equally atrocious with the foreign, and almost as cruel in its operations.

I accuse her of legalizing, on an enormous scale, licentiousness, fraud, cruelty and murder.

I accuse her of the horrid crime of kidnapping one hundred thousand infants annually, the offspring of slave parents.

I accuse her of stealing the liberties of two millions of the creatures of God, and withholding the just recompense of their labor; of ruthlessly invading the holiest relations of life, and cruelly separating the dearest ties of nature; of denying these miserable victims necessary food and clothing for their perishable bodies, and light and knowledge for their immortal souls; of tearing the husband from his wife, the mother from her babe, and children from their parents, and of perpetrating upon the poor and needy every species of outrage and oppression.

And, finally, I accuse her of being callously indifferent to the accumulated and accumulating wrongs and sufferings of her black population, assiduous in extenuating her oppressive acts, and determined to slumber upon the brink of a volcano which is in full operation, and which threatens to roll its lava tide over the whole land.

These are my allegations. And what is the defence which she puts forth? It is even as one has said . . . I mean the distinguished and eloquent O'Connell. . . .

'I come now to America, the boasted land of freedom, and here I find the slavery which they not only tolerate but extend, justified and defended as a legacy left by us! . . .'

. . . Whatever responsibility may attach to Great Britain for the introduction of slavery into the United States, (and to talk of robbery and kidnapping as things that may be entailed is precious absurdity,) the first moment the people of the United States published their Declaration of Independence to the world, from that moment they became exclusively accountable for the existence and continuance of negro slavery. The capital stock of slaves, at that period, was about 400,000. It has been traded upon until it now numbers about 2,200,000—an increase of more than five fold! . . .

The American Union originally consisted of thirteen States—it has at the present time twenty-four States, twelve of which are free States, and twelve slaveholding States. Slavery, therefore, is consolidated in the southern portion of the country. The laws which are now in force, for the subjection of the slave population, are unparalleled for their brutality. Draco's bloody code was as white as snow in comparison. Even the West Indian enactments are less despotic. But, as in the case of the Israelites in Egypt, the more our slaves are afflicted, the more they multiply and grow. Their increase is more rapid than even that of our white population; and in half of the slave States, the soil is so completely exhausted, and the market is so glutted, that slave labor is almost wholly worthless, and the planters are enabled to support themselves only by breeding slaves for sale in the extreme southern markets. Early alarmed at the frightful increase of the slave population, and at their great depreciation in value, the planters adopted the language and policy of Pharaoh:—and they said one unto another, 'Behold, the people of the children of Israel are more and mightier than we. Come on, let us deal wisely with them; lest they multiply, and it come to pass, that, when there falleth out any war, they join also unto our enemies, and fight against us. Therefore, they did set over them taskmasters to afflict them with their burdens.' The Egyptian Pharaoh, finding to his astonishment that his excessive cruelty produced an opposite effect from that which was intended, resorted to another expedient. He charged the Hebrew midwives, and all his people, saying, 'Every son that is born of the Hebrew women ye shall cast into the river, and every daughter ye shall save alive.' The American Pharaohs, equally surprised at the prolific result of their cruelty, but more ingenious than their prototype, interrogated each other in the language of Mr. Archer of Virginia, as published in the 15th Annual Report of the American Colonization Society:

'What course or remedy remained? Was open butchery to be resorted to, as among the Spartans with the Helots? Or general emancipation and incorporation, as in South America? Or abandonment of the country by the masters, as must come to be the case in the West Indies? Either of these was a deplorable catastrophe. Could all of them be avoided, and if they could, how? There was but one way, but that might be made effectual, fortunately! It was to *provide and keep open a drain for the excess of increase beyond the occasions of profitable employment!* This might be done effectually by extension of the plan of the Society. The drain was already opened. All that was necessary would be, to provide for the enlargement of the channel, as occasion might demand.'

We now come to the origin of the American Colonization Society. The motives, it seems, for its organization, were:—1st. To prevent a general emancipation and incorporation of the blacks with the whites—2d. To render unnecessary the abandonment of the country by the masters—3d. To render the slave system secure and lucrative—and lastly, To remove from the country 'those mirrors which reflect the light of liberty into the dark bosoms of the slaves'—namely, the free people of color.

. . . *It is the foulest conspiracy in the history of the world.* . . .

EXETER HALL MEETING—LONDON

The Liberator of this morning embodies all the *slanders* which I uttered in England against the American Colonization Society and the United States. The speeches which were delivered at the great meeting held in Exeter Hall, and which have caused so much excitement among the colonization crusaders and their backers the mobocracy, were all taken down by a skilful and accomplished reporter, expressly for publication in this country. So far from being ashamed of my language on that memorable occasion, I gave *eighty dollars* for a full report of all that was then uttered by myself and others, in order that I might faithfully present it to the public on my return. I wish neither to modify nor retract a single sentence. The other speeches will follow in their regular course. To that fearless and eloquent champion of liberty,—that first of Irish patriots,—DANIEL O'CONNELL, Esq., the colored population of this country and their advocates are under heavy obligations for his masterly vindication of their cause, his terrible castigation of American slavery, and his withering satire upon the colonization 'humbug,' at this meeting.

Now let the enemies of freedom foam and rage!—But the secret of their malice lies in the triumphant success of my mission. Had I failed to vanquish the agent of the American Colonization Society, or to open the eyes of British philanthropists to its naked deformity, there would have been no excitement on my return. These sensitive republicans, who are so jealous of the reputation of their country, be it remembered, are the most sturdy upholders of the slave system, and the most ardent sticklers for the banishment of our free colored population to the African coast. They esteem it no disgrace to debase, lacerate, plunder and kidnap two millions of slaves, and tread upon the necks of half a million free colored citizens; but it is foul slander, in their impartial judgment, to declare before a British audience that such conduct is in the highest degree hypocritical and tyrannical. But their iniquity is not done in a corner, nor can it be hid under a bushel; and I tell them that I will hold them up to the scorn and indignation of the world—I will stamp the brand of infamy upon their brow, which, like the mark of Cain, shall make them known and detested by the friends of freedom and humanity in every country and in every clime. 'Where there is shame, there may in time be virtue.' I have already crimsoned their cheeks with the bitter consciousness of their guilt; and through their shame I will never despair of seeing them brought to repentance. It is idle for them to bluster and threaten—they will find out, by and by, that I am storm-proof.

If I had outraged common sense and common decency, by throwing all the guilt of our oppression upon the British government; if I had dealt in the wretched cant, that slavery was an evil entailed upon us by the mother country; if I had been as dishonest, as hypocritical, and as pusillanimous as the agent of the American Colonization Society; if I had extolled that kind of philanthropy which calls for the banishment of every man, woman and child whose skin is 'not colored like my own'; if I had asserted that the stealers of human beings in the southern States were kind, liberal and paternal in their treatment of their victims, and anxious to abolish slavery;—in short, if I had sacrificed conscience, honesty and truth upon the altar of falsehood and prejudice; why, then the reputation of the United States would have been pure and spotless in the eyes of the English nation, and I should have received the applause, instead of the malediction of a senseless mob! But I was neither knave nor fool enough to do any such thing. I spoke the truth, in the love of the truth—the whole truth, and nothing but the truth. I freely acknowledged the guilt, the awful guilt of this boasted land of liberty, in holding one sixth part of its immense population in servile chains; and besought the sympathy of the friends of bleeding humanity in England, in behalf of our afflicted slaves. Nor did I fail to tear the mask from the brow of the American Colonization Society, so that it might be feared and loathed as a monster of cruelty, violence and blood. For this cause, 'the wicked have drawn out the sword, and have bent their bow, to cast down the poor and needy, and to slay such as be of upright conversation. Their sword shall enter into their own heart, and their bows shall be broken.'

The Reign of Terror

Garrison was now convinced that the cause of immediate emancipation was thriving on the dissent and upheaval it was provoking all over the North. To repeated warnings and pleading from his friends to trim his sails, he gave a firm no. Great Britain had recently emancipated the slaves in the West Indies (1833) and fulfillment of American emancipation seemed almost in sight. This, and Garrison's obvious success, began to further exacerbate the South and it increased its organizational drives to put down the Abolitionists, wherever they were. Conventions were held in the South to set up more effective counteraction, and the persisting mob action, which formerly had been pure rowdyism, was now being calculated and directed by men in broadcloth coats. It was almost impossible to mention slavery in New York. Colored churches were burned in New Haven. Assassins from New Orleans were reported to be stalking leading Garrisonians—and they were all burned, once a week, somewhere, in effigy. Instead of "going underground" at this time, as urged by his friends, Garrison initiated a daring new affront to those now in the leadership of the effort to stifle him. He invited George Thompson, an English Abolitionist and the leading figure in the Emancipation in the British islands, to visit him and address the local societies.

This enraged the merchants of Boston. They held Thompson personally responsible for the crippling decline in their West Indian trade. They arranged for a great Anti-Abolitionist meeting to be held in Faneuil Hall on August 21, 1835, at which the very top local leadership would appear. Harrison Gray Otis, who, as a Senator in 1820, had said that he would "strenuously and forever oppose the extension of slavery, and all measures which would subject a freeman, of whatever color, to the degradation of slavery," was to be the keynote speaker.

Garrison was greatly taken aback by this. He had felt that his moral suasion would finally touch men like Otis and carry the day. But the real blow to his hopes came when Otis, in his speech, said bluntly that even if freedom came to the Southern slave by peaceful means, it would change the civil polity of the South to an extent that would be unbearable for Southern whites and highly distasteful to the North. Here was obviously a dead end for Garrison, but he seemed to ignore its implication. He accused the sponsors of the Faneuil Hall meeting of trying to incite a lynching, and such a mob did materialize, with him as the proposed victim, not long after. On October 21 the Boston Female Anti-Slavery Society was to hold a meeting in the Anti-Slavery Hall. Although Garrison took the precaution of having Thompson leave the city *before the meeting, Bostonians assumed that Thompson would address the ladies and the combination of women in politics and an interfering Britisher was well calculated to bring about a mobocratic explosion. After the most serious threats had been made, Garrison put himself into the hot spot and came close to losing his life.*

The next day he left Boston by request of the city fathers, to lick his wounds, and discovered he cared more than he thought for the good opinion of his fellow citizens. He became very ill at a retreat in Brooklyn, Connecticut, while his partner at The Liberator, *Isaac Knapp, was shut out of their office and* The Liberator *foreclosed on by all its creditors. Somehow the paper was kept going and Garrison, coming back on November 4 to walk these streets of hate, found that a gallows had been erected in front of his house, saw remnants of mobs still carrying placards against him, and picked up a marked increase in subscribers to* The Liberator.

August 29, 1835

FORBEARANCE OF THE ABOLITIONISTS

. . . Utterly deprived of that protection and of those immunities which belong to them as citizens; and given up to be the prey of ruffians and assassins, the popular theory of self-defence and the example of worldly patriotism in all ages authorise them to resist unto blood—to proclaim a war of extermination—to light up the fires of a new revolution—and to rally together upon the 'tented field,' armed and equipped for mortal combat. As a body, moreover, they are numerous. In physical strength and courage, as well as morals, they are powerful. *The causes which induced our revolutionary fathers to rush to the strife of blood, were as dust in the balance, compared with the anguish, outrage and peril, to which abolitionists are subjected.*

Now, then, in view of this epitome of facts, let the inquiry be made, how have the abolitionists behaved under all these provocations, and exposed to all imaginable suffering? Have they, in a single instance returned evil for evil? Who, among them all, has given blow for blow? or who has girded on his sword? or who has recommended an appeal to force? . . . When rotten eggs and brick-bats have been hurled at their heads, what have they sent in return? *Forgiveness*. . . . When their private and public meetings have been ruthlessly invaded, what course have they adopted to prevent a repetition of the outrage? *Forgiveness.* When their property has been burnt in the streets, and their lives hunted like partridges upon the mountains, what have they manifested by way of retaliation? Still—*forgiveness!* Why? Are they pusillanimous? Do they lack nerve? No. But they fear Him who says—'Vengeance is MINE—I will repay,' and they can love their enemies, bless them that curse, do good to them that hate, and pray for them which despitefully use and persecute them. . . .

September 5, 1835

MR. OTIS'S SPEECH AT FANEUIL HALL

. . . It has of late become certain, though not perhaps generally known, that an association has been formed in a neighboring state for the avowed purpose of effecting the *immediate abolition of Slavery.* Their number is at present comparatively small and insignificant, but as they boast, augmented within the last year. Their printed constitution and proceedings, seen by me only within a few days, frankly develops their desire to establish auxiliary societies in every state and municipality, and to enlist in the service of the cause, man, woman and child. This simple statement shows it to be a dangerous association. . . . not only imminently dangerous, but hostile to the spirit and letter of the Constitution of the Union. . . .

Let us now consider whether the principles of the Anti-Slavery Associations do not conflict with the principles of this compact. In speaking of these associations, I rely entirely upon the account they give of themselves and their objects. I make no personal allusions, and impeach no man's motives. From some of their printed documents which have lately come into my hands, I find the names of persons, who are, I am told, of pious and respectable character; it would be strange were there not others (though I know nothing of them) of a different stamp. But let us look at their avowed and vaunted object, and if that be not unequivocally wrong and censurable in itself, their proposed means for the attainment of it are so altogether. The end of the institution is expressly stated to be the immediate abolition of slavery throughout the Union. They will have no temporising measures. Whatever is to be done, must be done quickly. They are in such haste that they cannot lose time in periphrase, and so they have enriched the nomenclature with a new word, *immediatism*. This comprehends every thing, and is the opposite of *gradualism,* another new coinage;—all which, being interpreted, means they intend to do immediately that which, by the Constitution, they are restrained from doing at all. All other persons who may be favorable to a more slow and gentle process are treated with sneers and contempt,—the Colonization Society especially, who are gradualists, and the greatest enemies to the African race.—Sir, I will not stop to debate the justifiableness of this end. Whether *immediate* abolition, if practicable, would be beneficial to master or man, is a theme I leave untouched, though I am entirely incredulous that it would be well for either. Still, for our present purpose, admit that it might be so, the associates will have found no justification unless their means are also free from objection. The first step adopted by them is to erect themselves into a *revolutionary society,*—combined and affiliated with auxiliary and *ancillary* societies, in every state and community, large or small, in the Eastern and Western States. All men are invited to join in holy crusade. The ladies are invoked to turn their sewing parties into abolition clubs, and the little children when they meet to eat sugar plums or at the Sunday Schools, are to be taught that A B stands for abolition:— Sir, I do not exaggerate—there is the book—[an anti-slavery pamphlet which lay on the table]—all I assert is there in substance: men, women and children are stimulated, flattered and frightened in order to swell their number.

This picture of the Society fully supports my assertion that it is revolutionary. It boldly professes its designs to be revolution in other States. The immediate abolition of slavery forced upon them by an extraneous pressure would be revolution in the strict sense of the word. *It would change the civil polity—it would give political power to those who have none, and the dominant power to them in all places where they happen to be a majority of the population. This would be inevitabl[e—*T.N.] *supposing*

the object to [*be*—T.N.] *attained without a servile war.* [Italics
mine.—T.N.] Now I deny that any body of men can lawfully
associate for the purpose of undermining, more than for overthrowing, the government of our sister States. There may be no
statute to make such combinations penal, because the offence is
of a new complexion. But they are not the less intrinsically
wrong. . . .

. . . who can calculate the amount of trouble and calamity
which will ensue, upon the perseverance of the Anti-Slavery Society? Are they aware of the pain and discomfort which they
excite in private families—of the interruption occasioned to domestic repose—of the cruel and unprovoked irritation, arising
from insult goading men to madness—and instigating them to
measures of precaution and severity towards the unfortunate race
which they pretend to serve? Are the ladies who have formed, or
may form the auxiliary clubs, mothers, or wives or maidens—and
can they from rural bowers and happy vales contemplate the
agonies of mothers who hear in their day and night dreams, the
shrieks of servile insurrection—the tears of the unconscious child
in sympathy with the mother—the horrors which petrify the
hearts of the delicate and pure! Surely the promise of good
should be great and certain, to balance against this violence to
the peace and happiness of our nation, even supposing their ap-
prehensions groundless. But looking further, a servile war must
have one of two issues. The citizens or the slaves must triumph.
If the former, and altogether the most probable . . . who does
not perceive the extermination of the blacks or a regime of the
most severe and rigorous vigilance should follow, and all chance
of emancipation postponed, perhaps forever? But suppose the
other issue, and that the slaves should conquer. The whites in
their turn must be exterminated. They could not remain at
home a conquered people. To say nothing of the accumulated
horrors of the process, Republics of the colored race will have
supplanted that of their masters, and we shall be brought into
proximity and perhaps alliance, or into constant war with those
who occupy the soil and the habitations of the good and the great
and the brave of our brethren. I drop a veil over the scene. . . .

September 19, 1835

Refuge of Oppression

A CALM APPEAL FROM THE SOUTH
TO THE NORTH

[From the Richmond Enquirer]

. . . The South has as deep an interest in the Union as the North. Certainly no State is more attached to it than Virginia; because the Potomac may be the dividing line, and she will become the border State. Her rivers would bristle with entrenchments, and her fields be turned into battle grounds. . . .

. . . nothing is so well calculated to inflame the sensibility of the South, as an interference with her domestic institutions. It is not a mere question of property . . . it *may* be her safety; the very lives of her wives and her children. . . .

. . . *The outrage is intolerable;* and it is without excuse. . . .

. . . we beseech you to *put down these Incendiaries.*—What would you say if your own *operatives* were to become discontented and rebellious[!!!]—threatening your houses with the torch and your families with the knife—and if we were to erect presses in our own bosom to print and circulate papers to blow them into a flame? . . .

. . . Why, above all, does not Massachusetts, with whom Virginia sympathised so keenly, in the days of her Boston Portbill, drive that *audacious* foreigner from her bosom, who is so grossly abusing the rights of hospitality, to throw our country into confusion? It is outrageous enough for Tappan and for Garrison to be throwing firebrands into the South—but for that impertinent intruder, Thompson, to mingle in our Institutions, for that foreigner, who, has nothing *American* about him, in name, interest, or principle—the outrage exceeds all the bounds of patience. . . .

The South, then, warns the North. The crisis may increase. The interests of the North may soon suffer as well as those of the South. The intercourse of her citizens, with the Southern States, will be submitted to unpleasant restrictions, from the effects of the suspicion which is now excited. The public Mail will be fettered. Our own safety will compel us to drive off the most obnoxious People of Color, who will become public nuisances in the northern cities. Commerce will be gradually fettered. It will first be prohibited with all the Abolitionists, and who knows but the indignant spirit of an incensed people may extend the restriction to all the merchants of the North?

Must we go on with this dark pencilling, until outrage being added to outrage, and excitement kindling with excitement, the feelings which bound us together like a band of brothers, may be ultimately exchanged for those of *deepest animosity,* and of *awful alienation?* When the South will be compelled to say to the North, as Mr. Jefferson's first draft of the Declaration of Independence said to our then British brethren: '. . . we must then acquiesce in the necessity which denounces our separation.' . . .

October 24, 1835

We give below, a copy of the inflammatory handbill, which was posted about the city on Wednesday. . . .

THOMPSON
THE ABOLITIONIST

That infamous foreign scoundrel THOMPSON, will hold forth *this afternoon,* at the Liberator Office, No. 48, Washington Street. The present is a fair opportunity for the friends of the Union to *snake Thompson out!* It will be a contest between the Abolitionists and the friends of the Union. A purse of $100 has been raised by a number of patriotic citizens to reward the individual who shall first lay violent hands on Thompson, so that he may be brought to the tar kettle before dark. Friends of the Union, be vigilant!

Boston, Wednesday, 12 o'clock.

November 7, 1835

Triumph of Mobocracy in Boston—Prostration of the Civil Power—Suppression of the Liberty of Speech—Ruffianism of the Press—Public Insult to Female Benevolence and Piety—

A Citizen, guiltless of crime, ignominiously dragged through the streets, and for self-preservation committed to jail, and finally obliged to leave the city to save his life—&c. &c.

I shall give, as far as I am capable, an exact and faithful account of the ruthless disturbance which took place in Boston on Wednesday afternoon, Oct. 21st, and by which this city was suddenly transformed into an infuriated pandemonium. It is the most disgraceful event that has ever marred the character of Bostonians, whether reference be made to the time of its occurrence, or to the cause which was assailed, or to those who stood obnoxious to violent treatment. The recent pro-slavery meeting in Faneuil Hall supported the *theory* of despotism, and the tumultuous assembly of Wednesday carried it into *practice*— trampling all law and order, the constitution and personal liberty, public decorum and private decency, common humanity and christian courtesy, into the dust. The light of day did not cause a blush, nor the certainty of exposure restrain from indecent and barbarous behavior, nor profession or station deter 'respectable, wealthy and influential citizens' from enacting the part of ruffians and anarchists. All distinctions (excepting that of *color,* to the honor of the BLACK MAN be it recorded) were blended, for the purpose of gagging the advocates of freedom, and infusing new strength into the arm of the remorseless scourger of *Woman* at the South. The merchant and the aristocrat—the wealthy and the learned—the 'respectable' and the 'influential'—the professor and the profane—all were huddled together in thick and formidable array, with every variety of feeling, but with one prevalent design, namely, to insult, annoy and disperse the Female Anti-Slavery meeting, (brave, gentlemanly, chivalric men!) and to tar-and-feather, or put to death, GEORGE THOMPSON or myself! Was it not a sublime spectacle to behold four or five thousand genteel ruffians courageously assembling together, to achieve so hazardous and glorious an exploit as the putting to flight one man and thirty defenceless females? . . .

As the meeting was to commence at 3 o'clock, P.M. I went to the hall about twenty minutes before that time. Perhaps a hundred individuals had already gathered around the street door and opposite the building, and their number was rapidly augmenting.

On ascending into the hall, I found about fifteen or twenty ladies assembled, sitting with cheerful countenances, and a crowd of noisy intruders (mostly young men) gazing upon them, through whom I urged my way with considerable difficulty. "That's Garrison," was the exclamation of some of these creatures, as I quietly took my seat. Perceiving that they had no intention of retiring, I went to them and calmly said—"Gentlemen, perhaps you are not aware that this is a meeting of the Boston *Female* Anti-Slavery Society, called and intended exclusively for *ladies,* and those only who have been invited to address them. Understanding this fact, you will not be so rude or indecorous as to thrust your presence upon this meeting. If, *gentlemen,*" I pleasantly continued, "any of you are *ladies*—in disguise—why, only apprise me of the fact, give me your names, and I will introduce you to the rest of your sex, and you can take seats among them accordingly." I then sat down, and, for a few moments, their conduct was more orderly. However, the stair-way and upper door of the hall were soon densely filled with a brazen-faced crew, whose behaviour grew more and more indecent and outrageous. Perceiving that it would be impracticable for me, or any other person, to address the ladies; and believing, as I was the only male abolitionist in the hall, that my presence would serve as a pretext for the mob to annoy the meeting, I held a short colloquy with the excellent President of the Society, telling her that I would withdraw, unless she particularly desired me to stay. It was her earnest wish that I would retire, as well for my own safety as for the peace of the meeting. She assured me that the Society would resolutely but calmly proceed to the transaction of its business, and leave the issue with God. I left the hall accordingly, and would have left the building, if the stair-case had not been crowded to excess. This being impracticable, I retired into the Anti-Slavery Office, (which is separated from the hall by a board-partition,) accompanied by my friend Mr. Charles C. Burleigh. It was deemed prudent to lock the door, to prevent the mob from rushing in and destroying our publications.

In the mean time, the crowd in the street had augmented from a hundred to thousands. The cry was for "Thompson! Thompson!"—but the Mayor had now arrived, and, addressing the rioters, he assured them that Mr. Thompson was not in the city,

and besought them to disperse. As well might he have attempted
to propitiate a troop of ravenous wolves. None went away—but
the tumult continued momently to increase. It was apparent,
therefore, that the hostility of the throng was not concentrated
upon Mr. Thompson, but that it was as deadly against the Society and the Anti-Slavery cause.—This fact is worthy of special
note—for it incontestibly proves that the object of the "respectable and influential" rioters was to put down the cause of emancipation, and that Mr. Thompson furnished merely a pretext
for five thousand "gentlemen" to mob thirty christian
women! . . .

. . . Notwithstanding the presence and frantic behaviour of
the rioters in the hall, the meeting of the Society was regularly
called to order by the President. She then read a select and an
exceedingly appropriate portion of scripture, and offered up a
fervent prayer to God for direction and succor, and the forgiveness of enemies and revilers. It was an awful, sublime and soul-
thrilling scene—enough, one would suppose, to melt adamantine
hearts, and make even fiends of darkness stagger and retreat. Indeed, the clear, untremulous tone of voice of that christian heroine
in prayer, occasionally awed the ruffians into silence, and was
heard distinctly even in the midst of their hisses, threats and
curses—for they could not long silently endure the agony of conviction, and their conduct became furious. They now attempted
to break down the partition, and partially succeeded—but the
little band of females still maintained their ground unshrinkingly,
and continued to transact their business.

An assault was now made upon the door of the office, the
lower panel of which was instantly dashed to pieces. Stooping
down, and glaring upon me as I sat at the desk, writing an account of the riot to a distant friend, the ruffians cried out—
"There he is! That's Garrison! Out with the scoundrel!" &c.
&c. Turning to Mr. Burleigh I said—"You may as well open the
door, and let them come in and do their worst." But he, with
great presence of mind, went out, locked the door, put the key
into his pocket, and by his admirable firmness, succeeded in
keeping the office safe.

Two or three constables having cleared the hall and stair-case
of the mob, the Mayor came in and *ordered* the ladies to desist,

assuring them that he could not any longer guarantee protection,
if they did not take immediate advantage of the opportunity to
retire from the building. Accordingly they adjourned, to meet at
the house of one of their number [Mrs. Chapman's, at 11 West
Street—T.N.], for the completion of their business; but as they
passed through the crowd, they were greeted with taunts, hisses,
and cheers of mobocratic triumph, from "gentlemen of property
and standing from all parts of the city." Even *their* absence did
not diminish the throng. Thompson was not there—the ladies
were not there—but "*Garrison* is there!" was the cry. "Garrison!
Garrison! We must have Garrison! Out with him! Lynch
him!" These and numberless other exclamations arose from the
multitude. For a moment, their attention was diverted from me
to the Anti-Slavery sign ["Anti-Slavery Rooms"—T.N.], and
they vociferously demanded its possession. It is painful to state,
that the Mayor promptly complied with their demand! So
agitated and alarmed had he become, that in very weakness of
spirit he ordered the sign to be hurled to the ground, and it was
instantly broken into a thousand fragments by the infuriated
populace. O, lamentable departure from duty—O, shameful outrage upon private property—by one who had sworn, not to
destroy but to protect property—not to pander to the lawless
desires of a mob, however "wealthy and respectable," but to preserve the public peace. The act was wholly unjustifiable. The
Mayor might have as lawfully surrendered me to the tender
mercies of the mob, or ordered the building itself to be torn down,
in order to propitiate them, as to remove that sign. Perhaps—
nay, *probably* he was actuated by kind intentions; probably he
hoped that he should thereby satisfy the ravenous appetites of
these human cormorants, and persuade them to retire; probably
he trusted thus to extricate me from danger. But the sequel
proved that he only gave a fresh stimulus to popular fury: and
if he could have saved my life, or the whole city from destruction, by that single act, still he ought not to have obeyed the
mandate of the mob—no indeed! He committed a public outrage in the presence of the lawless and disobedient, and thus
strangely expected to procure obedience to and a respect for the
law! He behaved disorderly before rebels, that he might restore
order among them!—Mr. HENRY WILLIAMS and Mr. JOHN L.

DIMMOCH also deserve severe reprehension for their forwardness in taking down the sign. The offence, under such circumstances, was very heinous. The value of the article destroyed was of no consequence: but the principle involved in its surrender and sacrifice is one upon which civil government, private property and individual liberty depend.

The sign being demolished, the cry for 'Garrison!' was renewed, more loudly than ever. It was now apparent, that the multitude would not disperse until I had left the building; and as egress out of the front door was impossible, the Mayor and his assistants, as well as some of my friends, earnestly besought me to effect my escape in the rear of the building. At this juncture, an abolition brother, whose mind had not been previously settled on the peace question, in his anguish and alarm for my safety, and in view of the helplessness of the civil authority, said —'I must henceforth repudiate the principle of non-resistance. When the civil arm is powerless, my own rights are trodden in the dust, and the lives of my friends are put in imminent peril by ruffians, I will hereafter prepare to defend myself and them at all hazards.' Putting my hand upon his shoulder, I said, 'Hold, my dear brother! You know not what spirit you are of. This is the trial of our faith, and the test of our endurance. Of what value or utility are the principles of peace and forgiveness, if we may repudiate them in the hour of peril and suffering? Do you wish to become like one of those violent and blood-thirsty men who are seeking my life? Shall we give blow for blow, and array sword against sword? God forbid! I will perish sooner than raise my hand against any man, even in self-defence, and let none of my friends resort to violence for my protection. If my life be taken, the cause of emancipation will not suffer. God reigns— his throne is undisturbed by this storm—he will make the wrath of man to praise him, and the remainder he will restrain—his omnipotence will at length be victorious.'

Preceded by my faithful and beloved friend Mr. J—— R—— C——, I dropped from a back window on to a shed, and narrowly escaped falling headlong to the ground. We entered into a carpenter's shop, through which we attempted to get into Wilson's Lane, but found our retreat cut off by the mob. They raised a shout as soon as we came in sight, but the workmen promptly closed the door of the shop, kept them at bay for a time, and thus kindly afforded me an opportunity to find some other passage. I told Mr. C. it would be futile to attempt to escape—I would go out to the mob, and let them deal with me as they might elect; but he thought it was my duty to avoid them, as long as possible. We then went up stairs, and finding a vacancy in one corner of the room, I got into it, and he and a young lad piled up some boards in front of me to shield me from observation. In a few minutes, several ruffians broke into the chamber, who seized Mr. C. in a rough manner, and led him out to the view of the mob, saying, 'This is not Garrison, but Garrison's and Thompson's friend, and he says he knows where Garrison is, but won't tell.' Then a shout of exultation was raised by the mob, and what became of him I do not know; though, as I was immediately discovered, I presume he escaped without material injury. On seeing me, three or four of the rioters, uttering a yell, furiously dragged me to the window, with the intention of hurling me from that height to the ground; but one of them relented and said—'Don't let us kill him outright.' So they drew me back, and coiled a rope about my body—probably to drag me through the streets. I bowed to the mob, and requesting them to wait patiently until I could descend, went down upon a ladder that was raised for that purpose. I fortunately extricated myself from the rope, and was seized by two or three powerful men, to whose firmness, policy and muscular energy, I am probably indebted for my preservation. They led me along bareheaded, (for I had lost my hat,) through a mighty crowd, ever and anon shouting, 'He shan't be hurt! You shan't hurt him! Don't hurt him! He is an American!' &c. &c. This seemed to excite sympathy among many in the crowd, and they reiterated the cry, 'He shan't be hurt!' I was thus conducted through Wilson's Lane into State-street, in the rear of the City Hall, over the ground that was stained with the blood of the first martyrs in the cause of LIBERTY AND INDEPENDENCE, by the memorable massacre of 1770—and upon which was proudly unfurled, only a few years since, with joyous acclamations, the beautiful banner presented to the gallant Poles by the young men of Boston! What a scandalous and revolting contrast! My offence was in pleading for LIBERTY—liberty for my enslaved countrymen, colored though they be—

liberty of speech and of the press for ALL!—And upon that 'consecrated spot' I was made an object of derision and scorn, and my body was denuded of a large portion of its covering, in the presence of thousands of my fellow-citizens! O, base degeneracy from their parent-stock!

Orders were now given to carry me to the Mayor's office in the City Hall. As we approached the south door, the Mayor attempted to protect me by his presence; but as he was unassisted by any show of authority or force, he was quickly thrust aside —and now came a tremendous rush on the part of the mob to prevent my entering the hall. For a moment, the conflict was dubious—but my sturdy supporters carried me safely up to the Mayor's room.

Whatever those newspapers which were instrumental in stirring up the mob may report, throughout the whole of this trying scene I felt perfectly calm, nay very happy. It seemed to me that it was indeed a blessed privilege thus to suffer in the cause of Christ. Death did not present one repulsive feature. The promises of God sustained my soul, so that it was not only divested of fear, but ready to sing aloud for joy.

Having had my clothes rent asunder, one individual kindly lent me a pair of pantaloons—another, a coat—a third, a stock —a fourth, a cap as a substitute for my lost hat. After a consultation of fifteen or twenty minutes, the Mayor and his advisers came to the singular conclusion, that the building would be endangered by my continuing in it, and that the preservation of my life depended upon committing me to jail, ostensibly as a disturber of the peace!! A hack was got in readiness at the door to receive me—and, supported by Sheriff Parkman and Ebenezer Bailey, Esq. (the Mayor leading the way,) I succeeded in getting into it without much difficulty, as I was not readily identified in my new garb. Now came a scene that baffles the power of description. As the ocean, lashed into fury by the spirit of the storm, seeks to whelm the adventurous bark beneath its mountain waves—so did the mob, enraged by a series of disappointments, rush like a whirlwind upon the frail vehicle in which I sat, and endeavor to drag me out of it. Escape seemed a physical impossibility. They clung to the wheels—dashed open the doors— seized hold of the horses—and tried to upset the carriage. They

were, however, vigorously repulsed by the police—a constable
sprang in by my side—the doors were closed—and the driver,
lustily using his whip upon the bodies of his horses and the heads
of the rioters, happily made an opening through the crowd, and
drove at a tremendous speed for Leverett-street. But many of the
rioters followed even with superior swiftness, and repeatedly attempted to arrest the progress of the horses. To reach the jail by
a direct course was found impracticable; and after going in a cir-
cuitous direction, and encountering many 'hair-breadth 'scapes,'
we drove up to this new and last refuge of liberty and life, when
another bold attempt was made to seize me by the mob—but in
vain. In a few moments, I was locked up in a cell, safe from
my persecutors, accompanied by two delightful associates, a good
conscience and a cheerful mind. In the course of the evening,
several of my friends came to my grated window to sympathise
and rejoice with me, with whom I held a pleasant conversation
until the hour of retirement, when I threw myself upon my
prison-bed, and slept tranquilly during the night. In the morning,
I awoke quite refreshed, and after eating an excellent breakfast
furnished by the kindness of my keeper, I inscribed upon the
walls of my cell the following items:

> Wm. Lloyd Garrison was put into this cell on Wednes-
> day afternoon, Oct. 21, 1835, to save him from the vio-
> lence of a 'respectable and influential' mob, who sought
> to destroy him for preaching the abominable and danger-
> ous doctrine, that 'all men are created equal,' and that
> all oppression is odious in the sight of God. 'Hail Co-
> lumbia!' Cheers for the Autocrat of Russia, and the Sul-
> tan of Turkey!
> Reader, let this inscription remain till the last slave in
> this despotic land be loosed from his fetters.

━━━

> When peace within the bosom reigns,
>   And conscience gives th' approving voice;
> Though bound the human form in chains,
>   Yet can the soul aloud rejoice.
>
> 'Tis true, my footsteps are confined—
>   I cannot range beyond this cell;—
> But what can circumscribe my mind?
>   To chain the winds attempt as well!

━━━

Confine me as a prisoner—but bind me not as a slave.
Punish me as a criminal—but hold me not as a chattel.
Torture me as a man—but drive me not like a beast.
Doubt my sanity—but acknowledge my immortality.

In the course of the forenoon, after passing through the mockery of an examination, for form's sake, before Judge Whitman, I was released from prison; but at the *earnest solicitation of the city authorities,* in order to tranquillize the public mind, I deemed it proper to leave the city for a few days, and accordingly took my departure, accompanied by Mrs. Garrison.

My thanks are due to Sheriff Parkman for various acts of politeness and kindness; as also to Sheriff Sumner, Mr. Coolidge, Mr. Andrews, and several other gentlemen.

I have been thus minute in describing the rise, progress and termination of this disgraceful riot, in order to prevent (or rather to correct) false representations and exaggerated reports respecting it and myself. It is proper to subjoin a few reflections.

1. The outrage was perpetrated in Boston—the Cradle of Liberty—the city of Hancock and Adams—the head-quarters of refinement, literature, intelligence and religion! No comments can add to the infamy of this fact.

2. It was perpetrated in the open daylight of heaven, and was therefore most unblushing and daring in its features.

3. It was against the friends of human freedom—the liberty of speech—the right of association—and in support of the vilest slavery that ever cursed the world.

4. It was dastardly beyond precedent, as it was an assault of thousands upon a small body of helpless females. Charleston and New-Orleans have never acted so brutally. Courageous cravens!

5. It was planned and executed, not by the rabble, or the working-men, but by '*gentlemen* of property and standing from all parts of the city'—and now, that time has been afforded for reflection, it is still either openly justified or coldly disapproved by the 'higher classes,' and exultation among them is general throughout the city! . . .

6. It is virtually approved by all the daily presses, except the Daily Advocate and the Daily Reformer. These independent

presses have spoken out in a tone worthy of the best days of the revolution.

7. It is evidently winked at by the city authorities. No efforts have been made to arrest the leading rioters. The Mayor has made no public appeal to the citizens to preserve order; nor has he given any assurance that the right of free discussion shall be enjoyed without molestation; nor did he array any military force against the mob, or attempt to disperse them except by useless persuasion; on the contrary, he complied with their wishes in tearing down the anti-slavery sign. He was chairman, too, of the pro-slavery meeting in Faneuil Hall, at which WASHINGTON was cheered for being a SLAVEHOLDER!

8. It is clearly approved by the courts. The proprietors and editors of the Commerical Gazette (to say nothing of the Atlas, Centinel and Courier) ought to have been indicted for attempting to stir up a riot. Sedition is the leading characteristic of that vile press. Where is the Grand Jury, that it does not present it for prosecution? . . .

WM. LLOYD GARRISON

Boston, Oct. 25, 1835

Garrison Blasts Beecher

When Garrison fled into the country from his prison cell after the attempted lynching, he was in a state of shock. He was newly married, and his wife was expecting a baby. He had begun his crusade orthodox in religion, conservative in politics. Two of his particular heroes had been Harrison Gray Otis, who had preserved some of the high-minded individualism of the old Federalists, but who had now revealed his non-acceptance of the true democratic process, and Lyman Beecher, the great Presbyterian preacher whose sermons on intemperance and dueling, masterpieces of forensic eloquence, had profoundly influenced Garrison. He had already, in a public letter, poured the full measure of his wrath out on Otis. A remark made by Lyman Beecher, widely quoted in the press, that Sunday was the "sun of the moral world," prompted him to open up with the big guns on him. In Brooklyn, Connecticut, where he was afflicted with a nervous rash and general debility, his meditations were taking him down into a Dantean hell of disillusion and disgust.

He began to think out another revolutionary contradiction, that everything that is condemned in the white Christian morality—adultery, neglect of the Bible and of the Sabbath, kidnapping, rape, theft, and all of the sins of the calendar—were not only permitted but encouraged in the relationship between the master and the slave. And then there was the further contradiction, that whereas everyone was constantly urged to follow Christ and be like Him, no one could do this without undergoing the most hateful persecutions. The more he kept hammering at these cleavages in the moral universe, the more the rocks of ages fell apart before his astonished eyes.

His attack on Beecher and orthodoxy, coming at this time, is a prime example of the natural revolutionary's compulsion to go further than he intended—to be seized by the logic of his position, and to propel himself toward conclusions more advanced than he had at the starting point. After Garrison had finished his attack on Beecher and published it, he told his wife shortly after, "I am conscious that a mighty sectarian conspiracy is forming to crush me, and it will probably succeed to some extent." The powerful attempt to ride Garrison out of his own movement was started by his review of Beecher's speech.

July 23, 1836

LYMAN BEECHER

At a public meeting held recently in Pittsburgh, 'to take into consideration the increasing desecration of the Sabbath day,' Dr. Beecher was one of the speakers. . . .

The Dr. asserts that 'the Sabbath is *the great sun of the moral world* . . . the cord by which heaven holds up nations from the yawning gulf of corruption and ruin.' Without controverting the duty of the religious observance of that day, we nevertheless object to the extravagant and preposterous language used by the Dr. It is not authorised by the gospel. It makes the outward observance of one day in the week . . . of paramount importance to every thing else in the moral or spiritual world, instead of being subordinate and co-operative. . . .

. . . Let men consecrate to the service of Jehovah, not merely one day in seven, but *all* their time, thoughts, actions, and powers. Now, too generally, their piety is marked by spasmodic action once a week, though they find it irksome even to secure that action uniformly. They have not yet entered into spiritual rest—they are still carnal. 'For we which have BELIEVED,' says the apostle, 'DO ENTER *into rest*.'

. . . 'For where the Spirit of the Lord is there is liberty'—liberty to pray in public or private, to worship any and every where, to break the fetters of mere outward observances, to set apart any portion of time for religious purposes; but never to be sectarian, or formal, or pharisaical. . . .

But we have been led into a course of remark, which we did not contemplate at the outset. Our chief design was to show the inconsistency of Dr. Beecher. . . . he assures us, that 'unless there is an immediate effort to preserve the Sabbath from desecration, we are undone.' Yet he is giving his protecting influence to a system of slavery, which, at a single blow, annihilates not only the fourth commandment, but THE WHOLE DECA-LOGUE! and which effectually excludes from the benefits of the Sabbath, two millions and a half of his fellow-countrymen!! He thinks if this system were let alone for two hundred years, it would come to an end! . . .

He oracularly asserts, in the style of our Fourth-of-July orators, that 'a great experiment is now making. It is the experiment of human liberty; and if it fails here, all hope will be
taken from the earth. If we cannot succeed, no nation will try
it again.'

The wonderful 'experiment' that we are now making is precisely this—to see how long we can plunder, with impunity, two
millions and a half of our population; how much labor we can
extort with the cart-whip, how near to a level with the brute
creation can we reduce every sixth man, woman and child in the
land; how large a commerce we can pursue as human flesh-
mongers; how tyrannical we may be without endangering our
safety!—By this 'experiment,' we are attempting to perform
impossibilities. '*If* it fails here,' says Dr. B.; but IT HAS FAILED
—we are not, we have never been, and while slavery exists we
can never be, a free people—we have not, we never have had,
never can have, until slavery is abolished, a union of the States
—and we are rushing down to destruction as fast as time will
allow us. Our 'great experiment' is for the purpose of proving to
an incredulous world, that liberty is best promoted by the
establishment and extension of slavery! . . . The delusion belongs to fatuity, it approaches to impiety! From the commencement, this 'experiment' has been absurd, impracticable, insane,
disastrous, diabolical! And yet Dr. Beecher dares to assert, that
'if it fails here, *all hope will be taken from the earth*(*!*) If *we*
cannot succeed, *no nation will try it again*'(*!!*) . . . As if God
had suspended the fate of all nations, and hazarded the fulfilment
of his glorious promises, upon the result of a wild and cruel
'experiment' by a land-stealing, blood-thirsty, man-slaying and
slave-trading people in one corner of the globe! As if God could
not easily dash this nation in pieces, as a potter's vessel is
broken, and thereby vindicate his eternal justice, advance the
cause of human liberty, promote his fear in the earth, and establish a kingdom of righteousness! And it seems probable that he
will do so—that he will cause it to fall, as did Lucifer, like
lightning from heaven—that he will make it a bye-word and an
astonishment through all time! For what are the United States
in the estimation of the Almighty? Do their dimensions excite
his wonder? Is he awed by the array of their naval and military

power? Is he impressed by their arts and sciences, their enterprise and opulence, their politics and religion, their high preten-
sions and solemn protestations? Does his throne tremble, is he
himself alarmed for the safety of the universe, lest this nation
should apostatize, and thus not only blot out that 'great sun of
the moral world,' the Sabbath, but make creation a blank? . . .
All nations before him are as nothing; and they are counted to
him less than nothing, and vanity.' And yet the fate of the world
is suspended upon the good behavior of this nation! . . . As if
down-trodden, benighted man, wherever pining in chains or
grovelling in degradation,—despite all the mutations of earthly
empires,—will not ultimately rise up in majesty, emerge into
light, and be 'redeemed, regenerated and disenthralled'! . . .

We have dwelt at some length on this infidel prophecy, because
the pride of this nation needs to be humbled; because it haughtily
imagines that it has a charmed life, an immortal existence; because it ought to be made to realize, that, were it a thousand
times more mighty and influential than it is, God can sink it as a
millstone in the depths of oblivion, and it shall never be missed,
nor shall its loss prevent the regeneration of the world, the complete enfranchisement of the human race; and because the 'experiment' we are now making is not such as is represented by
Dr. Beecher, but heathenish and inhuman. That our example
must be widely felt, for good or for evil—that our responsibility
is awful, our ability to do good to the whole world unequalled,
our influence commanding and prevalent, our success of amazing
consequence—these are self-evident truths. But, blessed be God!
it is not in our power, by any excess of wickedness, or suicidal
act of depravity, to prevent the coming of the millenial day.

The Dr. undertakes to 'glance at some of the perils which
threaten us,' but the existence of slavery is not in the catalogue!
He has no microscopic eye—he can behold mountains only—
and therefore so minute an evil must necessarily escape his
vision! 'The prevalence of Atheism,' first attracts his notice.
But is not the slave-system practically based upon Atheism?
Does it not, in effect, dethrone God, dehumanize man, blot out
free agency, and overturn the moral government of the universe? Yet Lyman Beecher stands as a shield before it, and
when he sees a slaveholder consents with him, and calls him a

'christian brother,' even though the man-thief claims a divine right to make merchandize of the members of Christ's body! . . .

Again, says the Dr.: 'There are men among us who volunteer to become ministers of sin; and there are women who pour their polluted breath against all the sanctities of social life; and there are women, too, who go and with greedy curiosity listen to invectives against the family state, and all that is pure, and lovely, and of good report in our social state. In this crusade against virtue and happiness, all that is odious, and all that is deadly, takes the specious name of some moral excellence. It is all done under the name of virtue.' Another graphic description of southern taskmasters, and their vast system of whoredom and adultery, and profitable bastardy, which is pouring a lava tide of desolation over all the land! Listen to the testimony of a minister, (George Bourne,) who resided many years at the South:

> '. . . Young colored women, stripped to a thin, scanty body garment, after the most offensively indecent examination, are publicly placed in scales, weighed, and sold by the pound.
>
> Breeding wenches, as they are shockingly termed in the slaveholder's ungodly and impure phraseology, are as regularly nurtured and trafficked, expressly to supply the human flesh market, as a northern farmer endeavors to improve and enlarge his stock of horses, cattle, hogs and sheep.
>
> On many plantations, bribes are offered expressly to encourage the most licentiousness, that children may be born; who are always for sale, provided rapacity can be satisfied; and thus all maternal and parental and pure domestic feelings wither and die.
>
> With comparatively few exceptions, the slave plantations are a scene of promiscuous uncleanness, of the most abhorrent character, which defies all attempts to preserve the existence of decency, personal or social. For this most frightful licentiousness, the [white] female slave-drivers are chiefly responsible. They would rather connive at the grossest sensuality in their husbands, sons, fathers, and brothers, than abandon the system which enables them to live in luxury and indolence. . . .'

Behold, what a Sodom slavery makes of one half of our country!—But the 'men among us who volunteer to become ministers of sin' and the 'women who pour out their polluted breath against all the sanctities of social life,' here alluded to, are not southern slaveholders; for Dr. B. seems not to be moved in view of a legalized system of prostitution by these *pious* prodigies of impurity. Who become 'ministers of sin,' if the southern clerical associates of Dr. Beecher do not, by claiming immortal souls as their property, and quoting Scripture for the deed? Who sanction and patronize lewdness, like the female slaveholders at the south? The Dr. says—'I have read the tracts of Fanny Wright and Robert Owen, and I felt ashamed, although I was alone. I believe I blushed, although no human eye was upon me.' Marvellous delicacy in view of a corrupt *theory!* But when has he blushed, either in private or in public, in view of the *practical* and *lawful* annihilation of the marriage institution among a sixth portion of our immense population, by the Presbyterians, Unitarians, Episcopalians, Methodists, Baptists, Catholics, &c, &c, &c.? Truly, 'the volcanic passions' of men, it would seem, are not hot and violent enough, but, like the furnace of Nebuchadnezzar, must be heated seven times' by the fires of southern slavery.

'Assassination,' says the Dr., 'in some parts of our country, is growing to be as common as it is in Spain.' In what part but in the slaveholding States, where violence and spoil are the order of the day!

Finally, we are told—'If we choose to give our honors and our trust to men who have made themselves wicked by the desecration of the Sabbath, we may expect to be filled with our own devices.' But we may give our honor and our trust to men who nullify the whole Decalogue, and expect to be filled with good things.

July 30, 1836

'Another alarming evil that threatens us,' he says, 'is *the breaking up of the family alliance,* and throwing all our property into common stock for infidels to handle. They, kind souls! will no doubt be honest, and give you the crumbs, and take *very good care of all the rest.*' It is marvellous to behold the anxiety and alarm of Dr. B. as he contemplates the possibility of the overthrow of the marriage institution, and the establishment of a

system of robbery, among our *white* population; while he is un-
moved, and as tranquil as a summer's twilight, in view of 'the
breaking up of the family alliance' among two millions and a
half of our *colored* population, and 'throwing all *their* property
into common stock for *slaveholders* to handle—who, kind souls!
give the *slaves* the crumbs, and take very good care of all the
rest.' What is slavery but a legalized system of agrarianism and
whoredom, incomparably worse than anything ever contemplated
by Robert Owen, or Fanny Wright, or even the Jacobins of
France? Why should not infidels have as much liberty to sub-
sist by plunder, by taking property which does not belong to
them, as professing christians and clerical robbers at the south?
Why should there be a monopoly of lewdness and incest among
church-going members and slaveholding believers, to the exclusion of those who deny the existence of a God, and the authen-
ticity of the Bible?—Neither Robert Owen nor Fanny Wright is
base enough to advocate the right to make merchandize of human beings; and both of them are more innocent and less dangerous persons, than that declamatory man-thief, Rev. Mr. Plumer
of Virginia, and that other clerical kidnapper, Rev. Mr. Winans
of Mississippi. We maintain, that the doctrines avowed by
southern ecclesiastical conferences, synods, presbyteries and
churches, in relation to the enslavement of almost one half of
the southern population, and the utter destruction of the 'family
alliance' among four hundred thousand colored families, are as
ruinous and diabolical, and as radically subvert the foundations
of God's moral government, as any which have ever been put
forth in the Free Enquirer, or Kneeland's Investigator. It is not
possible for human depravity to conceive or enforce a more hellish
system than American slavery. It is a troop of wolves preying upon defenceless lambs. It is a burning, ever-generating, all-
desolating Vesuvius of lust and impurity. It is a slaughter-house
of souls. It is a visible exhibition of Pandemonium.

Referring to those who are called agrarians, Dr. B. says—
'There are demagogues who seek to make our laboring population feel as if they were despised and wronged, and that there is
oppression in the fact that others should be richer than they.'
And is it not true that our laboring population are, to an alarming extent, despised and wronged? Is not honest labor becoming

more and more servile and despicable in the eyes of a growing aristocracy, both at the north and at the south? To say nothing of the treatment of the southern laboring population, (who have little or no share in the thoughts either of Dr. Beecher or the agrarian party,) our northern working-men have every reason to be alarmed at the prospect before them. There is a conspiracy all over the land against them. There is a proud aristocracy at the north, sympathizing with and publicly approbating a still more haughty aristocracy at the south; and, together, it is their aim, if possible, to degrade and defraud working-men of all classes, irrespective of color. The attempt at the north to subjugate the laboring population, may never succeed so far as to make merchandize of their bodies; but, unless this class arises in its might for the extirpation of southern slavery, it will be ground more and more to the dust, its time will be more and more limited, its wages more and more inadequate, its means of intelligence more and more circumscribed. What says Gov. M'Duffie on this subject?

'No community ever has existed without domestic servitude, and we may confidently assert, none ever will. In the very nature of things, there must be classes of persons to discharge all the different offices of society, from the highest to the lowest. Some of these offices are regarded as *degrading*, though they must and will be performed. Hence those manifold forms of dependent servitude, which produce a sense of *superiority* in the masters or employers, and of *inferiority* on the part of servants. *When these offices are performed by members of the political community, a dangerous element is obviously introduced into the body politic* . . . It will be fortunate for the non-slaveholding States, if they are not, in less than a quarter of a century, driven to the adoption of a similar institution, [slavery,] or to take refuge from robbery and anarchy under a military despotism . . . In a word, *the institution of domestic slavery supersedes the necessity of an order of nobility.*'(!!)

Mr. Hammond, of South Carolina, was not afraid to assert upon the floor of Congress, that

'The South had less trouble with the *slaves* than the North had with their *free laborers,* as the records of criminal justice and the newspaper accounts of the northern mobs fully showed.'

Mr. Leigh, in the Virginia Convention of 1829, said—

'There must be some peasantry; and as the country fills up, there must be more—that is, men who tend the herds, and dig the soil, who have neither real or personal capital of their own, and who earn their daily bread by the sweat of their brow. I ask gentlemen to say, whether they believe that those who depend on their daily subsistence, can or do ever enter into political affairs? They never do, never will, never can.'

Professor Dew, of William and Mary College in Virginia, speaks in defence of slavery in the following impious strain:

'I would say, then, let us cherish this institution which has been built up *by no sin of ours*—let us cleave to it as THE ARK OF OUR SAFETY. *Expediency*, MORALITY, and RELIGION, alike demand its continuance; and perhaps I would not hazard too much in the prediction, that the day will come when *the whole confederacy* will regard it as *the sheet anchor of our country's* LIBERTY.'

Again he says:

'Domestic slavery, such as ours, is the only institution which I know of, that can secure that spirit of equality among freemen, [i. e. among the aristocracy,] so necessary to the true and genuine feeling of republicanism, without propelling the body politic at the same time into the dangerous vices of agrarianism, and *legislative intermeddling between the laborer and capitalist.* The occupations which we follow, necessarily and unavoidably create distinctions in society. To say that all confer equal honor, if well followed even, is not true. The hirelings who perform all the menial offices of life, will not and cannot be treated as equals by their employers. And those who stand ready to execute all our commands, no matter what they may be, for mere pecuniary reward, cannot feel themselves equal to US in reality, however much their reason may be bewildered by the voice of sophistry. [Prof. D. then goes on to denounce 'universal suffrage in a state where there are no slaves.'] Political power [at the south] is thus taken from the hands of those who might abuse it, and placed in the hands of those who are most interested in its judicious exercise [i. e. the slaveholding tyrants.] How can he get wisdom that holdeth the plough, that glorieth in the goad, that driveth oxen and is occupied in the labors, and whose talk is of bullocks? . . . But whilst the *political* effects of our social system are so peculiarly beneficial, the *moral* effects are no less striking and advantageous (! !)—I have no hesitation in affirming, that the relation between the capitalist and laborer in the south is kinder, and more productive of genuine attachment, than exists between the same classes any where else on the globe (! !) Free from the constant feeling of insecurity which continually haunts the poor man of other countries, he moves on [like a horse in a bark-mill] in the round of his existence, contented and grateful'!

If there be any thing either in the spirit or doctrines of agrarianism more detestable and alarming, than is contained in the foregoing extracts, we have yet to make the discovery.

August 6, 1836

Again. 'When once the mass of our people,' says the Dr. 'shall come to feel that all property above them is held by oppression, the foundations of the nation are shaken, and nothing is before us but revolution and anarchy.' There is an insinuation in this extract which amounts to wholesale slander. There is no danger, whatever, that the 'mass of our people' will ever be carried headlong into excesses by cherishing such an opinion. The real danger is, that *they* will not long be regarded as men and as brethren, but as a servile and distinct race; that, as it respects their time, labor, improvement, and political and social equality, they will be defrauded by grinding monopolies, and reduced by systematic processes; and, hence, that they will have cause for complaint, and may be driven ultimately to revolution. We do not believe that there is any class of workingmen, however ignorant or depraved, who 'feel that *all* property above them is held by oppression'—but all classes *know,* and some *feel,* that there is a growing aristocracy in our land; that privileges are granted to the wealthy few, to the injury and impoverishment of the laborious many; that an equality of rights must beget an equality of conditions; that dissatisfaction arises, not because property is acquired, but on account of the manner of its acquisition; and that oppression, not wealth, excites to resistance, anarchy, and common plunder. How does it happen, that Dr. Beecher's sympathies and tears side only with the rich and the powerful? Is there no cause for anxiety, lest they may be tempted to keep back the hire of the laborers who reap down their fields, and regard the operative and mechanic as mere implements of industry? Shall they not be admonished at least as often as the poor and needy? If it is in the nature of destitution to be envious, is it not also in the nature of wealth to be extortionate? If the feeble covet strength, do not the strong incline to despotism? Our laboring population, whether white or colored, are not held in due estimation; they are generally overtasked; they are seldom adequately remunerated, according to the just rule, 'Thou shalt love thy neighbor as thyself,' and the other reasonable and disinterested requirement, 'Whatsoever ye would that men should do to you, do ye even so to them'; they are valued according to the strength of their bodies, rather than to the intelligence of their minds and the improvement of their hearts. The lower they are found in degradation, the nearer they approach to starvation, (even when owing to obscurity of birth or the fate of adversity!) the less sympathy is extended to them—the less aid do they find. Man is not regarded as man—his inherent and perfect equality is not understood—his princely and indestructible dignity is not recognised —even though the heavens and the earth were created for him, and though to him is given dominion over the beasts of the field and the fowls of the air, and though he is created in the image of God, and though Jesus, the Lord of Glory, descended from heaven, and died that he might live! When the abolitionists inculcate the duty of remunerating the colored laborer for his work, the cry is raised against them of 'fanaticism!' and when the white laborer protests against unrighteous monopolies, the same proud conservatives clamor about 'agrarianism,' 'levellers,' &c. As an apology for keeping our colored population in chains, we are referred to 'the scenes of St. Domingo!' although the struggle in that island was between an army of French invaders and an emancipated people. It was the consequence of an attempt to enslave freemen, not of liberating bondmen. So, whenever the workingmen strive to effect a just reform, they are made hideous, and driven back, by a fresh delineation of the horrors of the 'French revolution.' What has that dire tragedy to do with justice between man and man, or with equality between the employer and the employed? And were there no causes which produced it? It is popular to speak of the Goddess of Reason, of Robespierre and his vindictive associates, of the guillotine, and of the reign of atheism. But who dwells upon the fact, that a despotic government, a false religion, and a wicked priesthood, had conspired to crush, ruin and enslave the people, so that human endurance could bear no more, and all that was associated with the name of christianity became hateful? To a kingly and priestly despotism, long imposed and borne as long, must the origin of that tragedy be ascribed. Knowing nothing either of the character or the fruits of true religion,—detesting that which the Man of Sin forced upon their observance,—perceiving that they were made the victims of superstition and tyranny,—catching some faint glimpses of the natural equality of mankind,—and maddened to desperation by the wrongs heaped upon them,—they rose to obtain not only redress, but revenge, and in their blind fury made a sacrifice of the true with the false, of liberty with despotism, of all that was virtuous with much that was vile. But they were not made prodigies of impiety and cruelty in a day. They were trained to be atheists in the school of a false christianity. Yet the French revolution has been a fine windfall for the priesthood and the aristocracy in all countries. The causes of it are almost wholly forgotten—its terrible effects only are remembered. Both the aristocracy and the priesthood, however, need to be instructed by it more than the people.

Dr. Beecher proceeds:—'One of the most alarming indications of our day is, that men are too proud to be free under the law, and are beginning to turn the same glance upon the law, that they turn in Europe upon the despot . . . What is the meaning of those fearful heavings in our cities? There is already a power amongst us that can with difficulty be kept down.' Who are these men who are too proud to be free under the law, but the aristocracy and the rabble? Who composed the mob in Boston, but 'gentlemen of property and standing'? Who headed the disturbance at Utica, but officers of the law and members of Congress? Who plundered the public mail, in the open face of day, and burnt a portion of its contents, but the most respectable inhabitants of Charleston? Who have threatened the infliction of lynch law so daringly, as the southern representatives upon the floor of Congress? Who have winked at these and other violations of public order more approvingly than the great body of the clergy? And on what side is Dr. Beecher found, except on that which is supported by the lawless, the profane, the oppressive, the aristocratical? 'What is the meaning of those fearful heavings in our cities?' Let the pro-slavery associates of Dr. B. answer; let the Colonization Society answer . . . let the resolutions of certain presbyteries and synods and conferences answer; let the conduct of such papers as the Boston Recorder, Vermont Chronicle, Christian Mirror, New York Observer, Philadelphia Presbyterian, and Christian Advocate and Journal, answer!

Our remarks upon his late sabbatical speech, at Pittsburgh, are extending to a length which we did not originally contemplate. There are but two other points which challenge our notice. Having dwelt upon the prevalence of atheism, fatalism, and agrarianism in our land . . . Dr. Beecher says that a 'more serious evil than *all these* yet remains.' Imagine, if you can, what this is! But the Dr. shall tell you:—'Those silken ties, those soft but mighty bands which have held Christians of the *North* and of the *South* together, are beginning to break.' Those *silken ties* are literally *the chains of slaves*. The prospect of a purification of the northern churches and pulpits from the guilt of oppression, by excluding southern clerical slavites and men-stealers from church fellowship;—obedience to the apostolic injunction, 'Wherefore come out from among them, and be ye separate, saith the Lord, and touch not THE UNCLEAN THING, and I will receive you' . . . yes, this is something more deplorable than even atheism, fatalism or agrarianism! It matters not that southern churches are cages of unclean birds—clotted with innocent blood—full of violence, adultery and oppression—made up of traffickers in slaves and souls of men; not to be united with them in *christian fellowship*, would be a terrible catastrophe to virtue, republicanism, religion! 'Disunion is the key of death which will open Pandemonium upon us, and let in wide-spread, universal desolation'—disunion with those who make merchandise of Christ's body! with the scourgers and violators of helpless women! with the enemies of human rights! with the plunderers of the poor and needy! with the asserters of the divine institution of slavery! with the allies of the Man of Sin, who banish the bible and teach the sufficiency of oral instruction! Why, this is to use the dialect of heathenism, and to 'open Pandemonium' with a vengeance!

> 'Wherefore hear the word of the Lord, ye scornful men, that rule this people—Because ye have said, We have made a covenant with death, and with hell are we at agreement: when the overflowing scourge shall pass through, it shall not come unto us: for we have made lies our refuge, and under falsehood have we hid ourselves: Therefore thus saith the Lord God, Your covenant with death shall be disannulled, and your agreement with hell shall not stand; when the overflowing scourge shall pass through, then ye shall be trodden down by it.'

Dr. Beecher brings himself into awful condemnation, by giving the right hand of fellowship to *christian* thieves and adulterers, and by likening a separation from their vile company to 'the key of death,' the opening of Pandemonium. Most indubitably he refers to a prospective division between northern and southern churches on the ground of slavery; and he regards it as the worst of evils. Hence, he 'goes with the South,' in all its turpitude of crime, rather than peril the union between Christ and Belial! . . .

Only think of it, Baptists, Methodists, Episcopalians, Unitarians, &c. &c. 'our civil and religious liberties' depend upon the union of 'our beloved (Presbyterian) church' with southern whoremongers and men-stealers! Dr. Beecher seems to have forgotten, that the vitality and usefulness of a church do not depend upon numbers, but upon christian integrity and purity. Whatever religious denomination shall exclude slaveholders from their fellowship, and brand slaveholding as man-stealing, will be first

in real prosperity, and more perfect in union than any other.
Another alarming evil which the Dr. justly assails, is the prevalence of pollution:

> 'There is a systematized effort to pollute through the
> eye. The pencil, and the chisel, and the art of engraving,
> have prostituted their power to this bad end. Learning
> men wickedness by printing is too slow. We must have
> pictures to teach it through the eye.'

The mass of impurity which exists, both in the church and out
of it, and which has recently been brought to light by a few con-
temned pioneers in the holy cause of Moral Reform, is absolutely
appalling. If some of it be owing to painters, sculptors and en-
gravers, how much more is to be attributed to the criminal silence
of ministers respecting the seventh commandment! . . . No
wonder licentiousness abounds every where. But if, with all the
safeguards of virtue that surround us at the North—if, with
marriage made honorable and sacred, and with all our facilities
and opportunities to train up our children in the nurture and
ADMONITION of the Lord, lewdness is rolling in upon us like a
flood—what must be the state of things at the South, where
virtue is crucified by law, where two millions and a half of human beings are herded together as cattle or swine, where every
barrier against pollution is prostrated, where the marriage covenant is unknown, and where bribes are given to stimulate to an
unholy amalgamation! The system of slavery is essentially and
necessarily full of all uncleanness, incest, and adultery, without
let or hindrance, in the open face of day! Does Dr. Beecher oppose that system? Is his soul affected only in view of the profligacy which exists incidentally among our white population at
the North? Is the preservation of virtue among our colored
population a matter of no consequence? O that this talented
individual might be led to see and hate his present inconsistency,
and to forsake the company of lewd oppressors!

The Fanatics

In the fourth volume of The Liberator *Garrison had begun a very effective new department called "Refuge of Oppression." This usually occupied two or three columns at the left of page one of the paper and was intended as a regular feature "into which we propose to copy some of the choicest specimens of anti-abolition morality, decency, logic and humanity—generally without note or comment" (Lib., Jan. 4, 1834). It became, and still is, extremely valuable for the assessment of the weight and fury of the forces against Garrison. It makes one wince to think of him pouring over the abuse directed against him and his movement for these thirty years and conscientiously selecting those from which he took the worst floggings, to pass on to his readers, enemies and friends. The care with which he winnowed out those with the sharpest bite and the most crushing logic developed against him, the labor he put into setting them up in type, is the greatest proof of his firmness and resistant spirit. The selections themselves prove how widely* The Liberator *was read in "exchanges" and by the opposition. In one example that follows, references to "jacobinism and agrarianism" show how well known was Garrison's attack on Lyman Beecher. Here, also, is an excellent statement of the Southern boasts that their system would promote more "liberty and tranquillity" by insuring the absence of the early labor agitators and agrarian socialists, who came into prominence in the North in the wake of the great depression of 1837.*

January 28, 1837

Refuge of Oppression

THE FANATICS

[From the Richmond Enquirer]

. . . The public safety is the supreme law. The South must take her stand. Her safety calls for new and strong measures against the fanatics. The New York Journal of Commerce of the 5th states, that the Abolition Convention, which lately sat in that city, has broken up—but that its deeds are yet wrapt in darkness—and the only glimpse we catch of them is in 'the following outline from the Boston Liberator, leaving the imagination of the reader to fill up the details.'

[Here the Richmond Enquirer copies one of the most spirited paragraphs of the Liberator, which it professes to consider 'incendiary,' and throws it before the eyes of more slaves in one week than the Liberator ever visited since it was first published!] . . .

FANATICISM, EXTRA!

The following is taken from a communication to the Richmond Whig, and is republished in the United States Telegraph with approbatory comments! Sentiments so perfectly absurd, irrational, anti-republican and anti-American, were never before promulgated to the world; and yet the authors and approvers of such stuff are constantly clamoring against those who contend for universal freedom and equal rights, as fanatics! Oh! the times!

'There is an evident tendency to the excesses of jacobinism and agrarianism in the United States, created by that devotion to the person of a leader, which in its extravagant zeal has lost sight of principle. We have reason to know that many government men themselves are alarmed at the symptoms, and know not where nor how the distemper of the times is to end. We of the South have cause now, and will soon have greater, to congratulate ourselves on the existence of a population amongst us, which excludes that *populace* which, in effect, rules some of our Northern neighbors, and is rapidly gaining strength wherever slavery does not exist—a populace made up of the dregs of Europe, and the most worthless portion of the native population. We have been sometimes taunted, sometimes consoled with the remark, that our Northern brethren will step in to suppress domestic insurrections amongst us! Whoever lives to witness the first exchange of friendly offices between the North and South in this respect, will see the banner of the South crossing the Potomac and the Delaware to the relief of Northern property and constitutional liberty, against the fierce and exterminating aggressions of jacobins, levellers, and agrarians.

'Instead of rejoicing in the rapid emigration of slaves, which many do from the hope that the drain will at length relieve Virginia from that population, and make her what is called a free State, the far-sighted patriot ought to regret the circumstance as producing greater evils than it causes. We cannot attain so high a degree of prosperity as communities exempt from slavery; but we are better secured in our liberty and tranquillity.— We have no cause to fear agrarian and leveling licentiousness where slaves constitute the populace; and the tyranny of the mob is not only worse and more bloody than that of kings, but more immediately to be dreaded in this country. On these heads we confess our minds to have undergone, in five years, a total revolution, set in motion, at first, by the Northern Abolitionists, and completed by the scenes of the year. Let us hold to the slaves as a shield against levellers and agrarians, for which purpose they are far more valuable than for their labor. We were startled at the first annunciation of the proposition, that liberty cannot long exist without slavery. The seeming paradox overwhelms the mind at the first contemplation. But it is not truly philosophical. We will not stop to prove it; time will inscribe it as an infallible truth on the page of American history.'

The Children's Crusade

Frightening to many was Garrison's activity in forming children's groups of Abolitionists under the leadership of Henry C. Wright. Wright was perhaps the biggest contributor to The Liberator *after Garrison himself and was by far the most radical member of the Abolitionist movement. He was formerly an orthodox preacher, then became absolutely anticlerical and anarchistic. His position toward children was: "never teach your children, nor allow them to be taught, a religion that conflicts with their humanity. Never allow them to receive anything as from God, that conflicts with the facts of their physical, social, intellectual or moral being."*

Garrison's frequent publication of Wright's lectures to children aroused frantic opposition on the grounds that he was teaching innocent little souls "that no authority was to be obeyed but that which emanates directly from God." As a powerful and outraged opposition to Garrison began to develop in the ranks of the movement itself on account of his "sifting in these foreign matters," the worst thing they could say was that "I had as soon my son should be taught that the Bible is not true as that I have not the right, under God, to chastise him; for he understands that if done, it is done by the direct sanction of the Almighty."

Also in the following selections, there occur the names of the Grimké sisters, the first women to take a public platform for antislavery. They were thought to have been hopelessly corrupted by Garrison and Wright and a loathsome example to the good women of the land.

April 7, 1837

CHILDREN OF BOSTON

BOSTON, March 25, 1837

DEAR GARRISON,—Agreeably to notice, I met the Boston Juvenile Anti-Slavery Society this afternoon, at the Marlboro' Chapel. . . .

I addressed the children assembled, an hour and a half. Showed them—1. What is slavery. 2. In what consists the *sin* of slavery. 3. What to call the sin of slavery. . . . Children cannot conceive of a circumstance in which it can be right, in the sight of God, to hold a slave for one moment. Did I say children never offer an excuse? I am perhaps mistaken, for one boy in Boston asked me, 'Mr. Wright, would you have all the slaves set free now?' 'Yes—to-day.' 'I would not.' 'Why?' *They would cut all our throats.'* 'How do you know?' *'Father* says so.' How can a father dare to instruct his son in such wicked lies?

Those dear children would tell you that slavery is—*to hold and use a fellow man as property.* They would tell you what property is, what God allows us to hold and use as property, and what is meant by using a man as property—i. e. to kick or knock him about as you please. These children would tell you, that the essential sin of slavery consists in holding and using man as property. They would tell you that God never gave to man a right to have dominion over man—that he never designed it in the Gospel, *that man should coerce the will of man by physical force. Never*—under any circumstances. They would tell you, that slaveholding is theft and robbery, and slaveholders thieves and robbers.

Thus I instructed the children, that man is a man and that whoever would hold and use him as something else, is the vilest of robbers, and that those who claim a right of dominion over man, and enforce that claim by an appeal to physical force, and thus treat him as a brute, is a heaven-daring usurper of God's authority over us. For God, and God alone, has a right of dominion over man; and he has never delegated this right to another. The moment a man claims a right to *control the will of a fellow being by physical force,* he is at heart a slaveholder. All slaveholders do this. They are then hardened invaders of God's prerogative. They are robbers—men of violence and blood.

There are two Juvenile Anti-Slavery Societies in Boston—one of boys, one of girls. They are going to work for the overthrow of slavery. . . .   H. C. WRIGHT, Children's Agent

June 16, 1837

. . . 'Children, who catches children, and carries them off?' 'The black man.' 'Who told you so?' 'Our mothers and nurses.' 'Is it true, that black men steal little children, and carry them off?' 'No sir.' 'Who does?' 'White men.' These nurses and mothers do very wrong, and tell their children what is not true, when they would keep them still, and make them mind, by saying—'The black man will catch you.' It is false. The black man

never catches little children. The white men slaveholders steal
the children, and carry them off and sell them.

'Children, what color do you suppose the devil is?' 'Black.'
'What makes you think so?' 'Our parents and teachers told us
so, and the ministers always represent the devil as black. The
devil is always painted black.' 'The Chinese and Africans think
the devil is white. What makes them think he is white?' 'Because the white people hate the colored people so badly, and
steal them, and sell them, and make slaves of them.' 'If the devil
ever was black, I should think he was turning white, for he seems
to have a great affection for white people! He is entering into
the very hearts of the whites, exciting them to hate the blacks,
and to make them all slaves. It is time for our ministers and
painters to begin to represent the devil as *white*, unless they will
leave off stealing and enslaving the colored people. I hope the
mothers will no more frighten their children with a *black* man
or devil; they have much more reason to teach them to shun
the *white* man, and a white devil.' . . .   H. C. WRIGHT

Boston, June 8, 1837

July 21, 1837

A DOMESTIC SCENE

. . . It was a Sabbath eve. The table was spread, the lamp
lighted, and Bibles laid on the table. The family circle drew
around the table, each one with a Bible. In this domestic circle
of peace and love, were those devoted sisters, S. M. & A. E.
GRIMKE, whose writings breathe so much of the spirit of Heaven,
and are so adapted to lead the soul into the clear light and pure
atmosphere of the kingdom of God. Two questions of solemn
and mighty import were proposed for examination—questions
second to no others in their bearings on the condition and institutions of men on earth and their destinies in the eternal world.

1. *Has God given to man dominion over man?*
2. *Has God authorized man to control man by violence?*

. . . After a full investigation, after searching the old and the
new covenant, we came to the unanimous conclusion—*that God
never did give to man dominion over man*—that men, women or

children never should be subjected, in any kind or degree, to the will of man—that when one man, in any way or to any extent, subjects another man to his will, he invades the prerogative of God—that even a desire to hold dominion over man is rebellion against God and the very spirit of slaveholding, and that whoever, willingly or unwillingly, comes under the dominion of man and looks to the will of man for a law of life, becomes in manner, a slave. . . .

An inquiry was started—What Institutions among men *necessarily* tend to subject man to the will of man? Whatever they might be, it was concluded unanimously that they were *malum in se*—wrong in themselves. Our school system, from the infant school *down* to the University, as now constituted and managed, it was thought tended to enslave the mind of man to man, to alienate the soul from God and bind it in chains of human servitude. All civil governments are designed to subject man to the dominion of man and, of necessity tend to this result. Therefore, all human governments are usurpations; necessarily wrong, and no one who has entered into the kingdom of Christ should have any thing to do with them. This was a startling doctrine to some of our precious little circle, and efforts were made to show that such were not the design and necessary tendency of human governments. But like little children we were sitting at the feet of Jesus, learning of him and were determined to embrace the truth and do our duty and leave all consequences with God. 'Lord, what wilt thou have us believe and do?' was our only inquiry. The church and ministry were canvassed. Some of our circle thought . . . that many ministers preached themselves rather than Christ, and were more anxious to establish their own, rather than Christ's influence over men. The domestic institution [marriage—T.N.], though designed by God to establish his authority over the world, and peculiarly adapted to this end, yet, as now managed, it was an engine to crush the soul and subject it to man. At least, it does little towards conquering this world to Christ. We concluded, that even when our love for any fellow being, whatever the relation sustained to us, leads us to think, speak or act with reference to the will and pleasure of that being, our love was sin in the sight of God. Never to think, speak or act simply to please men, was our conclusion. . . .

Thus we settled the question that God alone has a right of dominion over man—that he has never authorized man to exercise dominion over man in any form—not even parents over their children, for their duty is to subject children not to their own will, but to God's. Nor man over woman. Thus did we conclude that no institution designed, or necessarily tending, like human governments and slavery, to subject man to the dominion of man, can be approved of God. They must be wrong. . . .

H. C. WRIGHT

Fourth of July in Providence

Another of Garrison's acts of heresy was provoked by a visit on March 30, 1837, from John Humphrey Noyes, who founded the Oneida Community in 1848. Garrison published a revolutionary letter from him, and they were like-minded in many ways. Garrison's approval of him as a revolutionary thinker led his clerical enemies to say that Garrison also endorsed a theory of Noyes that "one man had no more exclusive right to one woman than, when a number sat together at their dinner . . . one man had an exclusive right to the whole of one [serving] dish." But Garrison did not share Noyes's faith in revolution by sex; in fact, he was very conventional about sex, but he went far beyond Noyes in the frontal attack he made on American society in his Fourth of July address.

In it he considered the plight of the radical who believes that there is no hope for the health of a political system. What was the use of his efforts? His answer was: "to furnish proof through all time, that the nation did not perish in consequence of not having been duly warned." Here, again, he begins to develop more his tactic of the saving remnant, or revolutionary separatism.

July 28, 1837

FOURTH OF JULY IN PROVIDENCE

. . . Mr. Garrison read an extract from a letter in his possession from an esteemed friend, in which the following startling passage occurred:—*'My hope of the millenium begins, where Dr. Beecher's expires,* viz. AT THE OVERTHROW OF THIS NATION.' Tremendous thought! This passage had deeply affected his mind. Yet there was nothing treasonable in that hope—no want of true patriotism—no anti-republican malevolence. It was predicted upon the rise, progress, and actual character of this nation: it was uttered to dispel the impious and arrogant assumption, that the nation has a charmed life, is immortal, and therefore can never perish.

. . . In vain shall we depend upon our naval armaments, our strong fortifications, our military strength for these are sure evidences that our trust is not in the living God, but in an arm of flesh; *and the more they are multiplied; the more certain do we render our destruction.* Nor form of government, nor repre-

sentative body, nor written parchment, nor social compact, nor
physical preparation, can give us perpetuity . . . *The downfall
of the Republic seems inevitable.* We are waging war, not against
England or France, or the combined powers of Europe—but
against the Rights of Mankind, against the Image of God, against
Divine Revelation, against Life and Immortality . . .

Mr. Garrison next dwelt upon the barbarous treatment the
abolitionists had received at the hands of their guilty countrymen, and said that probably the end is not yet. It may be that
some of them will yet perish at the stake, or meet the fate of
the martyr Stephen. Thus far, swarms of calumnies have followed them, sucking the life-blood out of their reputations . . .
Like Paul, some of them have been cruelly beaten—others have
been stoned; and others have been in perils of robbers, in perils
by their own countrymen, in perils in the wilderness, in perils
in the city, in perils among false brethren. They are declared
to be outlaws on their native soil. The Constitution shields none
but those who wield the cowskin, or who consent with the thief,
the adulterer, and the oppressor. In one half of what is called
our 'glorious Union,' a fire is kindled to consume to ashes every
man who ventures south of the Potomac as an opponent of
slavery. This is American liberty!

. . . He then remarked, that with all our boasted security
and presumptuous self-confidence, we are continually betraying,
—in spite of our pride and at the expense of our veracity,—a
painful consciousness that the temple of our freedom is tottering
to its fall; that our Union is a rope of sand, which may be easily
severed by some chance wave of popular fury; that our Constitution is debilitated beyond all medical restoration; and that we
have built upon hay, wood and stubble, which need only a single
spark of the electric fluid to wrap the nation in one general conflagration. It is only for some few seditious hot-spurs at the
South to brandish their cowskins or bowie knives, and shout,
'We'll dissolve the Union!' and straightway we turn pale, our
knees smite together, our tongues cleave to the roofs of our
mouths! At every outbreak of real or imaginary fanaticism, we
are thrown into consternation. . . . Indeed, so feeble are the
bands which bind this nation together, and so general is the conviction of its instability, that even the speaker, though styled

a 'miserable fanatic and madman,' had been deemed capable of
effecting its utter overthrow! What did all this prove, but that
there is no moral or social cohesiveness to bind us together . . .

If (continued Mr. G.) History be not wholly fabulous . . .
the overthrow of the American confederacy is in the womb of
events, and it shall come in a manner that shall awe the nations
of the earth! . . .

. . . Why must it perish?

I. No superstructure, however beautiful, imposing or valuable, can remain long, which is not based upon a solid foundation. It is as true in morals as it is in mechanics. . . . He went
back to the first settlement of this country by the 'pilgrim fathers,' and found them laying its foundation in blood and violence—in slavery and the slave trade—in a war of extermination
with the proprietors of the soil—in cruelty, in bigotry, which
derided the claims of conscience, and whipped, banished or
hanged those whose religious views differed from their own . . .
We had enlarged, but not changed this foundation . . . we had
waxed worse and worse, having merely substituted Abolitionists
for Quakers and Baptists, upon whom to wreak our intolerance.

II. No nation, as such, can be judged and punished in a future
state. It must be visited, if at all, here—in a corporate form—
so that the nations of the earth may be instructed by 'terrible
things in righteousness.' What nation has ever sinned so fearfully as our own, according to the abundance of its light? We
are wholly oppression in the midst of us. We have waxed fat,
and kicked, and behaved abominably without let or hindrance.
. . . Our national transgressions remain to be avenged by Almighty God: not one of them is cancelled—not one repented of
—not one blotted out!

III. Neither sacred or profane history furnishes any example
of a nation of oppressors voluntarily surrendering their ill-gotten
power. Either the oppressed have been compelled to emancipate
themselves by revolution, or God has been necessitated to destroy
their oppressors by direct interposition—by blinding them with
his lightnings, and annihilating them with his thunder-bolts.
Wherein, then, do we hope for the salvation of this nation?

IV. This nation is destined to perish, because in wading
through blood and carnage to independence, *it at the outset dis-*

carded the Prince of Peace, and elected George Washington to be its Saviour; and it is now confidently relying upon its naval ships, its strong fortifications, its military prowess, for security from dangers without, from seditions within. It is a fruitless attempt at self-government, totally distinct from the government of God in Jesus Christ; while the fact is incontrovertible, that no man or body of men, have ever governed, or shall be able to govern themselves by any external restraints, or legislative enactments, or judicial penalties, or executive prerogatives; or by any military forces, or political checks and balances, or democratic creeds and forms; and hence this experiment, like all others which have preceded it, whether monarchical, aristocratical or republican, must sooner or later inevitably fail. For these outward contrivances to effect inward obedience,—these reliances upon the wisdom of man . . . do clearly show that *our trust is in each other,* and not in the living God. . . .

. . . we are an idolatrous people, and worship many gods. . . . 1st. The MOLOCH OF SLAVERY, in whose presence we tremble exceedingly, and to whom we cause our children to pass through the fire. 2d. PARTY, the Baal of Selfishness, upon whom we rely for all our honors, preferments, and successes. 3d. The GODDESS OF LIBERTY, an imaginary deity, to whom we pay superstitious honors, and whom we devoutly worship in the abstract. 4th. THE UNION, the Janus of Patriotism, having two faces, and thereby exciting continual strife between its northern and southern worshippers as to its real features. 5th. THE CONSTITUTION, a sacred oracle, alike infallible and immaculate, whom it is sacrilege to touch or examine. These be thy Gods, O Columbia!

To darken the aspect of our fate, it is only necessary to consider the appalling fact that we have A UNION OF CHURCH AND STATE IN SUPPORT OF SLAVERY. We have not only a President in the Chair of State, who unblushingly announces that . . . he knows not the Lord, neither will he set the captives free, even though a constitutional majority of the people should demand their emancipation at the Seat of Government; but we have Theological Professors . . . Doctors of Divinity, and Presidents of Universities, and Bishops and Ministers . . . in overwhelming proportion, some of whom are slaveholders, others maintain that slaveholding is by divine authority and in accordance with christianity, and others who take sides with the oppressor and against those who plead for the oppressed. . . .

The corruptions of the CHURCH, so called . . . are obviously more deep and incurable than those of the STATE; and therefore, the CHURCH, in spite of every precaution and safeguard, is first to be dashed in pieces. . . . Look at the ferocious spirit manifested last year in the Methodist General Conference at Cincinnati: what does it betoken? Look at the recent turbulent and despotic transactions in the Presbyterian General Assembly at Philadelphia: that mighty denomination is severed in twain at a blow. *The political dismemberment of our Union is ultimately to follow.*

Mr. Garrison spoke in indignant terms of the invasion of Texas by our countrymen, of the sudden recognition of its independence by our government, and of the prospect of its immediate annexation to our Union. It was in the confident belief that this unparalleled act of national profligacy would be perpetrated, and that the most dreadful consequences would follow in its train, that he had spoken so despairingly of the salvation of the country. . . .

If such be the dismal prospect before us, it might be asked,— What, then, have the abolitionists accomplished, after all their vaunted zeal and activity, their toils and sacrifices? . . . Much for themselves; much for the human race; much for the cause of God. They have won for themselves the gratitude of the perishing slaves, the respect and admiration of mankind, and the smiles of heaven. The 'blood of the souls of the poor innocents,' no longer stains their garments. It is through such instrumentalities as they have used,—it is by the victorious power of such examples as they have set . . . that the dominion under the whole heaven is ultimately to be transferred from human authority . . . to Him who is King of kings, and Lord of lords.

Still it might be asked,—If the pillars of our Union are to fall, and the nation itself is beyond redemption, why are we called upon to put forth confessedly unavailing efforts to prevent the direful catastrophe? . . . To exonerate our own souls from guilt, and to furnish proof through all time, that the nation did not perish in consequence of not having been duly warned. . . . Is it asked, of what avail will it be for any of us, in obedience to the command of heaven, to take a bunch of hyssop, and strike the lintel and side-posts of our dwellings with blood? Because the Lord is to pass through the land, to redeem the captives and punish their oppressors; and when he seeth the blood upon our lintel and side-posts, the Lord will pass over the door, and will not suffer the destroyer to come into our houses to smite us. By our fear, therefore, for his great name; by our hope of life and immortality; by all the ties which bind us to the universe of God; by the anguish, and blood, and groans of downtrodden, expiring humanity,—we may not suppress our voices, nor slacken our efforts, nor abandon the field of moral warfare, without committing high treason against heaven, and ranking ouselves among the enemies of our race. 'He that overcometh and keepeth my works unto the end, to him will I give POWER OVER THE NATIONS,' saith the Son of God.

A Colored Brother

Garrison's anger was intensified by the fact that the movement, in a mass form, was never healthier. Recruits were still coming in from all over the North. But the inevitable diluting of ideology began to take place as the cause became more and more popular and acceptable. It was becoming, in some quarters, a political advantage to be a bit of an Abolitionist and determined to "stand up to the South." Ironically, the more the ranks filled, the more necessary it seemed to some of the leaders to dump, or tame, Garrison. The New York State Anti-Slavery Society was particularly keen on going into politics; there was much anti-Garrison strength there. But the base he had among the Negroes was never undermined by these attacks as these perceptive remarks by a Negro preacher and political Abolitionist demonstrate.

October 13, 1837

SPEECH OF A COLORED BROTHER

Delivered at the late meeting of the N.Y. State Anti-Slavery Society at Utica

Rev. Theodore S. Wright, of New York, moved the adoption of the Annual Report, and said:

. . . Immediately after the insurrection in Virginia, under Nat Turner, we saw colonization spreading all over the land; and it was popular to say the people of color must be removed. The press came out against us, and we trembled. . . . Benj. Lundy, of Baltimore, nobly lifted up his voice. But he did not feel the vileness of colonization. A young man, for making certain expositions touching slavery, was incarcerated in a dungeon, where truth took a lodgment in his heart, where he avowed eternal hatred to slavery, and where, before high heaven, in the secresy [*sic*—T.N.] of his dungeon, with the chains upon him, he resolved to devote his life to the cause of emancipation. And when the president of the American Anti-Slavery Society stepped forward and paid the fine, we were crying for help, we were remonstrating.—We had no other means but to stand up as men, and protest. We declared, this is our country, and our home;—here are the graves of our fathers. But none came to the rescue. At that dark moment we heard a voice; it was the voice of Garrison, speaking in trumpet tones. It was like the voice of an angel of mercy. Hope, hope then cheered our path. The signs of the times began to indicate brighter days. . . .

Now, you would be considered as uncharitable towards pro-slavery men, whether editors of newspapers, presidents of colleges, or theological seminaries, if you advance the idea that they are not abolitionists, anti-slavery men.—Three years ago, when a man professed to be an abolitionist, we knew where he was. He was an individual who recognized the identity of the human family. Now a man may call himself an abolitionist, and we not know where to find him. Your tests are taken away. A rush is made into the abolition ranks. Free discussion, petition, anti-Texas, and political favor converts are multiplying. Many throw themselves in, without understanding the breadth and depth of the principles of emancipation. I fear not the annexation of Texas. I fear not all the machinations, calumny and opposition of slaveholders, when contrasted with the annexation of men whose hearts have not been deeply imbued with these high and holy principles. Why, sir, unless men come out and take their stand on the principle of recognizing man as man, I tremble for the ark, and I fear our society will become like the expatriation society; every body an abolitionist. These points which have lain in the dark must be brought out to view. The identity of the human family, the principle of recognizing all men as brethren, that is the doctrine, that is the point which touches the quick of the community. It is an easy thing to talk about the vileness of slavery at the south, but to call the dark man a brother, heartily to embrace the doctrine advanced in the second article of the constitution, to treat all men according to their moral worth, to treat the man of color in all circumstances as a man and brother, that is the test.

Every man who comes into this society ought to be catechised. It should be ascertained whether he looks upon man as man, all of one blood and one family. A healthful atmosphere must be created in which the slave may live when rescued from the horrors of slavery. I am sensible I am detaining you, but I feel that this is an important point. I am alarmed sometimes, when I look at the constitutions of our societies. I am afraid that brethren sometimes endeavor so to form the constitutions of societies, that they will be popular. . . .

. . . Our hearts have recently been gladdened by an address of the Annual Meeting of the Friends' Society in the city of New York, in which they insist upon the doctrine of immediate emancipation. But that very good man who signed that document, as the organ of that Society, received a man of color, a Presbyterian minister, into his house, gave him his meals alone in the kitchen, and did not introduce him to his family. That shows how men can testify against slavery at the south, and not assail it at the north where it is tangible. Here is something for abolitionists to do. What can the friends of emancipation effect while the spirit of slavery is so fearfully prevalent? Let every man take his stand, burn out this prejudice, live it down, talk it down, every where consider the colored man as a man, in the church, the stage, the steamboat, the public house, in all places, and the death-blow to slavery will be struck.

A Short Catechism

Garrison's thoughts at this time were never more dangerous and dire toward the church and the state. There was much bitterness, much hopelessness in them. He was acutely conscious of the frantic maneuvering going on behind his back to isolate him and defame him. One of the high points of his soreness and excoriation toward those who began to talk moderation and gradualism comes with this attack on the raw racism existing in this society. He is saying that with us, racism is a kind of religious exercise, and seems to be concluding that redemption by the ordinary forms of social transformation was out of the question.

November 17, 1837

A SHORT CATECHISM

Adapted to All Parts of the United States

1. Why is American slaveholding in all cases not sinful?
Because its victims are *black*.

2. Why is gradual emancipation right?
Because the slaves are *black*.

3. Why is immediate emancipation wrong and dangerous?
Because the slaves are *black*.

4. Why ought one-sixth portion of the American population to be exiled from their native soil?
Because they are *black*.

5. Why would the slaves if emancipated, cut the throats of their masters?
Because they are *black*.

6. Why are our slaves not fit for freedom?
Because they are *black*.

7. Why are American slaveholders not thieves, tyrants and men-stealers?
Because their victims are *black*.

8. Why does the Bible justify American slavery?
Because its victims are *black*.

9. Why ought not the Priest and the Levite, 'passing by on the other side,' to be sternly rebuked?

Because the man who has fallen among thieves, and lies weltering in his blood, is *black*.

10. Why are abolitionists fanatics, madmen and incendiaries?
Because those for whom they plead are *black*.

11. Why are they wrong in their principles and measures?
Because the slaves are *black*.

12. Why is all the prudence, moderation, judiciousness, philanthropy and piety on the side of their opponents?
Because the slaves are *black*.

13. Why ought not the free discussion of slavery to be tolerated?
Because its victims are *black*.

14. Why is Lynch law, as applied to abolitionists, better than common law?
Because the slaves, whom they seek to emancipate, are *black*.

15. Why are the slaves contented and happy?
Because they are *black!*

16. Why don't they want to be free?
Because they are *black!*

17. Why are they not created in the image of God?
Because their skin is *black*.

18. Why are they not cruelly treated, but enjoy unusual comforts and privileges?
Because they are *black!*

19. Why are they not our brethren and countrymen?
Because they are *black*.

20. Why is it unconstitutional to pity and defend them?
Because they are *black*.

21. Why is it a violation of the national compact to rebuke their masters?
Because they are *black*.

22. Why will they be lazy, improvident, and worthless, if set free?
Because their skin is *black*.

23. Why will the whites wish to amalgamate with them in a state of freedom?
Because they are *black!!*

24. Why must the Union be dissolved, should Congress abolish slavery in the District of Columbia?

Because the slaves in that District are *black*.

25. Why are abolitionists justly treated as outlaws in one half of the Union?

Because those whose cause they espouse are *black*.

26. Why is slavery 'the corner-stone of our republican edifice?'

Because its victims are *black*.

We have thus given twenty-six replies to those who assail our principles and measures—that is, one reply, unanswerable and all-comprehensive, to all the cavils, complaints, criticisms, objections and difficulties which swarm in each State in the Union, against our holy enterprize. The victims are BLACK! 'That alters the case!' There is not an individual in all this country, who is not conscious before God, that if the slaves at the South should be to-day miraculously transformed into men of white complexions, to-morrow the abolitionists would be recognised and cheered as the best friends of their race; their principles would be eulogised as sound and incontrovertible, and their measures as rational and indispensable! Then, indeed, immediate emancipation would be the right of the slaves, and the duty of the masters! . . .

The Lovejoy Climax

With all the turmoil going on as the Abolitionist ranks grew in power and strength, Garrison's now well-known nonresistant views had kept his followers from being badly hurt or harassed by serious legal action. Then editor Elijah P. Lovejoy, whom Garrison claimed never did advocate immediate abolition, was killed in Alton, Illinois, while defending his printing press, with a gun in his own hands, by a vicious proslavery mob. This shocking event aroused some hitherto reluctant liberals and individualists, like Reverend William Ellery Channing, who found Lovejoy much nearer their ideal as a reformer than Garrison and were greatly wrought up over the incident. They had regarded Garrison's verbal intemperance with annoyance and scarcely noticed his 1835 mobbing by the gentlemen in broadcloth.

Garrison published the story of Lovejoy's martyr's death in columns edged in black and went on to editorialize that in seven years' time there had really been no change in the status of the Negro, slave and free, and that the country seemed to be "diseased beyond the power of recovery." He condemned the whole American people, particularly since Faneuil Hall, hitherto "sacred to liberty and the rights of mankind," could not be obtained for a protest meeting against the slaying of a reformer upholding the freedom of the press.

Dr. Channing was equally aroused by this last irony and sent a vigorous and rare letter of public reproach to The Liberator, *which succeeded, along with many others, in opening the hall for the meeting.*

When the meeting took place, the Massachusetts Attorney General, James Austin, appeared on the platform, demanded the right to speak, and proved himself as willing to whip up a mob against the Abolitionists as the murderers of Lovejoy. Wendell Phillips, in one of his great spontaneous orations, easily put the attorney general to rout.

November 24, 1837

A MARTYR FOR LIBERTY

Slain by the Hands of His Own Countrymen!

An awful sensation pervades the land. It is one of shuddering horror, excited in view of a fearful and bloody spectacle, seldom equalled in atrocity, and never surpassed in infamy. The amiable, benevolent, intrepid LOVEJOY is no more! He fell overpowered by a band of assassins on the night of the 7th instant, and his mangled body lies covered by the sod! Thanks be to God, though being dead, he yet speaks!—for his spirit lives, and is walking abroad over the land, terrifying a guilty, conscience-stricken people by its presence; and from his grave is heard a cry of blood, in tones that pierce the heavens and shake the earth. The circumstances under which he was sacrificed make the deed one of loathsome turpitude, and must deservedly bring upon our country the worst reproaches of the civilized world,—ay, and the retributive judgment of Almighty God. In his martyrdom he died as the representative of Philanthropy, Justice, Liberty and Christianity; well, therefore, may his fall agitate all heaven and earth!

That his loss will be of incalculable gain to that noble cause which was so precious to his soul, is certain. In destroying his press, the enemies of freedom have compelled a thousand to speak out in its stead. In attempting to gag his lips, they have unloosed the tongues of tens of thousands of indignant souls. In murdering a loyal and patriotic citizen, in order to allay a petty local excitement, they have stirred up a national commotion which causes the foundations of the republic to tremble. O most insane and wicked of mankind! . . .

We cannot, however, in conscience delay the expression of our regret, that our martyred coadjutor and his unfaltering friends in Alton should have allowed any provocation, or personal danger, or hope of victory, or distrust of the protection of Heaven, to drive them to take up arms in self-defence. They were not required to do so either as philanthropists or christians, and they have certainly set a dangerous precedent in the maintenance of our cause,—though the fact does not in the least palliate the blood-thirsty conduct of their assailants. Far be it from us to reproach our suffering brethren, or weaken the impression of sympathy which has been made on their behalf in the minds of the people—God forbid! Yet, in the name of Jesus of Nazareth, who suffered himself to be unresistingly nailed to the cross, we solemnly protest against any of his professed followers resorting to carnal weapons under any pretext or in any extremity whatever.

December 8, 1837

APPALLING DEVELOPEMENTS

It required a sanguinary conflict of seven years, on the part of the American colonies with the mother country, to maintain the 'self-evident truths,' that all men are created equal, and endowed by their Creator with an inalienable right to liberty. That a people who had made such sacrifices, and suffered their blood to be so lavishly shed in the cause of HUMAN RIGHTS, might degenerate even to servility, within half a century, was deemed a possible, though not a very probable occurrence:—That, on achieving their independence, they would immediately begin to doubt or deny the soundness of the doctrines for which they had contended, as applied to all mankind, who would have ventured to predict?—That, instead of emancipating the four hundred thousand slaves whom they held in bondage, while they themselves were struggling for freedom, they would multiply them to MILLIONS within three-score years, and make their yokes heavier and their fetters more galling, was a supposition too absurd, too atrocious for human conception or utterance.

All these dreadful inconsistencies, however, are cherished realities. Nearly one-fifth part of the American people are at this moment held in chains and slavery! by their own countrymen! —and it is far more perilous to plead for their deliverance, than it was for the colonists to denounce the oppression of England We have been engaged in a moral campaign to redeem them from bondage, for a period equal in duration to the revolutionary war; yet they clank their chains, and their cries continue to enter into the ear of the Lord of Sabaoth!

When we first unfurled the banner of the Liberator, we anticipated a severe struggle with the foul Spirit of Slavery, whose name is BLASPHEMY. . . . We knew it would prove no childish controversy, and that the whole land would rock with the excitement. We were sure, that if a huge system of licentiousness, robbery and oppression could thrive on the American soil, it must be because there were deep corruption and almost total insensibility on the part of the people. But, we confess, of the awful state of this nation, which subsequent developements have made manifest, we had no adequate conception. Whatever scenes of violence might transpire in the slaveholding States, we did not anticipate that, in order to uphold southern slavery, the free States would voluntary trample under foot all order, law and government, or brand the advocates of universal liberty as incendiaries and outlaws. It did not occur to us, that nearly every religious sect, and every political party, would rally on the side of the oppressor; that Doctors of Divinity, Professors of Theology, Presidents of Colleges, and those who claim to be ministers of the gospel would have the impiety to justify the enslavement of men by the Bible; that public halls and meeting-houses would be closed against those who might wish to 'plead for justice, in the name of humanity, and according to the law of the living God'—and opened to those who were the deadliest enemies of freedom and Christianity; or that the right of petition would be denied to the people by Congress, respecting the existence of slavery in those portions of territory over which it holds entire jurisdiction. We did not dream that the free discussion of any system or institution, in the republic, would be regarded as dangerous or unconstitutional;—least of all that it would be necessary for any man to lay down his life, in a free State, in defence of the liberty of the press.

The whole land has been thoroughly proved, by a series of tests, to be diseased beyond the power of recovery. 'There is no healing of its bruise—its wound is grievous.' In the solemn language of another—'The violence of mobs—the fury of oppressors—the violence and madness of their protectors and apologists in Church and State, are but the tremendous convulsions, the fearful delirium, the dying throes of an expiring nation.' The American people are waging war, not against England or France, or the combined powers of Europe; but against the Rights of Mankind, against the image of God, against Divine Revelation, against Life and Immortality, against the Throne of the Eternal.

December 8, 1837

CHANNING'S LETTER

To the Citizens of Boston

I feel that I owe it to my fellow citizens and myself, to offer some remarks on the proceedings of the Board of Aldermen, in relation to a petition presented to them for the use of Faneuil Hall, in order that there might be an expression of public sentiment in regard to the late ferocious assault on the liberty of the press at Alton. . . .

This petition was rejected by the Board of Aldermen, on the ground, that the resolutions, which might be passed at the proposed meeting, would not express the public opinion of the city and would even create a disgraceful confusion in Faneuil Hall, or in other words, would excite a mob. . . .

. . . To intimate that such resolutions would not express the public opinion of Boston, and would even create a mob, is to pronounce the severest libel on this city. It is to assert, that peaceful citizens cannot meet here in safety to strengthen and pledge themselves against violence, and in defence of the dearest and most sacred rights. And has it come to this? Has Boston fallen so low? May not its citizens be trusted to come together to express the great principles of liberty, for which their fathers died? . . . Instead of this, what is Boston now doing? Into what scale is this city now thrown? Boston now says to Alton, go on; destroy the press; put down the liberty of speech; and still more, murder the citizen who asserts it; and no united voice shall here be lifted up against you, lest a like violence should break forth among ourselves.

It is this view of the rejection of the petition, which deeply moves me. That a petition, bearing my name, should be denied, would not excite a moment's thought or feeling. But that this city, which I have been proud to call my home, should be so exhibited to the world, and should exert this disastrous influence on the country, this I cannot meet with indifference.

I earnestly hope that my fellow citizens will demand the public meeting which has been refused, with a voice which cannot be denied; but unless so called, I do not desire that it should be held. If not demanded by acclamation, it would very possibly become a riot. A government, which announces its expectation of a mob, does virtually, though unintentionally, summon a mob, and would then cast all the blame of it on the 'rash men' who might become its victims.

But is there no part of our country, where a voice of power shall be lifted up in defence of rights incomparably more precious than the temporary interests which have often crowded Faneuil Hall to suffocation? Is the whole country to sleep? An event has occurred, which ought to thrill the hearts of this people as the heart of one man. A martyr has fallen among us to the freedom of the press. A citizen has been murdered in defence of the right of free discussion. I do not ask whether he was christian or unbeliever, whether he was abolitionist or colonizationist. He has been murdered in exercising, what I hold to be the dearest right of the citizen. Nor is this a solitary act of violence. It is the consummation of a long series of assaults on public order, on freedom, on the majesty of the laws. I ask, is there not a spot in the country whence a voice of moral reprobation, of patriotic remonstrance, of solemn warning shall go forth to awaken the slumbering community? There are, indeed, in various places, meetings of Anti-Slavery Societies, to express their sorrow for a fallen brother. But in these I take no part. What I desired was, that the citizens of Boston, of all parties, should join as one man in putting down the reign of terror by the force of opinion, and in spreading a shield over our menaced liberties. I felt, that the very fact that the majority of the people here, are opposed to the peculiar opinions of our murdered fellow citizen, would give increased authority to our condemnation of this ferocious deed. . . .   WM. E. CHANNING

December 15, 1837

PUBLIC MEETING IN FANEUIL HALL

Speech of Mr. Austin

. . . [Lovejoy—T.N.] resorted to violence, and he fell by violence. He excited the passions of men, by conduct unwise, impolitic, rash, extravagant and unchristian; and the consequence of his conduct was such as might have been anticipated.

Now he (M. A.) would ask, whether it may not be said, in the language of Scripture, "Died Lovejoy as a fool dieth!" He should have applied to the magistrates. He was the last man that ought to have been there, with a musket in his hand. . . .

Why then, asked Mr. A, are we called here to sympathize with the victim, or to say any thing about the mob at Alton, or why should the events there be the cause of special resolutions by the citizens of Boston? Have we no events of the like kind nearer home, to condemn? Yes, Sir, wherever the Abolition fever rages, there are mobs and murder. . . .

. . . what will be said to us by the citizens of Illinois and Missouri, whom it is our self-assumed prerogative to rebuke?

Will they not tell you that you yourselves have been instigated by the same passions, and have yielded to a like infirmity of human nature? . . . they will say,—'and do you not know that occasions have arisen in which your ancestors found it inevitable that they should take the law into their own hands—extreme cases, in which indeed there was no law reaching to their condition but the original and immutable law of self-preservation, and necessary self-defense?'

Will they not tell you that when your fathers were colonists, and as such under obligations to pay a tax levied upon them by the British Government, fatal to their liberties, their rights, their happiness—they implored, they besought its remission, and urged that their people should not be goaded into violence, and instigated to a madness which human reason could not control? And when these prayers, and entreaties, and supplications were vain, and there was no law that could protect them, and no middle path between ruin and resistance, did not they take their protection under the security of their own arm, and marching down from this Hall—*an orderly mob*—pour the disgusting instrument of their degradation into the sea? So will the people of Missouri claim to do, when their lives are threatened by the operations of these abolition conspirators. Do you suppose they will wait for the slow progress of the laws? They will tell you they will call on the God of Heaven, as your fathers did, and with his favor will defend themselves.

It is the natural operation of human passion, when stimulated, and goaded and urged to extremes, to pour out its resistance in ebullitions of ungoverned wrath. Lament it as we may, such is the constitution of mankind, and all the preaching of all the zealots of party will not produce a change.

Satisfy a people that their lives are in danger, by the instrumentality of the press, injudiciously and intemperately operating on the minds of slaves; give them reason to fear the breaking out of a servile war, in which their wives and daughters are to be the victims of that brutal ferocity that knows how to add horrors to death, and if you can keep such a people calm and tranquil, and quiet, obedient to the restraints of any law that can be made, or to any power that can enforce it, you must first beat out of them every vestige of humanity, and make them more abject than slavery itself.

It is the folly of the Abolition party that they will not learn this great truth.

. . . The best way to prevent mobs, is, to do nothing to excite a mob.

Extreme rights are not to be insisted on by peaceable men. . . .

The speech of the Attorney General produced a great excitement throughout the Hall. Wendell Phillips, Esq. who was to have followed Mr. Hillard in the arrangement, rose to reply. That portion of the assembly who sympathized with Mr. Austin, now became so boisterous, that Mr. Phillips could not proceed. . . .

Speech of Mr. Phillips

MR. CHAIRMAN:—We are met for the free discussion of these resolutions, and the events which gave rise to them. [Cries of question, hear him, no gagging, etc.] I hope I shall be permitted to express my surprise at the sentiments of the last speaker;—surprise not only at such sentiments from such a man, but at the applause they have elicited in these walls. A comparison has been drawn between the events of the Revolution and the tragedy at Alton. We have heard it asserted in this Hall, that Great Britain had a right to tax the Colonies, and we have heard the mob at Alton, got up to murder Lovejoy, compared to that band of our patriot fathers, who threw the tea overboard! [Great ap-

plause.] Fellow citizens, is this true? [No, no.] The mob at
Alton were met to wrest from a citizen his just rights; to resist
the laws. We have been told that our fathers did the same;
and the glorious mantle of Revolutionary precedent has been
thrown over the mobs of our days. . . . To draw the conduct of
our ancestors into a precedent for mobs; for a right to resist laws
we ourselves have enacted, is an insult to their memory. . . .
The men of that day went for the right. They were the people
rising to sustain the laws and constitution of the Province. The
rioters of our day go for their own wills, right or wrong. Sir,
when I heard the gentleman lay down principles which place the
rioters, incendiaries and murderers of Mt. Benedict and Alton,
side by side with OTIS and HANCOCK, with QUINCY and ADAMS,
I thought those pictured lips [pointing to the portraits in the
Hall] would have broken into voice to rebuke the recreant American—the slanderer of the dead. [Great applause and counter
applause.] The gentleman said that he should sink into insig-
nificance, if he dared to gainsay the principles of these resolutions. Sir, for the sentiments he has uttered, on soil consecrated
by the prayers of Puritans and the blood of Patriots, the earth
should have yawned and swallowed him up! [Here the agitation
continued for some time, before the speaker could be heard.] . . .

The Fire and Hammer of God's Word

The murderers of Lovejoy were never punished and the repression of Abolitionism by popular violence, by terror, continued, particularly in the Southern and border states. According to Judge Luke Lawless of Missouri, when a mob burned a Negro at the stake, such action was "not the act of numerable and ascertainable malefactors, but of congregated thousands seized by a mysterious, metaphisical and almost electric phrenzy, and thereby not indictable."

Garrison thought deeply about two problems: 1. That his policy of absolute nonviolence was better for the movement. 2. That the anger and retort in the North over the Lovejoy killing proved that the masses still felt a heroic martyrdom was better than a Christian turning of the other cheek—provided, of course, that it was a white man, and not a slave, meeting violence with violence.

He summed up this most exciting year (1837) with a new prospectus for The Liberator, *full of the most appalling "heresies." He called for the rejection of nationalism, of "human government," with its physical punishments and restraints against mankind, and for the ushering in of the Kingdom of God on earth. But his deepest thought went toward that uneasiness in his mind, that awful contradiction by which violence by a white man in defense of his liberty is noble, that by a Negro, unspeakable. If the Negro could not use physical force, no one could. His new call was for total human disarmament in the perfectly natural context of the Christian ethic which the "civilized" world pretended to follow with all its heart.*

December 15, 1837

PROSPECTUS OF THE LIBERATOR

Volume VIII

. . . In commencing this publication, we had but a single object in view—the total abolition of American slavery, and as a just consequence, the complete enfranchisement of our colored countrymen. . . .

In entering upon our eighth volume, the abolition of slavery will still be the grand object of our labors, though not, perhaps, so exclusively as heretofore. There are other topics, which, in our opinion, are intimately connected with the great doctrine of inalienable human rights; and which, while they conflict with no religious sect, or political party, as such, are pregnant with momentous consequences to the freedom, equality and happiness of mankind. These we shall discuss as time and opportunity may permit.

The motto upon our banner has been from the commencement of our moral warfare, 'OUR COUNTRY IS THE WORLD—OUR COUNTRYMEN ARE ALL MANKIND.' We trust that it will be our only epitaph. Another motto we have chosen is, 'UNIVERSAL EMANCIPATION.' Up to this time, we have limited its application to those who are held in this country, by southern taskmasters, as marketable commodities, goods and chattels, and implements of husbandry. Henceforth, we shall use it in its widest latitude: the emancipation of our whole race from the dominion of man, from the thraldom of self, from the government of brute force, from the bondage of sin—and bringing them under the dominion of God, the control of an inward spirit, the government of the law of love, and into the obedience and liberty of Christ, who is *the same,* yesterday, TO-DAY, and forever.' . . .

Next to the overthrow of slavery, the cause of PEACE will command our attention. The doctrine of non-resistance, as commonly received and practised by Friends, and certain members of other religious denominations, we conceive to be utterly indefensible in its application to national wars;—not that it 'goes too far,' but that it does not go far enough. If a nation may not redress its wrongs by physical force—if it may not repel or punish a foreign enemy who comes to plunder, enslave or murder its inhabitants—then it may not resort to arms to quell an insurrection, or send to prison or suspend upon a gibbet any transgressors upon its soil. *If the slaves of the South have not an undoubted right to resist their masters in the last resort, then no man, or body of men, may appeal to the law of violence in self-defence—for none have suffered, or can suffer, more than they.* [Italics mine—T.N.] If, when men are robbed of their earnings, their liberties, their personal ownership, their wives and children, they may not resist, in no case can physical resistance be allowable, either in an individual or collective capacity. Now, the doctrine we shall endeavor to inculcate is, that the kingdoms of this world are to become the kingdoms of our Lord and of his

Christ; consequently, that they are all to be supplanted, whether they are called despotic, monarchical or republican, and he only who is King of kings, and Lord of lords, is to rule in righteousness. The kingdom of God is to be established IN ALL THE EARTH, and it shall never be destroyed, but it shall 'BREAK IN PIECES AND CONSUME ALL OTHERS:' its elements are righteousness and peace, and joy in the Holy Ghost: without are dogs, and sorcerers, and whoremongers and murderers, and idolators, and whatsoever loveth and maketh a lie. Its government is one of love, not of military coercion or physical restraint: its laws are not written upon parchment, but upon the hearts of its subjects—they are not conceived in the wisdom of man, but framed by the Spirit of God: its weapons are not carnal, but spiritual: its soldiers are clad in the whole armor of God . . . Hence, when smitten on the one cheek, they turn the other also; being defamed, they entreat; being reviled, they bless; being persecuted, they suffer it; they take joyfully the spoiling of their goods; they rejoice, inasmuch as they are partakers of Christ's sufferings; they are sheep in the midst of wolves; in no extremity whatever, even if their enemies are determined to nail them to the cross with Jesus, and if they like him could summon legions of angels to their rescue, will they resort to the law of violence.

As to the governments of this world, whatever their titles or forms, we shall endeavor to prove, that, in their essential elements, and as at present administered, they are all Anti-Christ; that they can never, by human wisdom, be brought into conformity to the will of God; that they cannot be maintained, except by naval and military power; that all their penal enactments being a dead letter without an army to carry them into effect, are virtually written in human blood; and that the followers of Jesus should instinctively shun their stations of honor, power and emolument—at the same time 'submitting to every ordinance of man for the Lord's sake,' and offering no *physical* resistance to any of their mandates, however unjust or tyrannical. . . .

Human governments are to be viewed as judicial punishments. If a people turn the grace of God into lasciviousness, or make their liberty an occasion for anarchy,—or if they refuse to belong to the 'one fold and one Shepherd,'—they shall be scourged by the governments of their own choosing, and burdened with taxation, and subjected to physical control, and torn by factions, and made to eat the fruit of their evil doings, until they are prepared to receive the liberty and the rest which remain, on earth as well as in heaven, for THE PEOPLE OF GOD. . . .

So long as men contemn the perfect government of the Most High, and will not fill up the measure of Christ's sufferings in their own persons, just so long will they desire to usurp authority over each other—just so long will they pertinaciously cling to human governments, *fashioned in the likeness and administered in the spirit of their own disobedience.* Now, if the prayer of our Lord be not a mockery; if the kingdom of God is to come universally, and his will be done ON EARTH AS IT IS IN HEAVEN; and if, in that kingdom, no carnal weapon can be wielded, and swords are beaten into ploughshares, and spears into pruning hooks, and there is none to molest or make afraid, and no statute-book but the bible, and no judge but Christ; then why are not Christians obligated to come out NOW, and be separate from 'the kingdoms of this world,' which are all based upon THE PRINCIPLE OF VIOLENCE, and which require their officers and servants to govern and be governed by that principle? How, then, is the wickedness of men to be overcome? Not by lacerating their bodies, or incarcerating them in dungeons, or putting them upon tread-mills, or exiling them from their native country, or suspending them upon gibbets—O no!—but simply by returning good for evil, and blessing for cursing; by using those spiritual weapons which are 'mighty, through God, to the pulling down of strongholds'; by the power of that faith which overcomes the world; by ceasing to look to man for a redress of injuries, however grievous, but committing the soul in well-doing, as unto a faithful Creator, and leaving it with God to bestow recompense —'for it is written, Vengeance is mine; I will repay, saith the Lord.'

These are among the views we shall offer in connection with the heaven-originated cause of PEACE,—views which any person is at liberty to controvert in our columns, and for which no man or body of men is responsible but ourselves. If any man shall affirm that the anti-slavery cause, as such, or any anti-slavery society, is answerable for our sentiments on this subject, to him may be justly applied the apostolic declaration, 'the truth is not in him.' We regret, indeed, that the principles of abolitionists seem to be quite unsettled upon a question of such vast importance, and so vitally connected with the bloodless overthrow of slavery. It is time for all our friends to know where they stand. If those, whose yokes they are endeavoring to break by the fire and hammer of God's word, would not, in their opinion, be justified in appealing to physical force, how can they justify others of a different complexion in doing the same thing? And if they conscientiously believe that the slaves would be guiltless in shedding the blood of their merciless oppressors, let them say so unequivocally—for there is no neutral ground in this matter, and the time is near at hand when they will be compelled to take sides. . . .

The Non-Resistance Society

Garrison's new prospectus did not save him from the accusations that he was tainting the movement with extremism, and yet those he trusted most went along completely with his new ideas. Among the clergy, however, it was said about him that he openly advocated an equal division of property, the prostration of all law, the abrogation of marriage, and the promiscuous intercourse of the sexes—and this could all be proved, somehow, from his new prospectus. The pressure so built up that he decided to remove the peace question from abolition entirely by starting a Non-Resistance Society. In Tolstoy's brilliant Christian tract The Kingdom of God Is Within You, *Garrison and Adin Ballou become the seminal spirits. The Declaration of Sentiments which Garrison wrote for the Non-Resistance Society in 1838 is included. Tolstoy, indeed, was Garrison's last great convert and in the autumnal splendor of the Russian's passing came the end of the inspired line of Christian prophets. Tolstoy expressed his debt to Garrison with his usual elegance and precision as follows:*

The life work of Garrison, the father, his founding the Society of the Non-Resistants, and his Declaration, convinced me even more than my intercourse with the Quakers that the divergence of the Christianity of the state from Christ's law of non-resistance by violence has been long since noticed and pointed out, and men have laboured and still do labour to counteract it. But the fate of Garrison, and particularly that of Ballou, almost unknown, notwithstanding fifty years of active and persistent work in one direction, has confirmed me in the belief that there exists a certain inexpressed but fixed determination to oppose all such attempts by a wall of silence. . . . all the efforts of Garrison, the father, the foundation of his society, his periodical and his Declaration, as well as the life work of Ballou, are the same as if they had never existed.

September 28, 1838

DECLARATION OF SENTIMENTS
ADOPTED BY THE
Peace Convention
Held in Boston, September 18, 19, & 20, 1838

ASSEMBLED in Convention, from various sections of the American Union, for the promotion of peace on earth, and good will among men, we, the undersigned, regard it as due to ourselves, to the cause we love, to the country in which we live, and to the world, to publish a DECLARATION, expressive of the principles we cherish, the purposes we aim to accomplish, and the measures we shall adopt to carry forward the work of peaceful, universal reformation.

We cannot acknowledge allegiance to any human government; neither can we oppose any such government, by a resort to physical force. We recognize but one KING and LAWGIVER, one JUDGE and RULER of mankind. We are bound by the laws of a kingdom which is not of this world; the subjects of which are forbidden to fight; in which MERCY and TRUTH are met together, and RIGHTEOUSNESS and PEACE have kissed each other; which has no state lines, no national partitions, no geographical boundaries; in which there is no distinction of rank, or division of caste, or inequality of sex; the officers of which are PEACE, its exactors RIGHTEOUSNESS, its walls SALVATION, and its gates PRAISE; and which is destined to break in pieces and consume all other kingdoms.

Our country is the world, our countrymen are all mankind. We love the land of our nativity, only as we love all other lands. The interests, rights, liberties of American citizens are no more dear to us, than are those of the whole human race. Hence, we can allow no appeal to patriotism, to revenge any national insult or injury. The PRINCE OF PEACE, under whose stainless banner we rally, came not to destroy, but to save, even the worst of enemies. He has left us an example, that we should follow his steps. GOD COMMENDETH HIS LOVE TOWARD US, IN THAT WHILE WE WERE YET SINNERS, CHRIST DIED FOR US.

We conceive, that if a nation has no right to defend itself against foreign enemies, or to punish its invaders, no individual possesses that right in his own case. The unit cannot be of greater importance than the aggregate. If one man may take life, to obtain or defend his rights, the same license must necessarily be granted to communities, states, and nations. If *he* may use a dagger or a pistol, *they* may employ cannon, bomb-shells, land and naval forces. The means of self-preservation must be in proportion to the magnitude of interests at stake, and the number of lives exposed to destruction. But if a rapacious and bloodthirsty soldiery, thronging these shores from abroad, with intent to commit rapine and destroy life, may not be resisted by the people or magistracy, then ought no resistance to be offered to domestic troublers of the public peace, or of private security. No obligation can rest upon Americans to regard foreigners as more sacred in their persons than themselves, or to give them a monopoly of wrong-doing with impunity.

The dogma, that all the governments of the world are approvingly ordained of God, and that THE POWERS THAT BE in the United States, in Russia, in Turkey, are in accordance with his will, is not less absurd than impious. It makes the impartial Author of human freedom and equality, unequal and tyrannical. It cannot be affirmed that THE POWERS THAT BE, in any nation, are actuated by the spirit, or guided by the example of Christ, in the treatment of enemies: therefore, they cannot be agreeable to the will of God: and, therefore, their overthrow, by a spiritual regeneration of their subjects, is inevitable.

We register our testimony, not only against all wars, whether offensive or defensive, but all preparations for war; against every naval ship, every arsenal, every fortification; against the militia system and a standing army; against all military chieftains and soldiers; against all monuments commemorative of victory over a foreign foe, all trophies won in battle, all celebrations in honour of military or naval exploits; against all appropriations for the defence of a nation by force and arms, on the part of any legislative body; against every edict of government, requiring of its subjects military service. Hence, we deem it unlawful to bear arms, or to hold a military office.

As every human government is upheld by physical strength, and its laws are enforced virtually at the point of the bayonet, we cannot hold any office which imposes upon its incumbent the obligation to compel men to do right, on pain of imprisonment or death. We therefore voluntarily exclude ourselves from every legislative and judicial body, and repudiate all human politics, worldly honors, and stations of authority. If *we* cannot occupy a seat in the legislature, or on the bench, neither can we elect *others* to act as our substitutes in any such capacity. . . .

The history of mankind is crowded with evidences, proving that physical coercion is not adapted to moral regeneration; that the sinful dispositions of man can be subdued only by love; that evil can be exterminated from the earth only by goodness; that it is not safe to rely upon an arm of flesh, upon man whose breath is in his nostrils, to preserve us from harm; that there is great security in being gentle, harmless, long-suffering, and abundant in mercy; that it is only the meek who shall inherit the earth, that the violent who resort to the sword are destined to perish with the sword. Hence, as a measure of sound policy,—of safety to property, life and liberty,—of public quietude and private enjoyment,—as well as on the ground of allegiance to HIM who is KING OF KINGS, and LORD OF LORDS,—we cordially adopt the non-resistance principle; being confident that it provides for all possible consequences, will ensure all things needful to us, is armed with omnipotent power, and must ultimately triumph over every assailing force.

We advocate no jacobinical doctrines. The spirit of jacobinism is the spirit of retaliation, violence, and murder. It neither fears God, nor regards man. *We* would be filled with the spirit of CHRIST. If we abide by our principles, it is impossible for us to be disorderly, or plot treason, or participate in any evil work: we shall submit to every ordinance of man, FOR THE LORD'S SAKE; obey all requirements of government, except such as we deem contrary to the commands of the gospel; and in no case resist the operation of law, except by meekly submitting to the penalty of disobedience.

But, while we shall adhere to the doctrine of non-resistance and passive submission to enemies, we purpose, in a moral and spiritual sense, to speak and act boldly in the cause of GOD; to assail iniquity, in high places and in low places; to apply our principles to all existing civil, political, legal, and ecclesiastical institutions; and to hasten the time, when the kingdoms of this world will have become the kingdoms of our LORD and of his CHRIST, and he shall reign for ever. . . .

A Farce in One Act

It was not long before withdrawals and defections began to take place in the local antislavery societies. The Essex County Anti-Slavery Society was a Garrisonian stronghold, so an attempt to split it in favor of a new organization, with both local and national societies, was closely studied by both parties. Garrison's analysis of one abortive attempt reveals his mastery of the mass organizing process: "The true secret of the wonderful progress of our cause, aside from its intrinsic excellence, has been the entrusting of its management to THE PEOPLE . . ."

June 21, 1839

A FARCE IN ONE ACT

It is becoming more and more apparent, that the division in the anti-slavery ranks in this Commonwealth is confined to a very small number—a mere faction—as destitute of fair-mindedness and genuine abolition sympathy, as they are noisy and turbulent. A remarkable exemplification of this fact is seen in the result of the late annual meeting of the Essex County Anti-Slavery Society . . . That sly participant in the clerical appeal conspiracy, and vain and restless factionist, C. T. Torrey, has been the Recording Secretary of this society during the past year, and has spared no pains to mould it to his purposes. . . .

Mr. Torrey, as Recording Secretary, read the Annual Report, in which he had contrived to 'sift in,' as adroitly as he knew how, the new political dogmas, to which every abolitionist must subscribe implicitly, or be guillotined 'without benefit of *clergy*.' That portion of it, which related to this subject, was, on motion, stricken out, by a vote of 106 to 32. Mr. Torrey, we are told, instead of submitting the whole Report to the Society, took the unheard of liberty to cut out the rejected disquisition upon politics, and pocketed it or destroyed it upon the spot. Soon after, he requested all those who voted in the negative, and those only, to retire to a neighboring school-house, for the purpose of organizing another county society. Of the 140 or 150 delegates in attendance, it is said that not more than a dozen withdrew, in accordance with this invitation! These actually went through the farce of forming an 'Essex Co. *Abolition* Society' . . .

By the 4th Article of their Constitution, it is provided that 'each auxiliary shall be entitled to send *five* delegates to the meetings of the County Society; and every Society embracing more than fifty members shall be entitled to send *one* additional delegate for every twenty members.' Quite a select affair—as nice and aristocratical as priestly management could desire! . . . Hitherto, the utmost pains have been taken to secure a general attendance of abolitionists—and the more that came, the better for the cause, the more interesting and useful the convocation. But here we have the veritable iron bedstead of Procrustes, by which the bodies of abolitionists, in their individual and associated capacity, must be reduced or elongated to precisely the same dimensions! . . . *The people* are not to be trusted in the management of their own cause. Nearly every other moral and religious enterprise in the land is placed under the control of an almost self-elected, irresponsible body of men, who have little or no sympathy with the 'common people.' Hence it is, that the *republican* character of the anti-slavery cause, which allows people of both sexes, and of all classes and complexions—farmers, mechanics, workingmen, 'niggers,' women, and all—to stand on the same platform, and enjoy the same rights and privileges, to have the same freedom of speech and an equal amount of controlling power, has been from the beginning vulgar and odious in the eyes of chief priest, scribe and pharisee, those who are ever grasping for power, place, emolument. The true secret of the wonderful progress of our cause, aside from its intrinsic excellence, has been the entrusting of its management to THE PEOPLE —the bone and muscle of community—the unambitious, unaspiring, courageous, disinterested, true-hearted friends of bleeding humanity. It has thus fought its way to public respect and popular favor, and under the same auspices would still continue to advance in a geometrical ratio. But an example of this kind, it is clearly foreseen by the Doctors and Rabbis, if tolerated much longer, must prove fatal to their monopoly of power, and to the supremacy of a religious aristocracy. No marvel, now that ABOLITION is a prize worth seizing, that these proud men are eager to get possession of it. The pressure of public opinion against them is becoming more and more insupportable. They dare not so openly oppose, as they once did, an enterprise which they cordially hate; nay, they are compelled to acknowledge themselves abolitionists. Not 'Garrison abolitionists,' to be sure—for they are very pious men, and reverence the Sabbath, (though they are still unable to perceive how much better is a negro than a sheep,) and cherish a sacred regard for human governments, and believe in the divinity of politics, and are no radicals . . .

There Shall Be Division

Now, in 1839, the division was coming to a head. Zion's Herald, a Methodist paper, reported with some elation that within the movement, "THERE SHALL BE DIVISION. One party will set up independently of the other—of whom Mr Garrison, with all his no-government, no-clergy, no-Sabbath notions, will be the soul, the sun, the center and circumference. The other party, affiliated with kindred societies, and continuing with them in the GREAT NATIONAL SOCIETY, will go on its original basis."

This report released a wave of clerical abuse of Garrison. His intolerance of gradualism, his brutality toward those Christians "not ready" to attack slaveholders and their supporters as murderers, adulterers, thieves, barbarians, and kidnappers, his "anarchy, scheduling public lectures by females, his repulsive association with men like Noyes," all of which accusations had a basis of fact, made him a perfect target for the liberals and moderates. They charged that his attitude was "preventing many worthy men from appearing in favor of immediate emancipation."

The national Anti-Slavery office in New York had become almost wholly anti-Garrison. It was now regarded as a "worthy" public institution. Agents were being trained there not to emphasize Southern cruelties but to stress that this was an intellectual and religious crusade. They were talking softly there not of immediate emancipation but of "Immediate Emancipation, Gradually Accomplished," or "Gradual Emancipation, Immediately Begun." Their appeals were to be exclusively directed toward community leaders, professional men, men of property and influence. A typical modern writer on the movement, D. L. Dumond, says, "These men were offended and repulsed by Garrison's vagaries and vehemence, and above all, by his cheap cynicism toward political institutions."

Garrison could have made his peace with the front office, but he had had these offers before. When he had begun the crusade in Boston, Lyman Beecher had told him, "If you will give up your fanatical notions and be guided by us [the clergy], we will make you the Wilberforce of America." But Garrison would never give up working side by side with the slaves, the free Negroes, and the women, the three elements the New York clique wanted to drop. They were the sources of his strength. He believed profoundly in them—that the nonintellectual, the nonreligious, the despised men and women of no property and standing, would bring about the transformation. He had his answer carefully thought out: "Power is essential to creation, but the feeblest soul in the Universe may influence the most powerful body . . . God has chosen the foolish things of the world to confound the wise, and God has chosen the weak things of the world to confound the mighty."

James G. Birney, a former but now redeemed slaveowner, a lawyer,
publisher, and politician, was groomed to take Garrison's place. He
delivered a scathing attack on Garrison as a dangerous, irresponsible
radical whose excesses could only bring on a season of lust and blood.
Garrison printed this and his own reply in The Liberator. *The two*
versions have been abridged. The attack came on the single point that
all Abolitionists who could vote were morally obliged to do so, according
to the Birney faction. Garrison said, as a Non-Resistant, voting is "sin
for me, but I have no control over the consciences of others." Birney,
lawyer-like, based his whole argument on the wording of the original
Declaration of Sentiments of the American Anti-Slavery Society, which
Garrison had written.

June 28, 1839

VIEW

OF THE CONSTITUTION OF THE AMERICAN A.S. SOCIETY AS CONNECTED
WITH THE 'NO-GOVERNMENT' QUESTION

[From the Emancipator]

. . . ALL the action required by the constitution is MORAL.
Arguments addressed to the understandings and consciences of
members of Congress are as much *moral,* as when addressed to
our fellow-citizens generally. . . .

It is not unworthy of remark, that whilst our fellow-citizens,
generally, were to be *'addressed'*—Congress were to be *influenced.*
. . . They were 'also to endeavor, in a constitutional way, to
influence Congress,' &c, that is, by such considerations as are
usually found to have a *peculiar* influence on men enjoying *peculiar* stations at the will of the people. . . . if their action was
not responsive to our petitions, they were to be *influenced* by the
fear of incurring the displeasure of their constituents; consequently, of being removed from their places, that others might
occupy them;—the only 'constitutional way' of doing which was,
by the use of the Elective Franchise.

This action on Congress has been called, by way of distinction,
'political.' For several years after the organization of the American Society, our numbers were too few to attempt it. It was
therefore, generally, deprecated as inexpedient. Notwithstanding, however, on one occasion, if no more, the very next year after

the institution of the Society, when the moral propriety of abolitionists carrying out their principles at the ballot box was denied by some, it was strenuously upheld by the editor of the Liberator, who had aided in forming the Constitution—he himself setting the example of voting for a professed abolitionist, and encouraging others to do the same,—taking the ground, that, although the votes of all the abolitionists in Boston (where the election referred to took place) would not have been sufficient to elect the anti-slavery candidate on that occasion, the course recommended would, *if persisted in,* facilitate his election at some future period. (See Liberator, Dec. 1834.)

The constitutions of none of the State societies (and they are all auxiliaries to the American) contain any thing repugnant to political action. That of the Massachusetts Society declares in Art. 2, 'The objects of the society shall be, to endeavor, by all means, sanctioned by *law,* humanity and religion,' &c.

The Declaration of Sentiments, published simultaneously with the constitution by those who had subscribed the latter, contains the following passage.

'We maintain, that there are at the present time, the highest obligations resting upon the PEOPLE of the free States, to remove slavery by moral and *political* action, as prescribed in the Constitution of the U.S.'

After mentioning the pledge of the free States to put down servile insurrection—the danger, expense, and political inequalities produced by slavery, it proceeds to the conclusion that, 'IT MUST BE BROKEN UP.' How it was to be broken up, except by means of the Elective Franchise, does not appear. The Declaration of Sentiments, although possessing no *obligatory* force, is the highest evidence that can be had, apart from the constitution, of what was intended by the *body* of the abolitionists in that instrument.

It is not recollected, that any amount of opposition worthy to be mentioned was made to political action as inculcated (according to the foregoing interpretation) in the constitution—in the Declaration of Sentiments—in the State Societies' constitutions —and in the Editorials of the Liberator—till after political action was, in consequence of the increase of our numbers, decided upon. Within the last twelve or eighteen months, it is believed—after efforts, some successful, some not, had been begun to affect the elections—and whilst the most indefatigable exertions were being made by many of our influential, intelligent and liberal friends to convince the great body of the abolitionists of the necessity— the indispensable necessity—of breaking away from their old *'parties,'* and uniting together in the use of the elective franchise for the advancement of the cause of human freedom in which we were engaged;—at this very time, and mainly, too, in that part of the country where *political action* had been most successful, and whence, from its promise of soon being wholly triumphant, great encouragement was derived by abolitionists every where, a Sect has arisen in our midst, whose members regard it as of religious obligation, IN NO CASE, *to exercise the elective franchise.* This persuasion is part and parcel of the tenet which it is believed they have embraced,—that as Christians have the precepts of the Gospel to direct, and the Spirit of God to guide them, all Human Governments, as necessarily including the idea of *force* to secure obedience, are not only superfluous, but unlawful encroachments on the Divine government, as ascertained from the sources above mentioned. Therefore, they refuse to do any thing voluntarily, by which they would be considered as acknowledging the lawful existence of human governments. Denying to Civil governments the right to use force, they easily deduce, that family governments have no such right. Thus, they would withhold from parents any power of personal chastisement or restraint for the correction of their children. They carry out to the full extent the 'non-resistance' theory. To the first ruffian who would demand our purse, or oust us from our houses, they are to be unconditionally surrendered, unless *moral suasion* be found sufficient to induce him to decline from his purpose. Our wives, our daughters, our sisters—our mothers we are to see set upon by the most brutal, without any effort on our part, except argument to defend them—and even they, themselves, are forbidden to use in defence of their purity such powers as God has endowed them with for its protection, if resistance should be attended with injury or destruction to the assailant. In short, the 'No-Government' doctrines, as they are believed now to be embraced, seem to strike at the root of the social structure; and tend—so far as

I am able to judge of their tendency,—to throw society into entire confusion, and to renew, under the sanction of religion, scenes of anarchy and license that have generally heretofore been the offspring of the rankest infidelity and irreligion. . . .

. . . If the Constitution of the American Society requires, of those who subscribe to it, to use the elective franchise, for the abolition of slavery, and men join the Society knowing this, they are justly bound to vote. . . .

But there is no need of violating any one's conscientious scruples. If the No-Government men do verily believe that there rests on them the religious duty of directing their efforts to the annihilation (peaceable, of course) of all existing Governments, and that the abolition of slavery, by the use of the elective franchise, is inconsistent with it, they are certainly bound by their own rule as honest men to renounce the latter. But in doing so, they should remember, that they have ceased to 'consent' to one of the 'principles' of the Constitution, and are virtually no longer entitled to membership. In such a case, it would seem that the duty of withdrawing from the Society was altogether plain. *Justice* to those with whom they associated, and to the slave, requires it;—*self-respect* requires it—*the No-Government enterprise,* which they have nearest at heart, requires it. For what can be more unjust to those originally associated for the reasonable and single purpose of abolishing slavery, than the attempt to compel them into a crusade for abolishing Government? What more unjust to the suffering slave, than to tie on to his magnificent cause a project that is hopeless, because cast out by the common sense of the nations of the world? * What more prejudicial to the scheme of annihilating human governments, than to remain associated with those who are striving to purify, invigorate and immortalize their own?

For my part I can see no good reason why the No-Government party should *wish* to remain in the Anti-Slavery Association, see-

* The 'No-Government' theory is but a new growth of the *fungi* which sprung up in the early period of the Reformation when the minds of men were heated by the new ideas presented to them. It soon led to the most horrible excesses. Against it Luther spoke and wrote, and even invoked the civil authority—but all availed nothing. It ran its career through such scenes of lust and blood, that humanity could not but rejoice at its extinction.

ing it must be productive of endless dissentions;—especially, when, by withdrawing and forming on a platform of their own, they could conduct their enterprise vigorously and harmoniously, and permit the abolitionists, who are advocates of the elective franchise, to do the same with theirs. . . .

JAMES G. BIRNEY

REPLY TO JAMES G. BIRNEY
. . . . .

ABOLITION AT THE BALLOT-BOX

Once more, I beg not to be misapprehended. I have always expected, I still expect, to see abolition at the ballot-box, renovating the political action of the country—dispelling the sorcery influences of party—breaking asunder the fetters of political servitude—stirring up the torpid consciences of voters—substituting anti-slavery for pro-slavery representatives in every legislative assembly—modifying and rescinding all laws which sanction slavery. But this political reformation is to be effected solely by a change in the moral vision of the people;—not by attempting to prove, that it is the duty of every abolitionist to be a voter, but that it is the duty of every voter to be an abolitionist. By converting electors to the doctrine, that slavery ought to be immediately abolished, a rectified political action is the natural consequence; for where this doctrine is received into the soul, the soul-carrier may be trusted any where, that he will not betray the cause of bleeding humanity. As to the height and depth, the length and breadth of CHRISTIANITY, it is not the province of abolition to decide; but only to settle one point—to wit, that slaveholding is a crime under all circumstances, leaving those who believe in the doctrine to carry out their principles, with all fidelity, in whatever sphere they may be called upon to act, but not authoritatively determining whether they are bound to be members of the church, or voters at the polls. It has never been a difficult matter to induce men to go to the ballot-box; but the grand difficulty ever has been, and still is, to persuade them to carry a good conscience thither, and act as free moral agents, not as the tools of party.

EFFECTS OF NON-RESISTANCE UPON POLITICAL ACTION

I go still further. I do not only expect to see abolition at the polls, but I feel as sure as that day will follow night, that the political action of this country will be purified and renovated, in exact proportion to the prevalence of the great conservative doctrines of non-resistance! This may seem, to many, absurd, paradoxical, impossible; but it is strictly natural, rational, philosophical. As in the presence of Christianity, idolatry is made hideous even in the eyes of the idolators, and conscience is stimulated to put away the grosser forms of iniquity; so, revealed in the light of Non-Resistance, the kingdoms and governments of this world are seen in their real deformity, and those who sustain them are beginning to be ashamed of the work of their own hands, and to feel how awful are the responsibilities resting upon them, in assuming the power of life and death over each other. Non-Resistance measures every law of man by the law of God; and, already, the result of its examination is appalling. Suddenly there is a mighty stir in community! Priests have become politicians, and are holding up political action almost as the 'one thing needful.' Formerly, they shrunk from this work as from the touch of foul contamination. In their opinion, religion had the slightest possible connection with politics; and the christian who seldom ventured into the turbulent arena was deemed the wisest man. Between the Church and the State there was declared to be an impassable gulf. . . . Now the pulpit and the religious press are teeming with homilies upon the religious duty of going to the polls—upon the divine institution of human government—upon the criminality of those professedly good men, who neglect to use the elective franchise, or allow themselves to be made the tools of party—upon the solemn obligations resting upon the people, (in the language of Mr. Birney,) 'to sustain and purify governments and bring them into a perfect conformity with the principles of the divine government'! Men who refuse to meddle with politics are marked as dangerous citizens! Truly, we may exclaim, in view of this extraordinary change of sentiment, *'Mirabile dictu!'* And to what is it to be attributed, but to the preaching of the sublime doctrines of Non-Resistance? For it is certain that, as these doctrines have spread, our 'pro-government' brethren have obtained new views of duty at the polls, and are indebted for their awakened consciences and rectified vision to the despised and calumniated non-resistants. They are not prepared to adopt the theory of this humble class; they cannot wholly forsake houses and lands, relations and friends, and lose their lives, for Christ's sake; they are not willing, in all cases, to forgive evil-doers, and do not believe in overcoming evil with good, but rely upon physical force for protection and redress; yet they are forced to perceive how hideously defective is the government which they cherish, and to confess that it bears little or no resemblance to the gospel of Christ. Hence, in order to justify their conduct, and to refute the charges of non-resistants, they have set themselves to work in good earnest, (a small portion only,) to repeal wicked and oppressive laws, to soften the severity of the penal code, to elect better men to office, to obliterate the lines of party, and to make conscience and the fear of God attendants at the polls. In all this I rejoice. I hail such an altered state of political feeling as the harbinger of a mighty reformation.

That non-resistance will essentially aid, instead of injuring the anti-slavery cause, politically and morally, is proved to a demonstration.

In the first place, no person can be a non-resistant, without being a whole-hearted abolitionist—(the greater includes the less, always)—though a man may be an abolitionist, and not be a non-resistant.

Secondly, the principles of non-resistance have taken root more deeply, and spread more widely, in Massachusetts, than in any other State. All who embrace them are abolitionists. What State can compare with her for devotion to the cause of the slave,— for abolition integrity, activity, intrepidity,—in liberal contributions and self-sacrificing efforts to redeem the captives in our midst—in vigorous political action at the polls? To what State are the eyes of the South turned with so much anxiety and alarm, as to Massachusetts? Is she not regarded, every where, as the leader of the States in this great struggle? . . .

WM. LLOYD GARRISON

Against Nonresistance

Any hopes Garrison might have had that separating the pure pacifists from the rank and file of the movement could heal the dissension came to nothing. Many of the agents of the national society now unloaded abuse on the Garrisonians without a qualm. The beautiful Declaration of Sentiments for the Non-Resistance Society, which Garrison had struck off at a single sitting, itself one of the most remarkable documents of the emancipatory spirit in existence, one upon which all pacifist and civil disobedience movements since have been based, was regarded as something bordering on the obscene. The ministers particularly felt that Garrison was intruding into their realm, the moral kingdom, and that he had to be silenced. H. C. Wright, recording their quotes for The Liberator, *seems to be smacking his lips over the depravity of his old colleagues.*

August 30, 1839

Non-Resistance

LETTER FROM THE GENERAL AGENT

. . . R. R. GURLEY, minister, and general agent of the American Colonization Society. 'A millenium of rogues.' 'A blissful plan to extend protection to all kinds of malefactors, high and low.' 'Disorganizers and pickpockets.' 'Anarchy and despotism.' 'Aurora borealis.' 'Jack Cade come again.' 'A company of thieves and pickpockets, organized to protect themselves against the laws.'

ORANGE SCOTT, minister, and agent of the American Anti-Slavery Society. 'A proposition to abolish all laws.' 'Turning loose demons without restraint.' 'State of anarchy.' 'Destroy the marriage institution.' 'Mormonism.' 'A sin against God and humanity to adopt them.' 'A sin for which God might justly doom the nation to destruction, should these principles become general.' 'Loose and disorganizing views.' 'I hate them with a perfect hatred.'

JOSEPH TRACY, minister. 'Religious jacobinism run mad.' 'Blasphemy.' 'They lead to infidelity.'

JAMES G. BIRNEY, agent of the American A. S. Society. 'The principles of non-resistance strike at the root of the social structure.' 'Throw society into entire confusion.' 'Renew scenes of anarchy and bloodshed.' 'The offspring of the rankest infidelity and irreligion.' 'Non-resistants say, *all* governments are of the devil.'

DANIEL WISE, minister, and agent of the Mass. Abolition Society. 'Non-resistance principles tend to annihilate all marriage.' 'They tend to rape and adultery.' 'They directly tend to deluge the earth in blood.'

HIRAM CUMMINGS, minister, and agent of the Mass. Abolition Society. 'Non-resistance fosters despotism and tyranny.' 'These principles rivet the chains of the slave.'

C. T. TORREY, minister, and agent of the Mass. Abolition Society. 'The principles of non-resistance tend to infidelity.' 'They imbrute and crush humanity.' 'They destroy all government.' 'Lead to anarchy and blood.' 'Perpetuate tyranny and rapine.' 'Crush the last hope of the slave.'

Thus the above principles of non-resistance are ridiculed and condemned by ministers and editors. These are but specimens of the manner in which this class of persons are accustomed to speak of them in speeches and papers. . . .   H. C. WRIGHT

The Schism

The great struggle was to come at the annual meeting of the society in New York in May, 1840. Battle lines were closely drawn but the field of the struggle chosen by the political defectors did not materialize. Garrison wanted the fight to take place on the woman question, where he was very strong. His opponents tried to make it on Garrison's refusal to vote, or what was called his "No-Government position." Their plan was to get antislavery established as a party, or to form a bloc strong enough to wrest concessions from the major parties. However, Garrison knew that the New York board was so prejudiced by their Calvinism that they could not resist a baiting on the woman question and made the struggle come to a head on this rather than on his radicalism.

He published a letter from himself in The Liberator *describing with elation the throngs of women pouring in for his support. Then, at the meeting on May 12, he executed a brilliant parliamentary maneuver, having Abby Kelley, a Quaker girl from Lynn, Massachusetts, now an agent of the Massachusetts Society, appointed to the all-important Committee of Business. The vote to accept the committee as appointed came up. There were 557 for and 451 against her election. With this count, those opposed to Garrison's radical policies withdrew from the society, saying that serving with a woman on a committee was contrary to the Gospel and their consciences. They formed a new society known as the American and Foreign Anti-Slavery Society. While this was going on, the Garrisonians were driven by mobs from pillar to post. Their lodgings at Goss's Graham House were assailed with rocks, with windows and doors broken because of the "mixing of white and colored." Garrison could only get a place to rest his head on the fourth floor of a Wall Street cotton warehouse owned by a Negro, Thomas Van Rensalear.*

May 15, 1840

LETTER FROM THE EDITOR

New-York, *Tuesday noon, May 12, 1840*

DEAR FRIEND:

I hasten to send you a few lines, respecting our anti-slavery proceedings thus far, as the present anniversary of the National Society excites unusual interest in every quarter of the country.

I need not tell you—for you were present to behold the stirring scene with your own eyes—what a rallying there was at the Depot in Boston, yesterday noon, of the earliest, the truest, the most untiring and zealous friends of our old anti-slavery organization, in accordance with the arrangements that had been made to convey them to Providence, and from thence to this city. A few came from the land of 'down east,' and from the thick-ribbed hills of the Granite State;—but, especially from the counties of old Essex, and Middlesex, and Norfolk, and Plymouth, and Suffolk, in Massachusetts, they came promptly and numerously at the summons of HUMANITY, in spite of 'hard times' and the busy season of the year, to save our heaven-approved association from dissolution, and our broad platform from being destroyed. An extra train of cars had been engaged for the occasion; but, so numerous was the company, another train had to be started— our numbers continually augmenting at every stopping-place between the two cities. O, it was a heart-stirring and rare spectacle —such as has never before been witnessed in the progress of our all-conquering enterprise; and many were the spectators, who were looking on with wonder and surprise at such a gathering of fanaticism, and such a 'dying away' of abolitionism. On arriving at Providence, the company embarked on board of the steamboat RHODE-ISLAND, which had the American flag flying in the breeze, (the flag of LIBERTY has not yet been fashioned,) a considerable number of delegates from Bristol county and from the city of Providence joining us; so that, huge and capacious as were the dimensions of our chartered boat, it was very difficult to move about with facility, notwithstanding the *accommodating* disposition of all on board. On making an enumeration, it appeared that there were about 450 anti-slavery men and women in our company, of whom about 400 were from Massachusetts. [Probably another hundred went by other routes.] There never has been such a mass of *'ultraism'* afloat, in one boat, since the first victim was stolen from the fire-smitten and blood-red soil of Africa. There were persons of all ages, complexions, and conditions—from our time-honored and veteran friend SETH SPRAGUE, through ripened manhood down to rosy youth. They were, indeed, the moral and religious *elite* of New-England abolitionism, who have buckled on the anti-slavery armor to wear to the end of the conflict, or to the close of life. It was truly a great and joyful meeting, united together by a common bond, and partaking of *the one spirit of humanity.* Such greetings and shaking of hands! such interchanges of thoughts and opinions! such zeal, and disinterestedness, and faith! Verily, it was good to be there! And hundreds more, I am now confident, would have been with us, had the arrangement been made one week earlier, and the knowledge of it more widely conveyed; for it was, you know, entered into at a late hour. Some of the towns are remarkably well represented; but I believe our friends at Plymouth—the old PILGRIM ROCK—have surpassed all others. . . .

I have just come from the anniversary meeting. The meeting-house was crowded to excess with delegates alone! How many names will be enrolled I will not attempt to *guess;* but there is considerable excitement, and the new organization have rallied pretty numerously. This afternoon will probably determine the fate of the Parent Society. . . .

Yours truly, WM. LLOYD GARRISON

May 22, 1840

AMERICAN ANTI-SLAVERY SOCIETY

Business Meeting of the American Anti-Slavery Society

The seventh Annual Meeting, for business, was held, pursuant to the call of the Executive Committee, in the fourth Free Church in New-York, on Tuesday, May 12th, at 4 o'clock P.M.

The President being absent, Francis Jackson, of Massachusetts, one of the Vice Presidents, took the chair.

Prayer was offered by Benjamin Shaw, of Vermont.

On motion of the Recording Secretary, the following Assistant secretaries were appointed:

> CHAUNCY L. KNAPP, of Vermont
> WILLIAM BASSET, of Massachusetts
> WILLIAM F. GARDNER, of New Jersey
> SAMUEL D. HASTINGS, of Pennsylvania
> CHARLES L. REMOND, of Rhode Island

The call was then made for the names of members to constitute the roll.

On motion of C. W. Denison, Mr. Black, from Jamaica, W.I., was invited to a seat in the society.

The following persons were named by the chair, and appointed the Committee of Business:

William Lloyd Garrison, *Chairman,* Ichabod Codding, Thomas Davis, Rowland T. Robinson, Amos A. Phelps, Abby Kelley, William L. Chaplin, Lewis Tappan, Charles C. Burleigh, Charles W. Gardiner, and Charles W. Denison.

The vote appointing Miss Kelley being doubted, the house was divided, and on a count there appeared 557 in favor and 451 against her election.

Lewis Tappan, Amos A. Phelps, and Charles W. Denison, successively asked to be excused from serving on the committee, for reasons assigned; having reference to the appointment of Miss Kelley as a member. . . .

ANNUAL MEETING
OF THE
NATIONAL SOCIETY

We congratulate the friends of pure and undefiled abolitionism, in every part of the country, upon one of the most signal victories which has ever been achieved on behalf of our sacred enterprise from its commencement to the present hour. For a long time past, there has been a determination on the part of certain individuals to narrow by some means our noble platform,—to take the management of the American Anti-Slavery Society out of the hands of the single-hearted and faithful men and women who have hitherto constituted its life-guard, and to place it under the control of a *prudent, judicious* and *clerical* aristocracy, who would generously relieve the anti-slavery PEOPLE from all responsibility in its behalf. All that unrelenting prejudice and sectarian hostility within our ranks, combined with pro-slavery influences without, could do to accomplish an object so repugnant to every principle of freedom, has been done—but done in vain. . . . Such a gathering of true hearts and tried spirits as met at New-York the last week has not been known before, we venture to say, since the standard of IMMEDIATE EMANCIPATION was first unfurled to the breeze. They came, not from the Old Bay State alone, (although now, as in the times of that 'strife our sterner fathers saw,' she furnished the largest number of brave spirits,) but from the granite hills of New-Hampshire—from the mountains and vallies of Vermont—from Connecticut—from New-York, the seat of enterprise in every great and good work—from Pennsylvania, the home of *peaceful* Liberty—from the far West —and last, though not least, from Rhode-Island, made immortal as the refuge of the oppressed—came a noble and invincible band, actuated by a common principle, seeing eye to eye, and determined to rescue the ark of Liberty from the grasp of unworthy men, who were seeking to pervert it to unholy purposes. . . .

As all the resolutions and proceedings will be found on the preceding page, we refer our readers to that source for information as to what was done. They will perceive that the first vote which tested the relative numerical strength of the friends and opponents of the original anti-slavery platform, was taken upon the question of appointing our highly esteemed friend ABBY KELLEY a member of the Business Committee—she having been nominated to serve the Society in that capacity by the chair. The vote as declared was—557 in the affirmative, 451 in the negative—majority for the right 156! This result, considering the mighty efforts which had been made to procure the attendance of the clergy and a large delegation from the city of New-York, all of whom, with few exceptions, voted in the negative, can be regarded in no other light than as a glorious triumph of principle over party and faction. We believe, however, that if the votes could have been accurately counted, the majority would have been shown to be nearly, if not quite, a hundred more than appears by the record. The votes in the affirmative were so numerous, in fact, that the tellers found it impossible to ascertain the number with accuracy; while those in the negative, being fewer, were more readily counted. We regret that the vote could not have been taken by yeas and nays, so as to enable us to determine with certainty how many voted on each side from the different States. We cannot say positively, but it is our firm belief that a majority from every State, except New-York, voted in the affirmative.

The sectarian party having been thus signally defeated at the first onset, in their attempts to deprive women of their constitutional rights, did not deem it expedient to renew the siege upon the old platform. They immediately determined to secede, thinking no doubt that they could carry on the war against genuine abolitionism with more hope of success in a 'new organization,' than in a society open upon equal terms to every sincere hater of slavery, without regard to sex or official station. Accordingly, they met and formed an 'American *and Foreign* Anti-Slavery Society,' and placed at its head the unfaithful servants, who, by their attempts to rule the anti-slavery fraternity and concentrate power in their own hands, had shown themselves to be unfitted to take the lead in an enterprise whose object it is to break the bands of oppression, and extend the blessings of liberty to all, without distinction of sex, clime, color or condition. Of this 'new organization,' we shall say nothing at present, except to call attention to the verdict pronounced upon it by the American Anti-Slavery Society, and to register our testimony against it, as having originated in a spirit hostile alike to freedom and to the genius of our sacred enterprise. What else than a *pro-slavery* spirit, is that which refuses to labor in behalf of the oppressed by the side of any human being, merely on account of her sex? Wherein does such a spirit differ from that which dooms millions of the human race to chains and slavery on account of their complexion? Abolitionism *in its purity* can no more live in a soul which fosters this spirit, than in the heart of the slaveholder himself. Such being the spirit of 'new organization,' it must come to nought. It may seem to flourish for a time, and thousands may be enrolled in its ranks; but it has within itself the elements of its own destruction. In the only particular which distinguishes it from old organization, it is essentially and fundamentally *pro-slavery*. Bro. Lewis Tappan asserted that it was contrary to the rules of civilized society for women to act in a benevolent association in the same sphere with men! *Un*civilized, he should have said—for there is not a slaveholder or a ruffian in the world, who will not unite with him in denying the equal rights of woman! . . .—J.

The World's Anti-Slavery Convention

Immediately after his victory in New York, Garrison set sail for London, where there was to be a "World's Convention" of the anti-slavery forces. Unfortunately, the elements of division were there as well and some women delegates, chosen by the Garrisonian factions prior to the upheaval, were not allowed to be seated. Garrison arrived late and so did not take part in the debate on this, but when he found the exclusion in force he refused to take his seat on the platform, staying obdurately in the gallery with the rejected women.

When he returned to Boston after this much-publicized gesture, the Negroes gave him a reception on August 20. Some twenty-five hundred persons were reported in attendance. All the men on the platform but Garrison and his friend and traveling companion, Nathaniel Rogers, were black. J. T. Hilton welcomed Garrison, saying, "Wilst the pulpit was dumb, you, Sir, lifted up your voice . . . and lest editors may conceive themselves slighted, I will remark that they also were dumb; while your voice was raised in a manner the most determined and persevering. . . . The principles which characterized you here in the United States, you have nobly sustained in Europe. No change of country, or climate, or people, can make William Lloyd Garrison forget or deny his principles. . . ." (Lib., Aug. 28, 1840).

August 28, 1840

Mr. GARRISON arose amid the warmest greetings, and said . . . The object of our meeting is to hear tidings of the 'World's Convention.' I am sorry to be obliged to say so, but there has been none held. There has been one of an exclusive character, but we did not find it the one to which we were sent. The proposition to hold one originated in this country, and was first made in the Emancipator, the official organ of the American Anti-Slavery Society. It was for a WORLD'S CONVENTION—nothing less. The abolitionists of England endorsed the proposition. In the nature of things, there must be somebody to call it, and this service devolved upon the London Anti-Slavery Committee. They gave their notice to all climes and people. The American Society, in good faith, and upon the strength of that call, appointed delegates to attend the convention. Among others, I had the honor of an appointment; with several women, well known for devoted attachment to the cause, for eminent ability in its prosecution, and for great moral excellence and worth of character. It was our desire to have been there in good season, for we knew that the plottings of 'New Organization' would be unwearied; and, in fact, they were but too successful. . . .

. . . We found on our arrival in London, that the committee there had taken upon themselves to say who should be permitted to enter the Convention, and who should be excluded; and that the Convention had adhered to their decision by a large majority. Yes! the London Committee, who were but the instrumentality whereby the World's Convention was called, and who, after having called it, should have assumed no more authority than they might exercise as individual members in its ranks, decided that one half of the world should be excluded. . . .

And now, why did not that part of your delegation, to which no objection was made, enter the meeting? . . .

. . . We felt that in rejecting the credentials of those who were delegated with us, the London meeting did really dishonor our own. We felt that we had no more right there than was possessed by our rejected co-delegates; and we would not go in as a matter of favor. (Applause.) We felt that not only were your whole delegation dishonored by the exclusion of any of its members, but, in rejecting a part, they did also reject those who sent them.

And what was their plea? Why, it was contrary to British usage and custom. I would fain know what abolitionists had to do with that! Were they there from all kingdoms and nations to sustain *British* usage and custom? Neither is there any consistency in their plea. With a woman on the throne, a woman at the head of their established church, a woman commander-in-chief of the army and navy, a woman to address the house of lords, it ill becomes them to present their *usages* as an obstacle to woman's labors of benevolence—to woman's mission of mercy. (Applause.) But they have some very bad usages in Great Britain, and I wish to see those usages abolished. I have seen woman there, bearing burdens unsuited to her physical condition. I have seen woman breaking stone on the high-way, and laboring in the harvest-field, and the brick-yard. I have seen her, with her own hands, gathering dung in the street. And yet it would be contrary to British usage and custom to allow women to choose their sphere of usefulness in the field of morals and religion! (Continued applause.)

Now, I will not stop to inquire, whether we are sustained by you in the course we took. I never asked myself that question there; for I saw my duty in the light of the facts in the case, and could not hesitate to follow it.

But I cannot refrain from expressing my admiration of our friend Charles Lenox Remond. Though a warmer welcome than ordinarily awaits the white man was extended to him, as a man of color, he nobly refused to enter, where any of the advocates of human rights were thrust out. And, in thus deciding, he did more for our cause than he could possibly have done by neglecting to bear so emphatic a testimony. Indeed, it is far better for the cause of the slave that the Convention pursued the course it did. That course has raised discussion throughout England; and some, at least, who at first adopted it, have now repented. Nay, more; it has brought up before all Europe the question so important to the success of the anti-slavery enterprise, whether, in a moral cause, a woman may be a free moral agent. Not a doubt exists, in my mind, as to the ultimate affirmative decision of that question. I rejoice that it must be so, as it rouses a powerful influence, hitherto dormant, for the slave's cause—the cause of liberty and humanity.

And now I want the colored people to sympathise with all who need their sympathy. I want them to call on British abolitionists to sympathise with the oppressed and suffering classes in their own land. I beseech them to put forth the finger of warning and entreaty to their British friends, in view of all the sufferings of those at hand, even at their doors. I call upon the colored people to support every unpopular reform the world over—to pity and plead for the poor oppressed Irishmen; for all who suffer; whether at the south, or on the British shores, or in India—or numbered by the hundred millions. We should, as nations, reciprocate rebukes. And as we send our souls to theirs, freighted with reproof and exhortation, let them meet on the deep, and embrace as angel spirits, and pass on. (Applause.) When they rebuke our manifold national sins, let us also be faithful in rebuking theirs, and then we shall have cancelled the debt. (Applause.) . . .

Mr Rogers then came forward. He said . . . Garrison has

given you the gist and marrow of our experiences. I am witness
to his accuracy, for I accompanied him every where. I concurred
with all my heart in the views of our course which he has just
given you. I recollect, and you will also remember it, my exultation at the thought of a 'World's Convention.' I expressed all the
enthusiasm it kindled up in my soul; and in the little paper I
edited among the mountains, I spread out my expectations. I
was delighted, and I blustered out my feelings. I thought it was to
be a grand meeting of mankind—the first since the confusion of
tongues; and what were my emotions when I got there, and found
that Lucretia Mott, that devoted laborer in the cause, (applause)
had been excluded from that meeting on account of her sex! I
have the same credentials. If hers were dishonored, so were mine.
And was it for me to think that I could be of use where the services of such an advocate were rejected? Was it for me to suffer
this contempt to be cast upon those who sent me? I told them
No!

. . . I took myself up into the gallery, in company with Garrison and Remond, to overlook what remained of the proceedings.
The act was decisive in its effect. Haman never looked more
blank on seeing Mordecai sitting in the king's gate with his hat
on, than did this 'Committee in conference' on seeing us take the
position we did. Garrison was besought to come down. They
tried by every means in their power to seduce him down. Every
time he was mentioned, that whole conference would applaud,
as if they thought they could *clap* him down. We were beset with
entreaties and regrets; and, to crown the whole, at a special meeting of the Committee, the following letter and resolutions were
adopted and sent to us. [Here Mr. Rogers read the letter of the
London Committee.] This would have been very kind—flattering
in the extreme even, *if there had not been a motive for it*. It was
the winding up of their efforts to remove *that argument* against
their decision (pointing to Mr. Garrison,) out of the gallery.
(Applause.) But they might as well have expected to remove
the pillars upon which the gallery stood. They could not argue
away what they had done: they could not argue 'the seal off the
bond.' . . .

An Interesting Report

The schism of 1840 had pulled the props of money, prestige, and respectability out from under the American Anti-Slavery Society, leaving it shattered, gaping, and out of plumb. Garrison went to work to build it again, starting from nothing, by means of a speaking tour through New York State in the bleakest and rawest time of the winter of 1842. A revealing letter to his wife from Syracuse demonstrates perfectly his ability to get up off the floor, wash off the blood, and go forth to battle again, never abating in the least his revolutionary morality but, on the contrary, forcing it to the limit to build new forces, new strengths.

On Thursday forenoon, our convention opened in this place under circumstances by no means auspicious. Not a meeting house could be obtained for us, and we were forced to meet in a hall. . . . Handbills had been placarded about the town, announcing that Abby Kelley, C. L. Remond, Frederick Douglass and W. L. Garrison would be at the Convention, but, notorious as we are, and great as is the curiosity usually manifested to see and hear either of us singly, our meeting in the forenoon consisted only of eleven persons all told! These were nearly all of our own company.

In the afternoon, we had a small audience; but such was the feeling we excited in the meeting, by our scorching remarks and 'ultra' resolutions, the hall was crowded in the evening, when I opened my budget of heresies on the subject of temple worship, the church, the priesthood, the Sabbath, etc., which created no small stir. The next day Stephen S. Foster arrived, and we soon had the town in commotion . . . the discussions assumed so exciting an aspect that, at the close of the afternoon meeting, it became apparent that we should have a riot in the evening . . . all in defence of the clergy and the church. . . .

A footnote to this was that Foster was out on bail from the Boston jail, having assaulted (verbally) a constable who had just arrested a fugitive slave. He later (1843) published a book called The Brotherhood of Thieves: A True Picture of the American Church and Clergy.

December 30, 1842

INTERESTING REPORT
OF THE ANTI-SLAVERY CONVENTION

At Syracuse, N.Y. on the 22d, 23d, and 24th, Nov. 1842

Evening of 24th

. . . S. S. Foster then took the floor. After speaking ten minutes, with only the interruption of an occasional hiss, (a favorite logic with Syracuse outlaws,) he alluded to the fact of the Methodist Episcopal Church holding forty thousand females in the condition of harlots, or slave concubines; and said such a church was worse than any house of ill-fame or brothel in New-York. He would sooner go to a theatre than go into their churches—they were robbers and murderers.

At these words, a terrible yell broke out from the crowd in the back part of the house, and went up amid the stamping and dust of the excitement. Mr. Foster attempted to proceed, but his voice was drowned in the wild turmoil that filled the house. The President arose, and attempted to still the troubled waves, but his strong voice, even, could not be heard, and he sat down. Cries of . . . 'Hustle 'em out' were heard from different portions of the house, while the ladies near the speakers' stand and in the centre of the hall, were rushing to their friends, pale and with fear, for protection.

. . . The tumult increased, and threats and imprecations, amid the breaking of seats, windows, and other fixtures of the hall, combined in terrible harmony. . . . Among those who joined in the hissing, stamping, and outbreak, were found deacons of the church, sons of church members, and drunkards, all in sweet concord. 'My parents are Methodists,' roared out a sprig of slave-holding piety, 'and *I'll be dammed* if I'll hear 'em abused—hustle'm out—damm the niggers.'

. . . A rush was made for the speaker's stand, and attempts to seize Foster and Abby Kelley, tar and feathers being in readiness to clothe them, but they went out unperceived by the villains;

Mr. Foster under the protection of the sheriff, who kindly volunteered his services. Unmerchantable eggs were thrown at Garrison's head, and broke against the wall, causing the most loathsome smell, and injuring the garments of the innocent.

Thus broke up a meeting of free (?) citizens of the empire State, who had assembled to discuss one of the mightiest questions before the Union. Thus the citizens of Syracuse are taught that to question the sacredness of a religion and priesthood who sanction 'oppression, robbery and blood,' is fatal to the liberties and safety of those who do it! Thus the friends of human rights, for attempting to show how the American church, and her servile, time-serving priests, are standing in the way of human freedom, must be taught the danger of their course, by seeing their own liberties immolated upon the blood altar of Jesuitical domination! . . .

FRIDAY MORNING, 25th

On coming into the hall this morning, the Convention were informed that it could no longer be used, unless some person would become responsible for the damage that might be done; yet it might be occupied long enough to-day to decide this question.

Mr. Garrison moved that the Convention adjourn then, *sine die*. We should not feel justified, in remaining, under these circumstances, in the power of a mob.

Abby was surprised that the liberty of speech was stricken down in Syracuse, with none to defend it. She moved that we adjourn to some public square, and go on with the Convention. . . .

D. D. Hillis made a few remarks in extenuation of the conduct of the people. They were in favor of freedom of speech. No disturbance occurred last night, until Foster used language too abusive and indecent to bear. His language Mr. Hillis thought adapted to create indignation. Yet he was opposed to mobs. He thought the language of Foster unfit for the ears of ladies and virtuous gentlemen. . . .

Mr. Garrison thought a wounded bird most liable to flutter. Those are often the most vociferous in condemning reformers,

who are most in need of reform or reproof. Men often condemn
language employed in rebuking houses of ill-fame, who make
no cross of going there under cover of the night!

Mr. Hillis felt himself abused by these remarks, and came
forward with severe language, and violent attacks upon Garrison.
Said Garrison dared not to utter out doors what he had said
in the house. Called him a contemptible villain. There was
cheering from a number of persons during these remarks.

Mr. Garrison assured the gentleman he intended no personal
allusion. He was a stranger to him, and, of course, was not aware
of the applicability of his remarks to him.

Mr. Hillis apologized.

Mr. J. O. Bennett was opposed to the adjournment. Mr. Garrison and others had uttered sentiments insurrectionary and dangerous to the peace of community, in the garb of abolition. He
wished to exonerate abolition from the slander. He hoped the
Convention would remain until the public mind could be dis-
abused on this point. He thought the doctrines taught well
adapted to incense a mob.

W. O. Duvoll thought the gentleman did wrong in throwing
a salvo into the conscience of a lawless rabble, especially at such
a time as this, when liberty of speech was crucified between two
thieves—Church and State. . . .

AFTERNOON, 25th

S. S. Foster gave reasons for the severe language he had employed during his remarks the last evening. A great many facts
presented in support of his charges against the church, and in
favor of the resolutions under consideration last night at the time
of the mob. [These were for complete non-co-operation with
Church, or any political party not pledged to immediate emancipation, and not to aid any resistance to slaves attempting to gain
their liberty by a resort to arms—T.N.] . . .

The meeting adjourned to meet Saturday morning; but when
morning came, it was announced that the house could not be
obtained. Consequently, several resolutions which were before
the meeting, and others in the hands of the committee, were not
passed. . . .

The Fraternal Community

The split in the movement had the effect of freeing Garrison and his more devoted followers from some of the stultifying restraints imposed by the necessity of raising funds from men of property and influence. The movement began to turn toward utopianism. This was started by Adin Ballou, the Universalist preacher and pacifist. He had been greatly excited by Garrison's Declaration of Sentiments for the Non-Resistance Society, particularly the statement that its members would "obey all requirements of government, except such as we deem contrary to the commands of the gospel; and in no case resist the operation of the law, except by meekly submitting to the penalty of disobedience."

Ballou wrote a letter in March, 1839, to Garrison's close associate and sometime editor of The Liberator, *Maria Weston Chapman, saying he ascribed to almost all the sentiments in the Declaration and that he had "recently united with a little band of Christian brethren in forming a Society based on a declaration of principles and practices which embodies all the sentiments of yours. . . ."*

This was the beginning of the Hopedale Community, one of the first in that amazing rash of utopian-socialist experiments from 1841 to 1846. His colony persisted longer than most and he really crystallized the feeling of most of the Garrisonians at that time that some true separation from a tainted social system should be attempted. Even Brook Farm, the most urbane and sophisticated of the experiments, described itself as "Christ's view of Society," and most of them attempted to follow Ballou's try at "a civil state, a miniature Christian Republic, existing within, peaceably subject to, and tolerated by the governments of Massachusetts and the United States, but otherwise a commonwealth complete within itself . . . it asks of them no corporate powers, no military or penal protection. It has its own Constitution, laws . . . its own legislative, judiciary and executive authorities, its own education system . . . its own moral and religious safeguards."

Under the headline "Social Reorganization," The Liberator *printed, far more than any other contemporary source, the story of utopian socialism in the United States. Garrison never begrudged them space or sympathetic comment, although he realized this was a diversion from his main task of Negro liberation. It got so that the attendance rolls at Abolitionist and socialist conventions were identical; in fact, many conventions changed from one heading to the other without anyone leaving their seats.*

Ballou was a New Testament Fundamentalist and his constitution for the Hopedale Community was far too rigid for Garrison's taste.

February 26, 1841

CONSTITUTION
OF THE
FRATERNAL COMMUNION

• • • • •

DECLARATION, VIZ.

I believe in the religion of Jesus Christ, as he taught and exemplified it, according to the Scriptures of the New Testament. I acknowledge myself a bounden subject of all its moral obligations. *Especially* do I hold myself bound by its holy requirements, never under any pretext, whatsoever, to kill, assault, beat, torture, enslave, rob, oppress, persecute, defraud, corrupt, slander, revile, injure, envy, or hate any human being, *even my worst enemy:* never in any manner to violate the dictates of pure chastity: never to take or administer an oath: never to manufacture, buy, sell, deal out, or use any intoxicating liquor *as a beverage:* never to serve in the army, navy or militia of any Nation, State or Chieftain: never to bring an action at law, hold office, vote, join a legal posse, petition a legislature, or ask governmental interposition, *in any case involving a final authorized resort to physical violence:* never to indulge self-will, bigotry, love of pre-eminence, covetousness, deceit, profanity, idleness, or an unruly tongue: never to participate in lotteries, games of chance, betting, or pernicious amusements: never to resent reproof, or justify myself in a known wrong: never to aid, abet or approve others in any thing sinful: but, through divine assistance, always to recommend and promote, with my entire influence, the holiness and happiness of all mankind. . . .

ARTICLE IV

Sec. 1. The members of every Community in this Association shall, *if practicable,* dwell together, on their own soil, in a *compact neighborhood.* . . .

Sec. 3. All *Habitations,* with their surrounding lands and buildings, shall be owned and controlled *solely* by the community within whose limits they are comprised. . . .

Exposition

. . . Here, then, is the foundation of our superstructure—
☞ pure religion, morality, philanthropy. . . . The kingdom of
God and his righteousness take precedence of all other aims and
interests. Let not the uncircumsised soul, that disregards this
foundation, think to feel at *home* with us in rearing up our social
fabric.

Our second general object is to 'withstand the vices, and reform
the disorders of the present social state.' We feel that few as
we are, insulated, dependent for bread, hemmed in by the mighty
influences of both Church and State, necessitated to struggle
under disadvantageous economies, bound hand and foot in the
frame work of society, fettered by its corrupt customs, met every
where by its maxims and obliged to educate our children in
the midst of its evil examples—it is next to impossible for us to
triumphantly accomplish this object. . . . A living example of
reform—'a city set on a hill'—is now demanded, to convince
the unbelieving world that it is best and safest to do right. . . .
Society at large will not move with us; it only opposes and
hinders us; yet, if we cannot carry out our glorious principles,
single-handed under all our disadvantages, and against the whole
combined mass that either oppose or doubt it, it seems to be
taken for granted that those principles are impracticable. . . .
Give us a fair chance, we say, and we will reform the whole social state. At least, we will *try.*

Our third general object is, 'to secure to our posterity the
blessings of a more salutary physical, intellectual and moral education.' At present, the physical education of children, at least
among us common people, is left almost wholly to chance. . . .
Intellectual education has received the principal attention, both
of legislators and parents. But this is irregular, defective, and
in general, very far from accomplishing its professed ends. . . .
Health, knowledge and goodness are necessary to the full idea we
entertain of a well educated youth. . . . Our fourth general object is, 'to establish a more attractive, economical, and productive
system of industry.' By good company, pleasant well-contrived
work-shops, fields and gardens, convenient implements, enlightened methods of operation, a proper distribution of time between

the different occupations, and a choice of pursuits, it will be no difficult achievement to render industry at once honorable and agreeable. If honorable and agreeable, it will be attractive. It is now too often repulsive and tedious. . . . We shall be able to produce a great deal more than we now do, with much less of wearing effect to the body or mind, and consequently shall retain more power to promote the good of mankind at large.

Our fifth general object is, 'to facilitate the honest acquisition of individual property for laudable purposes.' In this we differ from the Shakers, and from all those Socialists, so called, who make the individual dependent on the mass of their associates (or too often, perhaps, on the will of the *few* who govern that mass) for their food, clothing, and other personal conveniences. We unite our property for certain great purposes, but hold it individually in negotiable shares. . . . We think this right and possession of individual property indispensable to a due degree of personal independence—and a great safeguard against the stealthy approaches of human despotism. If those who have *least* of this property are placed beyond the reach of want, and even enjoy great literary and religious privileges, we think no harm but much good will come of allowing others to hold and dispose of whatever they may acquire for laudable purposes. And we believe that the facilities and economies of a Fraternal Community will be such, that very nearly all its members can acquire an ample competence. They will be able to do this *honestly;* not by depressing or degrading others; not by taking advantage, either of their necessities or misfortunes. As they raise others, they themselves will rise; and thus, in the *true* social state, it will become comparatively easy to do what is now so difficult—i. e. to love our neighbor as ourself, to promote the good of each and of all by the same process.

Should these five general objects be successfully pursued, we can hardly conceive of the changes which must ultimately take place in society. The establishment of one Community will succeed another, till whole countries, and perhaps we ought not to hesitate saying the whole face of the globe, will be dotted with peaceful and happy habitations. Their healthful industry will subdue and beautify the earth which receives their cheerful sweat, and a generous husbandry be repaid with superabundant products of all that man or beast may need. War, oppression, intemperance, debauchery, and ten thousand hateful vices, now prevalent, will gradually disappear, and man return to his primeval Eden. . . .

Northampton

Garrison's brother-in-law, George W. Benson, was a leader in setting up a utopian-socialist colony in Northampton, Massachusetts. Its constitution bears strongly the mark of Garrison's thought and hand. He attended it briefly but could not keep away from the Abolitionist meetings in the surrounding area and never really pulled his weight, or became a true partisan of the utopian movement. However, it is refreshing to come across, in the Northampton constitution, a sentence which is the essence of Garrisonian thought: "To combine for the purpose of spreading speculative doctrines and ceremonial observances, forms of religious worship and discipline, is injurious to the welfare of mankind, because belief is constantly changing in every individual mind, according to the fresh accessions of light and knowledge it receives . . ."

The contrast between this constitution and Ballou's is striking upon close study. Ballou and Garrison never really hit it off, although they were coupled by Tolstoy as thinkers who had anticipated his "reconstructed" life almost word for word. Northampton was the only colony of this period where Negroes were residents consistently, and it was described by one of the most heroic and devoted Negro Abolitionists, David Ruggles, as "founded on the high idea of the EQUAL BROTHERHOOD OF THE RACE." Ruggles said also that he was being "sheltered here by friendship and cherished by love in this promising home for humanity, until health and sight shall allow me to re-enter the field of reform, for the regeneration of the race."

September 9, 1842

NORTHAMPTON ASSOCIATION
OF EDUCATION AND INDUSTRY

It is impossible to survey the present condition of the world, the institutions of society, the general character of mankind, and their prevailing pursuits and tendencies, without perceiving the great evils that afflict humanity, and recognizing many of them as the direct consequences of existing social arrangements.

Life is, with some, a mere round of frivolous occupations or vicious enjoyments; with most, a hard struggle for the bare means of subsistence. The former are exempted from productive labor, while they enjoy its fruits: upon the latter, it is imposed as a task with unreasonable severity and with inadequate compensation. The one class is tempted to self-indulgence, pride, and oppression: the other is debased by ignorance and crime, by the conflict of passions and interests, by moral pollution, and by positive want and starvation.

The governments of the world are systematically warlike in their constitution and spirit, in the measures they adopt, and in the means they employ to establish and support their power, and to redress their real and alleged grievances, without regard to truth, justice or humanity; and political parties are notoriously and characteristically destitute of all principle, except the love of place and the emoluments which it bestows, without consideration for the true advancement of society.

Religion, whose essence is perfect spiritual liberty and universal benevolence, is prostituted into a device for tyrannizing over the minds of men, by arraying them into hostile sects, by substituting audible and visible forms for the inward power of truth and goodness, and by rendering the superstitious fear and irresponsible dictation of men paramount to the veneration and authority that belong only to God.

For these evils, viz. extreme ignorance and poverty in immediate juxtaposition with the most insolent licentiousness; adverse and contending interests; war, slavery, party corruption, and selfishness; sectarian exclusiveness and spiritual tyranny,—society, as at present constituted, affords no remedy. On the contrary, it has sprung out of these evils, is maintained by them, and has a direct tendency to re-produce them in a constantly increasing progression; and the human mind is driven to the conclusion, either that the infinitely wise and benevolent Creator of the world designed to produce a state of things subversive of moral goodness and destructive to human happiness, which is a contradiction in terms; or that man, necessarily imperfect, and therefore liable to err, has mistaken his path by neglecting the light which Nature and Religion were intended to afford for the attainment of Truth and Righteousness, Purity and Freedom.

No believer in God can doubt that it is not He who has failed in his purpose, but man who has wandered from his true course, and after the perception of this truth, and of the insufficiency of existing institutions to correct the manifold evils of society, and promote its further progress, it is the duty of all to endeavor to discover and adopt purer and more salutary principles, and to apply them individually and collectively to the regulation of their conduct in life. The vices of the present forms and practices of civilization are so gross and palpable, that no apology is required for the honest attempt to escape from them, even although it should not be accompanied with the pretence of peculiar wisdom and virtue, and should not be followed by the complete success which is both desirable and attainable. The following principles, indicating dangers to be avoided, duties to be performed, and rights to be maintained, are adopted as a bond of union and basis of co-operation.

I. Productive labor is the duty of every human being, and every laborer has the exclusive right of enjoying and disposing of the fruits of his labor.

II. The opportunity of self-improvement in all knowledge is the right of every human being.

III. It is the right of every human being to express the dictates of his conscience on religious and all other subjects, and to worship God under any form or in any manner agreeable to his convictions of duty, not interfering with the equal rights of others.

IV. Fair argument is the only legitimate means of controlling the opinions or belief of another, and no praise or blame, no merit or demerit, no reward or punishment, ought to be awarded for any opinions or belief, for which every human being is responsible to God alone.

V. The rights of all are equal, without distinction of sex, color or condition, sect or religion.

VI. The family relation, the relation between husband and wife, and between parents and children, has its foundation and support in the laws of Nature and the will of God, in the affections of the heart and the dictates of the understanding. Other and wider relations may be formed for the purposes of social improvement, but none that are inconsistent with this, which is sacred and permanent, the root and fountain of all human excellence and happiness.

VII. The combination of individuals and families is an evil

or good, according to the objects to which it is directed. To combine for the purpose of inflicting an injury, is evil: to combine for the purpose of protecting from injury, or conferring a benefit, is good. To combine for the purposes of war, aggression, conquest, tyranny, and enslavement, is evil: to combine for the purpose of living in peace and amity towards all, and in the exercise of mutual benevolence and friendly offices, is good. To combine for the purpose of spreading speculative doctrines and ceremonial observances, forms of religious worship and discipline, is injurious to the welfare of mankind, because belief is constantly changing in every individual mind, according to the fresh accessions of light and knowledge which it receives, and because a fixed profession is not, and cannot be the true index of a varying belief, and because such combinations therefore necessarily tend to produce habits of insincerity, to restrain freedom of thought and expression on the most momentous subjects, to cause the outward show of religion to take the place of its practical and spiritual influences, and to afford an instrument to priests and tyrants to enslave the mind and the body. On the other hand, to combine for the purposes of counteracting, within a greater or less sphere, the causes which have produced ignorance and vice, oppression and crime, bigotry, fanaticism and intolerance; of raising labor to its true dignity, and giving to it its just rewards; of economising labor, and increasing its productiveness by means of machinery, of co-operation, and of a wise division of the departments of industry; of securing the full enjoyment of liberty in thought, in word, and in action; and of promoting the progressive culture and full development of all the capacities of human nature by the union of spiritual, intellectual, and practical attainments, is conducive to the happiness and improvement of the world, promotes the cause of freedom, of truth, and of goodness, and according to their means and opportunities is the right, the duty, and the interest of all.

Such are the principles and objects of the Northampton Association of Education and Industry, and it is the full and distinct recognition of their truth and obligation, and with the view of applying them in practice, that the following regulations are adopted. . . .

Social Reorganization

The notion that antislavery was not enough and that the slaves them-
selves needed some better form of society to escape to began to grow
among the Garrisonians. A series of letters appeared in The
Liberator *for 1843 and 1844 urging the expansion of abolition into the*
whole field of human transformation. Garrison allowed and supported
this, although he never stopped his own denunciations of slavery as it
was, as the worst of all human evils. The names of these letter writers,
with the exception of John A. Collins, are not traceable.

John A. Collins was the chief agent of the Massachusetts Anti-Slavery
Society, working with the great Frederick Douglass, also a paid agent.
Collins became obsessed with pure communism and used most of his
time advocating it. However, much of what he said came almost directly
from Garrison's remarks on "the existing system of physical force."

Garrison's most typical comments on utopian socialism came in January
and August of 1844. It was left to Henry C. Wright to really blast away
the nationalism and fraud which the Garrisonians fought all their lives.

February 9, 1844

ON THE REFORM POLICY OF ABOLITIONISM

. . . it may be asserted that the Abolition party in the United
States has within it all the elements which are necessary to a
thorough reform; that is to say, a reform which shall be personal,
social, political and religious; and the proofs are as follows:

. . . There is in Abolitionism a perseverance which no obstacles can weary, and a courage and fearlessness that no opposition can subdue, or persecution affright:

A broad and sweeping flood of thought marks the progress of
Abolitionism, exhibiting a disposition to leave no error unde-
tected, nor any abuse unremedied:

Abolitionism began to struggle with *a partial evil,* and has
arrived at that stage of progress when the mediate causes of
that evil, namely, a corrupt church, a wicked government, and
a falsely organized society, are perceived and denounced:

Abolitionism has helped to bring forth, and is serving as a
nursing-mother to theories which point out the more secret

causes of individual and public depravation and wrong-doing; and, in so doing, has furnished undeniable proof that the period of negative action, which has hitherto been its principal characteristic, is fast drawing to a close, and will be succeeded by positive declarations, in reference to the new personal, social, and divinized order, together with action conformable thereto. . . .

It is the duty of Abolitionists to help on the grand design of social reorganization, by ceasing to exact or render service for hire, *which is slavery,* though under another guise than that of personal servitude, and by aiding to plant Communities or Phalansteres, parallel, and as near as possible to the line which divides the Slave from the Free States, so that the slaveholders may learn the true position which they ought to occupy towards their fellows whom they now hold in bondage, and also that these latter may find close to them safe asylums, sympathizing friends, and social conditions, altogether vastly superior to those which are now obtainable in competitive society. . . .

SAMUEL BOWER

Boston, Feb. 3, 1844

March 24, 1843

LETTER FROM DR. BROOKE, OF OHIO

OAKLAND, (Ohio,) March 4, 1843

DEAR BROTHER GARRISON:

. . . A subject in interest far transcending the anti-slavery question, begins to occupy the attention of many of our friends in the West. It is an inquiry into the cause of, and proper remedy for, the various evils that afflict mankind, and of which chattel slavery is comparatively but an insignificant portion. For the existence of war, either in its most horrible aspect, or the modified term of it called government—of slavery—of ignorance, poverty, distress and degradation in the majority, or unprivileged class—of partial intellection, wealth, luxury, *distress and degradation* in the minority of mankind, or privileged order, there must be a cause. *What is that cause?* Many believe it to exist in the property system, or system of individual accumulation, a part of our social arrangement, at war with man's nature and God's government, consequently a prolific parent of misery to the race. Jesus taught, 'It is easier for a camel to go through the eye of a needle than for a rich man to enter the kingdom of heaven.' Why is this? Because no man can accumulate wealth which shall be the product of his own labor alone. If he acquires riches, it must be by the uncompensated labor of others. This is unjust in him, and no unjust man can enter the kingdom. He also taught, as had been taught before his appearance, 'Thou shalt love thy neighbor as thyself.' Every one knows he cannot do this and practise the present competitive system, therefore nearly every one construes the command to suit himself. Why were these teachings given by Jesus? Because they had been previously written into the constitution of man by his Creator. Human happiness can never be complete, while this or any other natural law of our being is violated. God has given to man no arbitrary laws to be obeyed, simply because he has so willed it. His laws are immutably and unchangeably ordained in the creation. The teachings of the prophets, the apostles, and of Jesus, point men to these laws, while *we* have unhappily adopted the view that they were true because they were taught, instead of perceived that they were taught because they were true, and pre-ordained from the beginning. . . .

Yours for all reform, A. BROOKE

October 11, 1844

SOCIAL REORGANIZATION

CUMMINGTON, (Mass.) Sept. 8, 1844

FRIEND GARRISON:

The following thoughts, in substance, I intended to have made at the Convention of the Northampton Association . . .

As a non-resistant, I have no where to stand but on community ground, or *common possession.* All else to me is sectarian ground, or *associated wealth,* and must be defended by deeds, constitutions and creeds. On community or Humanity's ground, none are needed—all share *equally* in the great blessings of the great Father of the great community.

If I voluntarily practised the holding of individual or associated wealth, I should endorse Henry Clay's sentiment, that 'that is property which the law makes property.' What of earth or its products, but what is holden by this tenure?—terms which inhuman laws prescribe. It matters not if *six thousand* years of legislation have sanctioned the holding of Heaven's equal bounty to man. If the landholder has a warrantee 'from the Almighty,' his claim is good; otherwise, he is a slaveholder and a robber. The idea of individual property-holding in earth and its produce, is the basis of all slaveholding; man-holding is subsequent. Remove the former, and the latter is abolished at once.

Hence arises the (seeming) necessity of civil government, with its paid minions and hired assassins, to enforce obedience. Most of this splendid array is to protect *our property*. To hold exclusive possession is immoral. If man could create or produce any thing, he might price and traffic in it. To price and traffic in another's products is taking what is not our right, (excepting what we need and this we have, 'without money and without price,') and making merchandise of what is others'. The earth and its rich bequests should be enjoyed in common with the blessings of air and sunshine—all sharing equally, and each enough. The right to hold one foot of earth implies the right to hold every foot of it. The right to price one thing implies the right to price every thing. The right to price a thing low implies the right to price it high. Now, if I have the power to enjoy the extent of these assumed rights, I may make my brothers as miserable as I please. And who can tell what degradation and misery is now endured by the rigorous enforcement of the law that might makes right? This seems to be the highest idea, the ruling principle in society, that the end sanctifies the means; the best passport imaginable that selfish men can have to the practice of immorality.

It is contrary to the teachings and practice of Jesus. 'Lay not up for *yourselves* treasures on earth.' If not for *ourselves,* who then? Acknowledge the brotherhood of the race, and labor for *humanity.* Practically saying, I am laboring thus. If you will be my disciple, do so too. Let this single reference to the sayings and practice of Jesus suffice. I sincerely hope that friend Ballou and all others who think they ought to do as he said and did, *because* he said and did so, 'will take heed to their steps.' Let their practice 'be *consistent*' with their profession.

The followers of Jesus *established a community of property.* 'And the multitude of them that believed were of one heart and of one soul; neither said any of them that aught of the things he possessed was his own, but they had all things common.' If brother Ballou and his brethren at Hopedale think their (the disciples') course was right, and they intend to have theirs a 'model community,' let them do likewise. Be consistent.

Individual possession is the great entering wedge, which has split society into eight hundred million fragments. While it remains as it does, there will be no more affinity or harmony than exists between antagonistic elements. It virtually, practically and theoretically denies the brotherhood of man. Thence follow untold evils. Here my heart sickens—it feels for others' woes. Had I tongue and utterance,* for Humanity's sake I would not rest, and for Community's sake I would not hold my peace, until this wedge was out. My own motto would be—Pull out the wedge.

I perceive, in the efforts to reorganize society, the germ of a truer, better life, which will hasten the *dis*-organization of all existing institutions; and the great *fact* will be apprehended, that man was not made for institutions, but that institutions were subordinate to man. . . .   HIRAM STAFFORD

February 24, 1843

.   .   .   .   .

Resolved, That we look upon the existing system of physical force, the standing armies, navies, bulwarks and battlements, prisons and gibbets, penitentiaries, pillories and whipping posts, but as so many causes to perpetuate the evils they are designed to prevent; that the evils and their intended remedies existing, each in the relation of cause to the other, can never come to an end, except by the action of causes external to themselves, and we believe that so long as society recognizes the right of an individual to hold property in the soil, or the products of human

---

* I was educated a farmer, among the green hills of Vermont. My means of information have been very limited; self-esteem and language small; not much practice in speaking or writing.

industry, separate from the whole human family, the evils above enumerated must, from the necessity of the case, exist, in some form or other.

Resolved, That history and philosophy teach us, that men embrace the theories inculcated by the institutions which surround them, and since the characters of men are moulded by those institutions, it becomes us, as practical friends of humanity, and philosophical reformers, to endeavor to supersede these institutions, which degrade man's nature by establishing such as will tend to call out the higher faculties of the soul. . . .

A. BROOKE, *President*

JOHN A. COLLINS, *Cor. Secretary*
J. LUKINS, *Rec. Secretary*

Rights of Property and Co-operative Associations
PROCEEDINGS of the Oakland Meeting
[CONCLUDED]

April 28, 1843

PROPERTY CONVENTION

BOSTON, April 24, 1843

DEAR GARRISON:

Time will not allow me to give the readers of the Liberator a detailed account of the 'Property Convention' recently held in Worcester. . . . The meetings continued for four days and evenings, and the interest continued to increase, as well as numbers, up to the last session. Many individuals, who were at first either indifferent or hostile to a re-organization of society on a community of interests, became exceedingly interested before the meetings were brought to a close. The right of individual property must soon command the attention of the enlightened and the benevolent, however much reformers may strive to give it the go-by. Every movement throughout the civilized world is forcing the masses to investigate the claims by which the apparently favored few hold their hoarded wealth. The inventions of the age are fast throwing out of employment millions, whose daily labor was their only means to secure an apology for a living. Every labor-saving machine now introduced into society is an engine of oppression. Governments and men of wealth have monopolized all the land, and capitalists convert all the benefits of machinery to their own use, so that when its multiplication throws the masses out of employment, they have no means either to get into the country or to purchase the soil. They are driven into the poor-house or the prison. Men might as well attempt to outrun a locomotive, as it speeds itself over the railroad track, as to endeavor to compete with these iron automatons placed in our factories. The people have it in their power to convert this land into a paradise, if they will. If they allow capitalists to fatten upon their toil, the fault must be their own. . . .

Yours for the truth, J. A. COLLINS

January 5, 1844

SOCIAL REORGANIZATION

. . . Several 'Associations' have been formed in this country, within the last five years, as experiments by which to solve, if possible, the great problem of social co-operation; and others are in process of formation. Many conventions have been held in various parts of the free States, (for in the slave States, nothing is tolerated which militates against their slaveholding despotism,) to investigate the subject, and these have been generally well attended, and of a highly interesting character. One was held in this city last week, the proceedings of which may be found in a subsequent column. It was numerously attended each day by as intelligent, respectable, virtuous and philanthropic persons as we ever saw convened together; and more interesting meetings we never witnessed, for any purpose whatever. . . . 'Free discussion' was carried to its utmost latitude. All sorts of notions, opinions, doctrines and propositions were advanced for the consideration of the convention; and though some of these were very absurd, some very visionary, some very fallacious, and some very impracticable, yet a great deal of wholesome, robust, world-saving truth was enunciated, much light was thrown on many important points, the advantages of a social organization were set forth in a captivating manner, the causes of human degradation were traced to their source, and the brotherhood of the human race was seen with joy, and expatiated upon with great power and eloquence. . . . Yet, important and interesting as was the convention, not one of the daily papers has made any allusion to its proceedings, though in their columns room has been found for the insertion of all sorts of trash . . .

The various 'Associations' in this State were ably represented by those who are identified with them:—that at Northampton, by George W. Benson, David Mack, and James Boyle; that at Hopedale, by Adin Ballou and D. S. Whitney; that at Brook Farm, West Roxbury, by George S. Ripley, Charles A. Dana, and C. List. John A. Collins appeared in behalf of the Skaneateles 'Community,' which is essentially different from any 'Association.' Albert Brisbane and William H. Channing of New-York, advocated the views of Charles Fourier—the former without modification.

How could a meeting fail to be interesting, where minds like these were called into earnest activity? In many important points, the several speakers were in perfect agreement; on some, perhaps not important, they disagreed; on a few which were deemed of vital consequence on both sides, they were widely divided. Mr. Collins stood alone in the advocacy of his peculiar views, though there were probably some in the audience who embraced them. These he defended with great ingenuity, readiness and eloquence. He attempted to vindicate the doctrine of philosophical necessity, his deduction from which was, that no man is responsible for his thoughts, his opinions, his belief, or his acts; that all men do as well as they can in the circumstances under which they are placed; that society is the great dragon of iniquity, who is guilty of all the crimes and outrages that are perpetrated, and not the people in their individual capacity; that no one is deserving of praise or blame for what he does. He argued that no man may justly claim a right to individual property, either in land, houses, cattle or anything else; that no one has any more right to the productions of his own brains or hands than any other person; that 'love-relations' require that all property should be held in common; that all buying and selling is selfish and sinful; and that it is wrong to take animal life or eat animal flesh.

From these views, every other speaker dissented. How the

world could be filled with robbery, oppression and villainy, and yet there be no robbers, oppressors, or villains, it was difficult to comprehend. It was fatalism to say that no man is responsible for his conduct, and a doctrine which would gratify corruption and profligacy universally. The root of evil was in the heart of man, and not in external circumstances, though these often operated disastrously on the manners and morals of the truly unfortunate. . . . It was contended that every man had a right to the products of his own toil, superior to that of any other, but not in a selfish or covetous sense; and these he was bound to distribute as the law of brotherly kindness should demand in all cases of human necessity. The debate covered a wide field; but as we took no notes, we are unable to give any report of the speeches.

This question of social reorganization is evidently destined to produce a great sensation in the country, if nothing more. We have been able, as yet, to examine it only very superficially. Of Fourier's plan, we know nothing accurately, though we intend to give it a full and speedy examination. Of one thing we feel certain: an internal regeneration must precede the external salvation of mankind from sin and misery. The chief obstacles to the success of these communities or associations will lie in the breasts of their members and not in the present state of society. If they will dwell together in love, having the same mind that was in Christ Jesus, they will surely prosper. If they attempt to walk by sight, and not by faith, they will perish. No theory or plan of association can save them from themselves, though it may aid them in the work of human redemption.

August 9, 1844

REORGANIZATION OF SOCIETY

I believe that society, as it now exists, is radically false in its structure—the embodiment and supremacy of all the selfish passions and propensities—at war with the rights and interests of mankind—and as unnatural as it is iniquitous. I believe, moreover, (for truth and love must finally prevail throughout the earth,) that it ought to be REORGANIZED, from the foundation to the roof, and must be, before peace and good will can prevail, to any considerable extent. I *do not* believe, however, that this mighty change is to be effected by any mere external arrangement or artificial contrivance, or by the adoption of any written creed, however excellent in itself, but by a regeneration of mind and a oneness of spirit in righteousness, which shall 'overturn, and overturn,' all that is oppressive and unjust, until the form of society shall be simple, beautiful, the outward symbol of an inward redemption. But this redemption must exhibit itself in a practical manner, and it seems to me must ultimately lead to such an organization as has been alluded to. The subject is one of vast importance, and I hope will be investigated with zeal and courage by all who claim to be reformers, and who profess to deplore the present frightful condition of our race. The attention of all such is directed to the Convention which has been called by the Northampton Association of Education and Industry, and which is to be held in that place on the 31st inst. Delegates will probably be present from Hopedale, Brook Farm, and other 'Communities,' and the proceedings cannot fail to be equally interesting and important. It is my intention to be there, to do all in my power to help the glorious cause of social organization along.

> 'It's coming yet, for a' that,
> When man to man, the world all o'er,
> Shall brother be, for a' that.'

September 27, 1844

Letters from Henry Wright. No. II

GRAEFENBERG, (Austria,) March 30, 1844

NATIONALISM

DEAR GARRISON:

At the supper table this evening the subject of Inspiration came up, and I happened to remark, that God holds intercourse with men, and communicates his will to them, and holds them responsible not as NATIONS but as INDIVIDUALS. . . .

'What do you think of national combinations?' asked M.

'As now organized and managed, they are the most formidable

obstacles to the regeneration and redemption of mankind. Every step made by man in the path of improvement, must be made in spite of them.'

'It is strange that the character of these organizations should never have been known before, (said A.) but that it was left for you to discover it and make it known.'

'Not at all. I may as well be the discoverer as another. And as to the world being so long in ignorance of their true character, that is no more strange than that they should be ignorant so long of the true character of sectarian and priestly combinations. The great object of these organizations seems to have been to enable the few to rule and murder the many, systematically, respectably, and legally, and, as it were, by their own consent. For, as wolves and tigers gorge themselves with flesh and lick their gory chops, so do nations gorge themselves with human victims, not in detail, but in masses, by wholesale. States and Nations are to be regarded as we regard combinations of men to pick pockets, to steal sheep, to rob on the road, to steal men, to range over the sea as pirates—only on a larger and more imposing scale. When men steal, rob and murder as states and nations, it gives respectability to crime—the enormity of their crimes is lost sight of, amid the imposing number that commit them, and amid the glitter and pomp of equipage. The little band of thieves is scorned and hunted down as a felon; the great, or governmental band of thieves, is made respectable by numbers, and their crimes cease to be criminal and hateful in proportion to the number combined to do them. If a community of ten commit piracy, they are all hung, and a man is made infamous if he joins this *little* band of pirates; but if a community of 25,000,000, called Great Britain or Austria, do the same deed, it is all right, and Christian, and heaven-ordained, and a man is made infamous if he refuses to join this *great* band of pirates. Such reasoning is most false. I cast it from me. I can no more join a community of 25,000,000, that exists by plunder and murder, than I can join one composed of ten.'

'Do you think it right for men to combine as states and nations?' asked G.

'It is right for men to combine, and call their combinations by what names they please, provided the name does not deceive the

people as to the real nature and designs of the combination, and
provided, also, the object of the combination be good.'

'Is the object for which the existing national combinations are
formed, one which you approve?' asked M.

'What is that object? Perhaps I am not fully aware of it.'

'PROTECTION,' said M.

'From whom or what?'

'From the assaults and insults of human beings, of course,'
said M.

'By what means?'

'By military power, of course,' said M.

'That is, by inflicting starvation, nakedness, disease and death
upon their enemies?'

'Just so,' said M.

'All such combinations are condemned by the voice of God and
Humanity. Those who thus combine give the strongest proof of
their intention to act the part of villany to the rest of mankind,
and of their utter destitution of love and principle. They combine to defend themselves against the vengeance of those whom
they expect to injure. Thus the Puritans of New-England combined and armed to defend themselves against the Indians, because they were conscious of an intention to do to them what
they would have resented and taken vengeance for, had the
Indians done it to them. They knew that their conduct would
provoke the Indians to retaliate, because they knew that if the
Indians had done the same to them, they would have retaliated.
Hence, from the first, they combined and armed, to protect themselves from the Indians' wrath and revenge, whom they intended
to injure. Then, when they did arise to protect their wigwams,
their council fires, their sepulchres, their wives and children and
country, against the avarice and ambition of the Puritans, the
Puritans denounced the Indians as savage murderers, and had
the impudence to look to God to save them from the wrath which
their own injustice and bloody cruelty had provoked. So with
the republican, (?) praying (?) slaveholders of America. They
combine to protect themselves against the slaves. Why? Solely
because they know the slaves are wronged, and that, if they were
thus wronged, they should seek every opportunity to destroy
their oppressors. Those who are conscious of a desire to injure

none, and of a willingness to make restitution if they should injure any, have no need of armed combinations for defense.'

'But men must be restrained by *social influence,*' said S.

'But not by swords and guns; and these governmental combinations cannot wield any other influence, for, like the eagle, the lion, the bear, the leopard, and other beasts that represent them, they have no souls, no consciences, no responsibility.'

'But is it not better to restrain men by the gallows, swords and guns, than not at all?' asked M.

'No. Let every nation be blotted out, that cannot exist without shedding blood. There is no anarchy, no disorder, no cruelty like a battle-field. To resort to armies and navies to protect from anarchy, is to leap into the mouth of a shark to escape the jaws of a wolf.'

'But, national combinations are necessary to regulate the intercourse of men in distant lands,' said G.

'The very worst means possible to effect such an object. National truth, justice, honor, honesty, responsibility, are *names—* nought else. As well expect honesty and justice of wild beasts as of nations. No—let states and nations cease to meddle with individual intercourse—let men meet and deal, one with another, the world over; then would there be some hope that truth and justice might be done. Every interference of states or nations to regulate commerce has been a curse to all concerned. Commerce is an inter-individual affair, and should rest solely on the character of individuals, and not on the swords and guns of nations. The day is coming when men will deal with one another around the world, without the pernicious influence of these soulless, irresponsible bodies called nations.'

'But nations have religion to guide them,' said A. 'England is guided by a religion.'

'Yes. England has a religion. England is full of religion, and of priests to carry it on; but a religion that lives by plunder, and is consistent with national robbery and murder. Let the plains of India, let China, let Van Dieman's land, let Waterloo, let her cowering, ignorant, prostrate millions, tell what kind of a religion she has. It is a religion without conscience, without truth, or justice, or honesty.'

'A religion without justice, truth, or honesty!' exclaimed A. 'What sort of a religion is that?'

'Just the sort that guides England and America and all nations, in the commission of robbery and murder—a religion that licenses slavery, war, drunkenness. To baptize every act of injustice which the State sees fit to legalize, is the object of all State religions. A man or a nation may be very wicked, yet very religious. The greatest villains on earth are often very religious. Slaveholders are often very religious. So are soldiers—so are pirates—and will pray most devoutly while stealing and murdering men.'

'Do you say that a nation may be *Christian*, and steal, vote and murder?' asked A.

'NO. Christianity and religion *may* be very different. No nation can be *Christian*, without being pure, honest, loving, forgiving; but a nation may be *religious*, and full of wrath, revenge and murder. Therefore I say of England as a nation, she has much religion, but no honesty.'

Thine, H. C. WRIGHT

The Constitutional Argument

The real conflict between the Garrisonians and the political Abolitionists was over whether or not the Constitution was a proslavery document. Both sides of the argument were reiterated over and over again in The Liberator. *One of the best expressions of the political side that it was not came with a memorial of the Massachusetts legislature to Congress calling for the three-fifths slave representative clause to be abrogated. This was in Article I, Section 2 of the Constitution, viz: "Representatives and direct taxes shall be apportioned among the several States which may be included within this Union according to their respective numbers, which shall be determined by adding to the whole number of free persons, including those bound to service for a term of years, and excluding Indians not taxed, three-fifths of all other persons. . . ." This gave the South a considerable edge over the North; the more slaves, the more votes. It put a political advantage into the institution. Garrison obligingly printed the entire memorial in the paper. It occupied nine and a half columns. Garrison answered it, holding to his position that the Constitution was fatally flawed from the beginning.*

May 3, 1844

MASSACHUSETTS RESOLUTIONS

House of Representatives, April 4, 1844 . . .

. . . It is said that the slave representation in the government of the United States was a concession made to the South in the formation of the Constitution. It is also said that it was an acknowledgment that slaves are property, and that their owners are entitled to the protection of that clause of the Constitution which provides that private property shall not be taken, unless for public uses. In these positions, the subscribers believe there are several grave errors; for, first, they consider the slave representation clause as a concession, not to the South, but to a small minority of the people of the South—owners of this species of pretended property; who, having, by means of this unnatural wealth, monopolized to themselves all the political power of the States in which they live, to the utter prostration of the rights, not only of the slaves, but of the laboring poor *free* population of their own

States, claim to be exclusively the *people*, of whom they form perhaps not a tenth part, and to concentrate in themselves all the rights and interests of the South.

Secondly, it is a grave and gratuitous error to assume that the Constitution of the United States acknowledges slaves to be property. The truth is, that the words slave and slavery are studiously and purposely excluded from that instrument. Why was it that, in declaring *numbers* to be the standard of representation in the House and of direct taxation, it was provided that those numbers should be *determined* by adding to the whole number of *free persons,* including those bound for a term of years, all excluding Indians not taxed, three-fifths of *all other persons?* . . . JOHN QUINCY ADAMS

J. R. GIDDINGS

Garrison on the Constitution as Pro-Slavery

. . . It is absurd, it is false, it is an insult to the common sense of mankind, to pretend that the Constitution was intended to embrace the entire population of the country under its sheltering wings; or that the parties to it were actuated by a sense of justice and the spirit of impartial liberty; or that it needs no alteration, but only a new interpretation, to make it harmonize with the object aimed at by its adoption. As truly it might be argued that because it is asserted in the Declaration of Independence that all men are created equal, and endowed with an inalienable right to liberty, therefore none of its signers were slaveholders, and, since its adoption, slavery has been banished from the American soil! The truth is, our fathers were intent on securing liberty to *themselves,* without being very scrupulous as to the means they used to accomplish their purpose. They were not actuated by the spirit of universal philanthropy; and though *in words* they recognized occasionally the brotherhood of the human race, *in practice* they continually denied it. They did not blush to enslave a portion of their fellow men, and to buy and sell them as cattle in the market, while they were fighting against the oppression of the mother country and boasting of their regard for the rights of man. Why, then, concede to them virtues they did not possess? *Why cling to the falsehood, that they were no respecter of persons in the formation of the government.*

Revolutionary Separatism and Protest

Shortly after this, Garrison put before his wing of the movement his long-held belief that to co-operate with the federal government was an accommodation to evil. Thus, ten years after its founding, the American Anti-Slavery Society took a most revolutionary step, separating peacefully from the Government of the United States: "ours must be a bloodless strife, excepting our blood be shed . . ." The Society called on the whole American people, all who were not slaveholders, to secede from the government with them, to "pay it no allegiance, and give it no voluntary aid." Garrison called the secession "a revolution without taking up arms."

This action of "No Union with Slaveholders" caused another split in the movement. However, the comment of three of the dissenters, one being the distinguished Whig historian Richard Hildreth, seemed to prove that in the long run, and in terms of the way things happened, this separatism was the ultimate element bringing Emancipation.

May 31, 1844

ADDRESS

TO THE

FRIENDS OF FREEDOM AND EMANCIPATION IN THE UNITED STATES

At the Tenth Anniversary of the American Anti-Slavery Society, held in the city of New-York, May 7th, 1844,—after grave deliberation, and a long and earnest discussion,—it was decided, by a vote of nearly three to one of the members present, that fidelity to the cause of human freedom, hatred of oppression, sympathy for those who are held in chains and slavery in this republic, and allegiance to God, require that the existing national compact should be instantly dissolved; that secession from the government is a religious and political duty; that the motto inscribed on the banner of Freedom should be, NO UNION WITH SLAVEHOLDERS; that it is impracticable for tyrants and the enemies of tyranny to coalesce and legislate together for the preservation of human rights, or the promotion of the interests of

Liberty; and that revolutionary ground should be occupied by all
those who abhor the thought of doing evil that good may come,
and who do not mean to compromise the principles of Justice
and Humanity.

. . . It matters not what is the theory of the government, if
the practice of the government be unjust and tyrannical. We rise
in rebellion against a despotism incomparably more dreadful than
that which induced the colonists to take up arms against the
mother country; not on account of a three-penny tax on tea, but
because fetters of living iron are fastened on the limbs of millions of our countrymen, and our most sacred rights are trampled
in the dust. As citizens of the State, we appeal to the State in
vain for protection and redress. As citizens of the United States,
we are treated as outlaws in one half of the country, and the national government consents to our destruction. We are denied
the right of locomotion, freedom of speech, the right of petition,
the liberty of the press, the right peaceably to assemble together
to protest against oppression and plead for liberty—at least in
thirteen States of the Union. If we venture, as avowed and unflinching abolitionists, to travel South of Mason and Dixon's line,
we do so at the peril of our lives. If we would escape torture and
death, on visiting any of the slave States, we must stifle our
conscientious convictions, bear no testimony against cruelty and
tyranny, suppress the struggling emotions of humanity, divest
ourselves of all letters and papers of an anti-slavery character,
and do homage to the slaveholding power—or run the risk of a
cruel martyrdom! These are appalling and undeniable facts.

Three millions of the American people are crushed under the
American Union! They are held as slaves—trafficked as merchandize—registered as goods and chattels! The government
gives them no protection—the government is their enemy—the
government keeps them in chains! There they lie bleeding—we
are prostrate by their side—in their sorrows and sufferings we
participate—their stripes are inflicted on our bodies, their shackles are fastened on our limbs, their cause is ours! The Union
which grinds them to the dust rests upon us, and with them we
will struggle to overthrow it! The Constitution which subjects
them to hopeless bondage, is one that we cannot swear to support! Our motto is, 'NO UNION WITH SLAVEHOLDERS,'

either religious or political. They are the fiercest enemies of mankind, and the bitterest foes of God! We separate from them not in anger, not in malice, not for a selfish purpose, not to do them an injury, not to cease warning, exhorting, reproving them for their crimes, not to leave the perishing bondman to his fate—O no! But to clear our skirts of innocent blood—to give the oppressor no countenance—to signify our abhorrence of injustice and cruelty—to testify against an ungodly compact—to cease striking hands with thieves and consenting with adulterers—to make no compromise with tyranny—to walk worthily of our high profession—to increase our moral power over the nation—to obey God and vindicate the gospel of his Son—to hasten the downfall of slavery in America, and throughout the world!

We are not acting under a blind impulse. We have carefully counted the cost of this warfare, and are prepared to meet its consequences. It will subject us to reproach, persecution, infamy—it will prove a fiery ordeal to all who shall pass through it—it may cost us our lives. We shall be ridiculed as fools, scorned as visionaries, branded as disorganizers, reviled as madmen, threatened and perhaps punished as traitors. But we shall bide our time. Whether safety or peril, whether victory or defeat, whether life or death be ours, believing that our feet are planted on an eternal foundation, that our position is sublime and glorious, that our faith in God is rational and steadfast, that we have exceeding great and precious promises on which to rely, THAT WE ARE IN THE RIGHT, we shall not falter nor be dismayed, 'though the earth be removed, and though the mountains be carried into the midst of the sea'—though our ranks be thinned to the number of 'three hundred men.' Freemen! are you ready for the conflict? Come what may, will you sever the chains that bind you to a slaveholding government, and declare your independence? Up, then, with the banner of revolution! Not to shed blood—not to injure the person or estate of any oppressor—not by force and arms to resist any law—not to countenance a servile insurrection—not to wield any carnal weapons! No—ours must be a bloodless strife, excepting *our* blood be shed—for we aim, as did Christ our leader, not to destroy men's lives, but to save them—to overcome evil with good—to conquer through suffering for righteousness' sake—to set the captive free by the potency of truth!

Secede, then, from the government. Submit to its exactions, but pay it no allegiance, and give it no voluntary aid. Fill no offices under it. Send no Senators or Representatives to the national or State Legislature; for what you cannot conscientiously perform yourself, you cannot ask another to perform as your agent. Circulate a declaration of DISUNION FROM SLAVEHOLDERS, throughout the country. Hold mass meetings—assemble in Conventions—nail your banners to the mast! . . .

The form of government that shall succeed the present government of the United States, let time determine. It would be a waste of time to argue that question, until the people are regenerated and turned from their iniquity. Ours is no anarchical movement, but one of order and obedience. In ceasing from oppression, we establish liberty. What is now fragmentary, shall in due time be crystallized, and shine like a gem set in the heavens, for a light to all coming ages.

Finally—we believe that the effect of this movement will be—

First, to create discussion and agitation throughout the North; and these will lead to a general perception of its grandeur and importance.

Secondly, to convulse the slumbering South like an earthquake, and convince her that her only alternative is, to abolish slavery, or be abandoned by that power on which she now relies for safety.

Thirdly, to attack the slave power in its most vulnerable point, and to carry the battle to the gate.

Fourthly, to exalt the moral sense, increase the moral power, and invigorate the moral constitution of all who heartily espouse it.

We reverently believe that, in withdrawing from the American Union, we have the God of justice with us. We know that we have our enslaved countrymen with us. We are confident that all free hearts will be with us. We are certain that tyrants and their abettors will be against us.

In behalf of the Executive Committee of the American Anti-Slavery Society,   WM. LLOYD GARRISON, *President*

WENDELL PHILLIPS }
MARIA WESTON CHAPMAN } *Secretaries*
Boston, May 20, 1844

June 14, 1844

NO UNION WITH SLAVEHOLDERS!

The following resolutions, after a protracted and able discussion, were adopted at the late New-England Anti-Slavery Convention by a vote of 250 to 24.

1. Resolved, That no equal union can exist between a slaveholding and a free community; that under any form of government, a large body of slaveholders must necessarily control the policy and character of the nation; and that it is the great fault of the United States Constitution, that it assists and facilitates this result.

2. Resolved, That for this reason, as well as for other reasons, no abolitionist can consistently swear to support the Constitution; that it is, in the opinion of this Convention, a gross departure from abolition principle for abolitionists to throw a ballot for any office under the State or United States Constitution, which requires such oath; and that we deem it a first duty for them to agitate for the dissolution of the Union.

June 7, 1844

PROTEST

We, the undersigned, members of the New-England Anti-Slavery Convention, assembled in Boston on the 28th of May, 1844, and the following days, do hereby protest against the first and second resolutions passed in the said Convention, and also against the preamble and resolution offered by Wm. Lloyd Garrison, which resolutions declare it to be the duty of abolitionists to repudiate the Constitution of the United States and to agitate for the dissolution of the Union,—on the following grounds . . .

4. That the abjuration of the Constitution of the United States, and the dissolution of the Union, do not seem to us to tend in the slightest degree towards a peaceful abolition of slavery; but, rather, to its abolition by force on the part of the free States, thus released from their connexion with the South, or by

means of a servile insurrection, countenanced and sustained by
the North. . . .   WILLIAM A. WHITE
                                          RICHARD HILDRETH
                                          DAVID H. BARLOW

August 16, 1844

PRESENTATION OF THE STANDARD

Last Evening of the New-England Anti-Slavery Convention, 1844

At 8 o'clock, Mr. Walcott entered . . . with the banner in his
hand which he had designed and executed for the New-England
Convention. It bore, in a red field, an eagle preying upon a fettered and prostrate slave, illustrative of American liberty, while
the reverse, in gold letters, ran thus: 'Immediate and Unconditional Emancipation' . . .

Mr. CHARLES C. BURLEIGH took the Standard from the artist,
and advanced towards Mr. Garrison, speaking as follows:

In the name of the New-England Convention, I present this
banner to the President of the American Anti-Slavery Society . . .

Mr. Garrison . . . spoke as follows:

. . . Now will rise the cry of traitor; and let it come, I say—
let it come! I acknowledge its truth in reference to a slaveholding Constitution and a slaveholding government—to slavery and
a slaveholding oligarchy. . . . This is our treason—thus far we
are traitors. . . .

We have commenced a mighty moral revolution, which must
roll onward and onward till it is crowned with complete and
triumphant success. It is now incomprehensible to the people at
large. They know not what we mean by talking of a revolution,
without taking up arms; but we are teaching them how incomparably more glorious, triumphant and permanent is the revolution of opinion, than the revolution of arms and blood. . . .

The Anti-Texas Movement

Garrison's call for a Northern secession did not seem so fanatical a few months later as the North became incensed over the proposed annexation of Texas. Northern secession became a common topic, verging on a mass movement of protest at the Administration's boldness in the Texas situation. Garrison himself became very popular and was chosen as a delegate to an enormous meeting of protest at Faneuil Hall in January, 1845. Charles Sumner, in a letter to Judge Story, commented, "The debates in the Convention were most interesting. I never heard Garrison before. He spoke with natural eloquence . . . It seemed doubtful, at one time, if the Abolitionists would not succeed in carrying the convention . . ."

Garrison characteristically printed an account in The Liberator *taken from the reactionary New York* Herald, *so critics could not say he was giving himself the best of it. But when the Editor of the Boston* Daily Mail *accused him of crashing the convention, he defended himself with unusual zeal for a man not concerned with routine political arrangements. At a February 4 meeting of the colored citizens of Boston, Garrison's position on Texas and secession of the North was unanimously upheld (Lib. Feb. 7, 1845). But the secession movement ran its course and before the summer of 1845 had ended, it had entirely collapsed. Garrison reacted bitterly and cried out, "I am for revolution, were I utterly alone."*

January 31, 1845

GREAT ANTI-ANNEXATION MEETING
IN FANEUIL HALL

The delegates elected to the convention, on the subject of Texas, assembled in Faneuil Hall . . .

There was a large and respectable body of delegates in attendance, comprising much of the moral worth and talent of the State. We noticed among the delegates, men who have been known to the citizens of Massachusetts, both as State and national Legislators, who have occupied seats upon her Judicial benches, lawyers of eminent standing, divines, men of letters, with others who have made themselves more or less distinguished in the various walks of life. . . .

Evening Session

. . . Wm. Lloyd Garrison came upon the stage amid deafening cheers, and said he rose to second the motion of Rev. Mr. Lovejoy,* and also to offer the following in amendment or rather, in connection and addition:

'That in view of the fact, that two branches of the Government have already declared their wish and concurrence in the project of annexation, we deem it our duty distinctly to declare what ought to be, and what we have faith to believe will be, the course of Massachusetts, should the infamous plan be consummated. Deeming the act utterly unconstitutional and void, we declare that the people of this Commonwealth will never submit to it as the law of the land, but look upon the Union as dissolved, and proceed to form a new government for herself and such of the free States as will aid her in carrying out the great purposes of our fathers in behalf of civil liberty. And we call upon the several towns of the Commonwealth, whenever the President shall announce that Texas is annexed to this Union, immediately to assemble and choose delegates for a second session of this Convention, which shall take measures for the formation of a new Union with such States as do not tolerate domestic slavery—the Union of 1789 having ceased to exist.'

In the maintenance of his course, Mr. Garrison made a lengthy and characteristic speech, during which he was interrupted with cheers and hisses.

Ebenezer Hussey of Lynn, then addressed the Convention, in favor of the Union, followed by Hon. L. Child, of the Massachusetts Senate, who closed his remarks with a motion to lay the resolution of J. C. Lovejoy, and the amendment of W. L. Garrison, on the table, which was carried.

---

* The resolution read: "Resolved, That in case the area of slavery be extended by the annexation of Texas to the United States, the free States will be released from any obligation which may be supposed to have bound them in any manner to support Slavery—and that it will become their duty to treat slaveholding on land, no less than on sea, as a species of piracy—at variance with all just laws and constitutions, and not to be countenanced in any way whatever, either by restoring fugitive slaves, or furnishing military aid to suppress servile insurrections."—T.N.

February 7, 1845

I find in the New-York Herald, the following report of the speech which I made on the proposition submitted by me to the Convention. . . .

> This proposition of Mr. GARRISON was received with great applause, and a few hisses. Referring to the latter, he said, he learned by that noise he had hit the nail on the head, and he called on the brave hearts before him to see that the nail was clenched. (Shouts of approbation; one chap called out treason.) Mr. G. said he represented 3,000,000 of slaves, in the Convention; all the free blacks, and the abolition party of the Union. . . . He would never uphold the unholy compromise of the Constitution with slavery, for his motto, as was well known, was—'No union with slaveholders!' (Prolonged and deafening applause.) . . .

'TREASONABLE PROJECT OF MR. GARRISON'

To the Editor of the Daily Mail:
    . . . My object, however, is not to defend myself against your absurd charge of treason, but to repel an insinuation which severely reflects on my honor and honesty as a man. You say— 'Mr. Garrison was not, we understand, a delegate to the Convention, and he professes to believe in the principle of no-human government. He had, therefore, no right to intrude himself, for good or evil, upon the deliberations of that body.' . . . My right to sit as a member of that Convention was as valid as that of any other member. I was chosen as one of the delegates from Ward 10, (in which I reside,) with seven others, without a dissenting vote; and my certificate of membership, signed by the chairman and secretaries of the meeting, was duly presented to the Convention. It was, I have reason to believe, the most numerously attended Ward meeting in the city. I submit to your sense of propriety, whether you were justified in giving this libellous accusation to the public, without further inquiry. . . .

WM. LLOYD GARRISON

Boston, Feb. 1, 1845

October 3, 1845

MIDDLESEX COUNTY ANTI-TEXAS AND ANTI-SLAVERY MASS MEETING AT CONCORD

. . . Mr. Garrison . . . arose and spoke as follows:

. . . Sir, I know how nearly alone we shall be. An overwhelming majority of the whole people are prepared to endorse this horrible deed of Texan annexation. The hearts of the few who hate it are giving way in despair; the majority have got the mastery. Shall we therefore retreat, acknowledge ourselves conquered, and fall into the ranks of the victors?—Shall we agree that it is idle, insane, to contend for the right any longer?

. . . I will be frank with you. I am afraid you are not ready to do your duty; and if not, you will be made a laughing-stock by tyrants and their tools; and it ought to be so.

I have nothing to say, Sir—nothing. I am tired of words— tired of hearing strong things said, where there is no heart to carry them out. When we are prepared to state the whole truth, and die for it, if necessary—when, like our fathers, we are prepared to take our ground, and not shrink from it, counting not our lives dear unto us—when we are prepared to let all earthly hopes go by the board—*then* let us say so: *till* then, the less we say, the better, in such an emergency as this.

'But who are we,' will men ask, 'that talk of such things? Are we enough to make a revolution?' No, Sir; but we are enough to *begin* one, and once begun, it never can be turned back. I am for revolution, were I utterly alone. I am there because I *must* be there. I *must* cleave to the right. I cannot choose but obey the voice of God. Now, there are but few who do not cling to their agreement with hell, and obey the voice of the devil. But soon the number who shall resist, will be multitudinous as the stars of heaven. . . .

Twenty Years of *The Liberator*

The sudden collapse of the anti-Texas movement did not mean that Garrison was cast out into the outer darkness of the social pariah. On the contrary, there was no one respected and sought after more than Garrison by the moral and intellectual leaders of the time. He was on the list of Transcendentalist Bronson Alcott's proposed "select company of gentlemen" who were to "diffuse" the best ideas of the century, along with Emerson, Theodore Parker, Wendell Phillips. He was one of Parker's "Council of Reformers," meeting with Charles Sumner, Dr. and Mrs. Samuel Howe, the Channings, James Freeman Clarke. He had the unquestioning loyalty of many noble women, Abby Kelley Foster, Maria Weston Chapman, Lydia Maria Child, Lucretia Mott, personalities that in a more rational form of society would be in the first order of intellectual and social rank. People he had quarreled with and cast off, Frederick Douglass, Elizur Wright, Nathaniel Peabody Rogers, and even the defectors of 1840, still appeared at his meetings and paid him homage for leading them into a life of purpose and principle. His quarrel with Frederick Douglass, a tragic event in his life, came out of Douglass's adopting the position, upon moving to Rochester in 1847 and starting his own paper, that the Constitution was an antislavery document and abolition could be brought about solely by political action and the manipulation of political expediencies.

January 31, 1851

LIBERATOR SOIREE

IN

COCHITUATE HALL

Agreeably to public notice, a Social Festival was held by the Friends of Emancipation . . . to celebrate the completion of the second *decade* since the publication of the LIBERATOR was commenced. . . .

[After the supper was disposed of, Mr. Quincy (the chairman —T.N.) continued:]

I give you joy on this happy occasion of our assembling ourselves together. . . . It is often our lot to weep with those that weep. It is our felicity to-night to rejoice with those that rejoice.

And who, I should like to know, have a better right to rejoice than the American abolitionists? Who have a better right to look upon the world with eyes of joy and gratitude, than they who are attempting to rescue the slave from his despair, and the country from its disgrace? I hold that we, of all men and women in this broad land, are those who have a right to rejoice, and to thank God for the lot which he has appointed us. And although our usual course lies in different paths from this, although it is not often that we find ourselves assembling on a festive occasion like the present, I am sure that we are not of those who, 'When God sends a cheerful hour, refrain!' . . .

[Garrison is given a gold watch—T.N.]

Mr. GARRISON,—taken wholly by surprise at the proffered gift, —rose with much embarrassment, and said—

Mr. PRESIDENT—if this were a rotten egg, [holding up the watch,] or a brickbat, I should know how to receive it. (Laughter and cheers.) If these cheers were the yells of a frantic mob seeking my life, I should know precisely how to behave. But the presentation of this valuable gift is as unexpected by me as would be the falling of the stars from the heavens; and I feel indescribably small before you in accepting it. A gold watch! Why, I have been compensated in this cause a million times over. In the darkest hour, in the greatest peril, I have felt just at that moment that it was everything to be in such a cause. I know that the praises which have fallen from the lips of my beloved brother and faithful coadjutor have been spoken in all sincerity; otherwise they would be intolerable. I know that I am among those not accustomed to flatter, and who do not mean to flatter. I know how to appreciate such demonstrations as greet me here to-night. Had it not been for such as are here assembled, we should not have had an anti-slavery struggle. I am sorry, my friends, that I have not a gold watch to present to each one of you. (Laughter.) You all deserve one! . . .

The period may have been when I was of some consequence to the anti-slavery movement; but it is not so now. The cause is safe in the hands of its friends. I owe so much to them all—so much to this dear friend, [Mr. Phillips,] and to you, [Mr. Quincy,] and to others whose names I need not to call, that it is impossible for me fully to express it. (Cheers.) . . .

Speech of Wendell Phillips

. . . John Foster used to say, that the best test of a book's value was the mood of mind in which one rose from it. To this trial I am always willing the most eager foe should subject the Liberator. I appeal to each one here, whether he ever leaves its columns without feeling his coldness rebuked, his selfishness shamed, his hand strengthened for every good purpose; without feeling lifted, for awhile, from his ordinary life, and made to hold communion with purer thoughts and loftier aims; and without being moved, the coldest of us, for a moment, at least, with an ardent wish that we, too, may be privileged to be co-workers with God in the noble purposes, for our brother's welfare which have been unfolded and pressed on our attention? Let critics who have time settle, after leisurely analysis, the various faults, which, as they think, have marred our friend's course, and denounce, as suits them, the other topics which he has chosen to mingle with his main subject; enough for us, in the heat of our conflict, to feel that it has always 'been good for us to have been' with him. How can we ever thank him for the clear atmosphere into which he has lifted us! If of the abolitionist it may be said, with such exceeding measure of truth, that he has broken the shackles of party, thrown down the walls of sect, trampled on the prejudices of his land and time, risen to something like the freedom of a Christian man, something of that perfect toleration which is the fruit only of the highest intellectual and moral culture—how much is all this owing to the influence of such a leader! My friends, if we never free a slave, we have at least freed ourselves, in the effort to emancipate our brother man. (Applause.) From the blindness of American prejudice, the most cruel the sun looks on; from the narrowness of sect; from parties, quibbling over words; we have been redeemed into full manhood—taught to consecrate life to something worth living for. Life! what a weariness it is, with its drudgery of education; its little cares of to-day, all to be lived over again to-morrow; its rising, eating, and lying down—only to continue the monotonous routine! Let us thank God that he has inspired any one to awaken us from being these dull and rotting weeds—revealed to us the joy of self-devotion— taught us how we intensify this life by laying it a willing offering on the altar of some great cause! . . .

Resistance to Tyranny

He still would not retreat a single inch. In 1850, the last great compromise was attempted to hold a country together which was rotten at the core. Every possible attempt was made to stifle controversy and division between the sections. The yearly convention of the American Anti-Slavery Society was to be held as usual in New York City on May 7, 1850. James Gordon Bennett of the proslavery New York Herald *worked with might and main to turn the whole city into a lynch mob directed against Garrison's meeting. "Go on Tuesday morning to the Tabernacle and there look at the black and white brethren and sisters, fraternizing, slobbering over each other . . . cursing the Constitution of our glorious Union . . . The Union expects every man to do his duty; and duty to the Union, in the present crisis, points out to us that we should allow no more fuel to be placed on the fire of abolitionism in our midst, when we can prevent it by sound reasoning and calm remonstrances."*

Bennett kept the war drums beating for days on end, incessantly urging that the meeting be broken up, that "public opinion should be regulated," that New York should not be "misrepresented" by these lunatics who will destroy this city's prosperity and make it an arena of blood and murder. On the day of Garrison's arrival, he was the target of the attack. He had "boldly urged the utter overthrow of the Churches, the Sabbath and the Bible. Nothing has been sacred with him but the ideal intellect of the Negro race. To elevate this chimera, he has urged the necessity of an immediate overthrow of the government . . . actual disruption and annihilation of the Union, and a cessation of all order, legal or divine, which does not square with his narrow views of what constitutes human liberty. Never, in the time of the French Revolution and blasphemous atheism, were there more malevolence and unblushing wickedness avowed than by this same Garrison. . . ." And so on, all more or less true, in substance.

The meeting was held on schedule, and it was crowded. Antislavery had now become so popular that a joke went that years ago it was difficult to get a hall to get into, now it was difficult to get into a hall.

Garrison stood calmly, benignly, in his accustomed place as chairman, wondering just how bad things were going to be. Deftly, he smoked out the power and character of the opposition. It appeared to be a motley group of hired disrupters under the command of a political hack named Captain Isaiah Rynders, and not the "merchants, men of business, and men of property" the Herald *had urged to do their duty there. Garrison was at his most infuriating. "In this country," he said, "Jesus has become obsolete. A profession in Him is no longer a test. Jesus is the most respectable person in the United States. (Great sensation, and*

215

*murmurs of disapprobation.) Jesus sits in the President's chair of the
United States. (A thrill of horror here seemed to run through the assembly.) Zachary Taylor sits there, which is the same thing, for he believes
in Jesus. He believes in war, and the Jesus that 'gave the Mexicans hell.'
(Sensation, uproar and confusion.)"*

*In the midst of a pandemonium of opposition and threat, the meeting
went on to its scheduled conclusion. A noted minister, Dr. William Henry
Furness, stepped blandly up to Rynders on his way out and said, "How
can we thank you for what you have done for us today." Rynders was
dumbfounded, not knowing what he had done to be thanked for—which
was, to Furness, provoking "a simple assertion of the right of the people
to think and speak freely."*

*Another of Garrison's shocking demonstrations was in a picnic grove
in Framingham, Massachusetts, on the Fourth of July, 1854, with Henry
Thoreau on the platform with him as another speaker.*

> Mr. Garrison said he should now proceed to perform an action
> which would be the testimony of his own soul to all present, of
> the estimation in which he held the pro-slavery laws and deeds
> of the nation. Producing a copy of the *Fugitive Slave Law,* he
> set fire to it, and it burnt to ashes. . . . Then holding up the
> U.S. Constitution, he branded it as the source and parent of all
> the other atrocities,—'a covenant with death, and an agreement
> with hell,'—and consumed it to ashes on the spot, exclaiming,
> 'So perish all compromises with tyranny! And let all the people
> say, Amen!' A tremendous shout of 'Amen!' went up to heaven
> in ratification of the deed, mingled with a few hisses and wrath-
> ful exclamations from some who were evidently in a rowdyish
> state of mind, but who were at once cowed by the popular
> feeling" (*Lib.*, July 7, 1854).

*But in 1856, his whole position was shattered by the Negro slaves
themselves rising and attempting to win their freedom in suppressed and
aborted acts of revolt. Because of the Frémont presidential campaign of
1856, for the first time since Nat Turner slave resistance was reported,
luridly and at length, in the Southern press. "Black Republican" campaign
orators were being blamed for "inciting Negro insurrections," with their
criticism of the slave system and the election of Frémont, if achieved, was
said by the South to be a signal for the slaughter of every white man,
woman, and child south of the Mason-Dixon line.*

*Henry C. Wright, his revolutionary soul ablaze from the sparks of
small, sporadic, but continuing acts of slave rebellion, began to urge a
new line for the American Anti-Slavery Society. He began this with a
letter in* The Liberator *of January 23, 1857, in which he said that he felt
the North was ready to accept without cavil the possibility that the slaves
were ready to strike for their own freedom in the best revolutionary tra-
dition. This letter served notice on the members of the pacifist-oriented*

American Anti-Slavery Society that the violent vs. non-violent method of emancipating the slaves would have to come up for reappraisal at the twenty-fifth annual meeting of the Massachusetts Anti-Slavery Society held on January 29 and 30.

Many of the old-time Abolitionists of the Quaker persuasion objected strenuously to Henry Wright's call for the endorsement of slave insurrections by the society—a position directly counter to all the early affirmations on this ticklish subject. In a spirited debate of two days, every variation on the violence-nonviolence theme was played out with eloquence and penetration. It was a time of great crisis for the society, and for Garrison himself. He let Wright lead the discussion and become the dominant figure at the convention.

Wright and Garrison finally came up with an ideological resolution of the dilemma which was not quite honest, but there was no other way to do it. This was, generally, that no man had a right to be a slave by consent, that he was dutybound to seek his freedom and in a manner that would be consistent with his own ideas of right. If he believed, with the great majority of the American people, that he could do it by the shedding of his oppressor's blood, then he should do it. On the other hand, if he believed, along with Wright and Garrison, that life was so sacred that no power in the universe had the right to take it away, he could not shed blood without destroying himself. However, since Garrison and Wright were in such an infinitesimal minority on this question, it was not fair for them to insist that the embattled slave follow their scruples, but, in Wright's words: "Every man must actualize his resistance and rebellion—his treason—by such means as he thinks right and most efficient. Would you deem it right —a duty—to kill the man who would enslave you? Then, you being judge, it is your right and duty to kill the man who would enslave your brother."

Thus, by falling back on the ethics of Transcendentalist individualism, Garrison and Wright prepared their pacifist society to swallow John Brown, Harper's Ferry, and Gettysburg without feeling any real impairment of their deeply rooted "peace principles." This most significant meeting, accurately reported by practitioners of "phonography," an early form of shorthand by that time in general use, marked another shattering in the ranks of the faithful. However, like the others, it released more and more of the revolutionary essences of antislavery which were penetrating deeper and deeper into the mass American consciousness, without the masses themselves being aware of it.

January 23, 1857

RESISTANCE TO TYRANTS
OBEDIENCE TO GOD

NEW GARDEN, (Ohio,) Jan. 8, 1857

DEAR GARRISON:

Few axioms are more clearly established in my mind than this: i. e., that resistance to tyrants is obedience to God. . . .

These thoughts are suggested by the present panic at the South, touching slave insurrections. Before me are extracts from various papers in Virginia, South Carolina, Georgia, Florida, Alabama, Louisiana, Mississippi, Tennessee, Arkansas, Missouri, Kentucky and Maryland, referring to *intended* insurrections among the slaves, and to the murder of the slaves for such supposed, but unproved insurrections. The entire slaveholding population is in the greatest alarm, lest their throats should be cut, their families destroyed, their wives and daughters violated, and their houses burned, by the outraged and long-suffering victims of their tyranny. Well may they tremble. BLOW FOR BLOW—a just and righteous *retribution,* is the cornerstone of their Church and State. Four millions are in their midst, whose wives and daughters they have ravished, whose hearthstones they have polluted with innocent blood, whose domestic relations and affections they have despised and crushed, whose husbands and wives, parents and children, mothers and sisters, they have scourged and sold; and whose bodies and souls they have tortured and imbruted. The cry of vengeance from these victims of inhumanity, is ever sounding, like a midnight cry of blood and rapine, in their ears. But for the momentous issues involved, it would be ludicrous enough to see these slaveholding Governors, Legislators and Judges, the Brookses, the Butlers, the Masons, the Toombs, and all the slaveholding tyrants of the South, pale and trembling like the meanest and most groveling cowards, at the first whisper of an *intended* insurrection of their slaves.

Poor creatures, they have their reward. They flee when no man pursueth, as the consciously guilty ever do. One ominous feature of this affair—ominous to the South—is that, during all this excitement, not a paper nor pulpit, not a judge, legislator or governor, in the North, so far as I know, not even Bennett's *Herald*, the New York *Observer*, nor *Journal of Commerce*, has expressed one word of sympathy for the pale, trembling and guilty slaveholder. I say, this absence of expressed sympathy in the North, even by the Northern wing of the Border Ruffian, Gutta Percha Democracy, is ominous to the slaveholders. Does it not prove that the North is fast verging to a position when an insurrection of slaves against the tyrants that crush them will be most welcome news—as welcome as would an effort of the serfs of Russia to cast off the tyranny that crushes them? Does it not prove that the feeling is fast gaining at the North, that resistance to their masters, on the part of the slaves, is obedience to God? and that, in the final struggle—which must come—the North will be on the side of the slave, and against the slaveholder? . . .

HENRY C. WRIGHT

February 13, 1857

ANNUAL MEETING OF THE MASSACHUSETTS ANTI-SLAVERY SOCIETY

SKETCHES OF DISCUSSIONS, CONTINUED

On Thursday evening, at Mercantile Hall, HENRY C. WRIGHT offered some resolutions, and said before reading them—

I believe that resistance to tyrants is obedience to God; and the man who believes in fighting at all, is a traitor to his principles if he does not assert the right of the American slave to armed resistance. To prevent misconception, it should be understood that non-resistance is not the doctrine of the Abolitionists generally, nor of the disunionists generally.

I furthermore believe that this Union has proved an utter failure in regard to the preservation and extension of liberty, and a great calamity to the human race. Man cannot reconcile moral contradictions; and he who attempts it, loses the power of correct discrimination in matters of conscience. Thus, this nation has lost the power to discriminate in relation to liberty and slavery.

In no nation of the world are theft, and robbery, and falsehood, so prevalent and so popular as in this nation. The clergy and the politicians uphold all these; and the people do not distinguish either the guilt or the disgrace of them. The American Union is at this hour one of the deadliest enemies of freedom.

I hope that our last Presidential election has been held. We can never reach slavery through the national organization, though we may through the State organization.

Wisconsin has placed herself, in this matter, far in advance of every State, having decided the following points by the unanimous voice of her Supreme Court.

1. Every State has a right to sit in judgment on the constitutionality of acts of Congress, relating to citizens of that State.

2. The Fugitive Slave Law is not constitutional.

3. Wisconsin will protect her citizens in violations of the Fugitive Slave Law.

4. Congress has no power to pass a Fugitive Slave Law at all. Each State must decide for itself whether any of its citizens are to be delivered into the hands of the slave power.

Now, I want the State of Massachusetts to come up to this ground. I ask—can it protect its citizens against kidnappers? *Will* it do so? If not, what is your republicanism good for? Down with it, I say, and the sooner the better.

4. Resolved,* That the American Union, as might have been anticipated from the antagonistic nature of the parties to it, has proved a sad and total failure, having, from its formation to the present day, directly tended to the moral degradation and ruin of the American people, and the extension and perpetuity of the most dreadful form of bondage now known to mankind.

5. Resolved, That the present American Government has proved a curse and calamity to the cause of Human Freedom throughout the world; and, therefore, it is the right and duty of the people at once to alter or forever abolish that government.

6. Resolved, That the people of the non-slave States owe it to themselves and to their posterity, and to justice, liberty and humanity, to call town, county and State Conventions to consider

* The resolutions that follow were printed in *The Liberator* on Feb. 6, 1857.—T.N.

the expediency and duty of forming a Northern Republic on the principle of No UNION WITH SLAVEHOLDERS.

Whereas, the fundamental, organic law of Massachusetts is, that 'all men are born free and equal, and endowed by their Creator with an inalienable right to liberty'; therefore,

7. Resolved, That, to allow a man to be arraigned and tried before *any* tribunal on the issue, Is he a freeman or a slave—is he a man or a chattel? is an atrocious violation of the fundamental law of the State.

8. Resolved, That it is the duty of Massachusetts to execute this fundamental law of her government, and to forbid, by such laws as shall be deemed just and necessary, the arrest and trial of any persons living under her jurisdiction, on an issue so insulting to God and so derogatory to man.

9. Resolved, That we recognize it, as a fixed law of our being, that 'Resistance to tyrants is obedience to God,' and that, under this law, it is the right and duty of the slave to deny the authority and resist the power of the slaveholder.

10. Resolved, That, in every effort of the slave to obtain his freedom, whether by flight or insurrection, our sympathies are, and ever must be, with him, and against his oppressor; and we pledge ourselves that we will do all in our power which we, as individuals, deem right and most fitting, to aid the enslaved in their struggle for liberty.

11. Resolved, That those who hold to the right of armed resistance to oppression, and glorify their Revolutionary sires for their bloody conflict with the British tyrants, are recreant to their own principles if they do not recognize this right on the part of the slaves against their tyrant masters, and assist them to achieve their complete enfranchisement.

12. Resolved, That the people of the North have long since passed the point where passive endurance of Southern insult, oppression and outrage is a virtue, even were there no inherent criminality in the Union itself: and we regard any further delay of the dissolution of the Union, especially when based on nothing better than the action, or the hopes of political parties pledged to the support of slavery in the States, as not only delusive, but criminal in the very highest degree.

JAMES N. BUFFUM. I protest against the official recognition, by this society, of the use of violence, of arms and bloodshed, among its means of opposing slavery. I understand the original doctrine of the Anti-Slavery Society to be, that its end is to be sought by moral and peaceful means. Hitherto, we have acted upon this principle. I approve the principle, and, am not prepared for any change in the prudent policy to which we have hitherto adhered; neither do I understand how the non-resistance which Henry C. Wright has so long and energetically professed, can give birth to such resolutions as we have just heard.

Mr. GARRISON. It seems to me that our friend Buffum has not correctly apprehended the spirit and meaning of the resolutions. In them, we are taking the American people on their own ground, and judging of them by their own standard. We have a right to demand that a nation shall act in consistency with that which it avows to be its rule of faith and practice.

Our friend, Mr. Wasson, thought that he might properly wait in slavery twenty-five years, to avoid the horrors of a bloody insurrection. But the voice of God in the soul cries aloud—'Give me liberty, or give me death.' A man has *no right to consent* to be a slave, either twenty-five years or twenty-five seconds, to avoid consequences.

(Mr. Wasson here asked if Mr. Garrison would counsel a slave to kill his master.)

That is not the question. A man has no right to consent to be a slave. He is bound in duty to seek freedom; and he must seek it in a manner accordant with his own ideas of right, deciding that point for himself.

ABBY KELLEY FOSTER. Mr. Wasson forgets that the question is not whether we shall counsel the slave to forsake peace, and commence war; *the war exists already,* and has been waged unremittingly ever since the slave has been in bondage. Four millions of slaves are disarmed warriors to-day; and all the evils of war, violations of life, liberty, property and every other right, are *now going on,* and *increasing.* The war is going on, with or without our consent, and we are looking to see whether right or wrong shall be victorious. Certainly every friend of liberty here would rejoice to hear to-night that the slaves of Louisiana or of Tennessee had risen against their masters.

Mr. Buffum. Our friend Garrison ought not to recommend the *false* standard used by other men.

Henry C. Wright. I will read again those expressions in the resolutions to which friend Buffum objects, and I think that if he will attend carefully to their phraseology, he will be obliged to give his assent to them.

Is it not true that resistance to tyrants is obedience to God? (Mr. Buffum replied—Yes.)

Is it not true that whether they obtain their liberty by flight or insurrection, our sympathies are with the slaves? (Yes.)

Is it not true that those who allow themselves to fight for their own liberty are traitors to their own doctrines if they refuse to fight in behalf of the slaves?

Parker Pillsbury—We may have to look this subject of violence very seriously in the face, and may as well familiarize our minds with it. We must abolish slavery. If by peace provisions in the Constitution, we have tied our hands from the use of *any needful instrumentality,* we had better untie them.

Our people have been so long familiarized with slavery that they have forgotten the duty of not consenting to be a slave. It is as well a sin to be a slave as to hold a slave.

Our friend Wright asked the question, Will Massachusetts protect the slave? A fugitive is in Boston who arrived yesterday. Perhaps he is an impostor. If so, he is a good actor; for he looks just as the real slavery which exists in our country makes a man look.

I wonder—will Massachusetts protect that slave? I think not. If he is arrested, he is lost. I wish she might prove her disposition and ability to protect him, though blood should run from Beacon Hill to Broad Street.

We have had the annexation of Texas—and the war with Mexico—and the passage of the Fugitive Slave Law; and the South proceeded to put this law in force here in Boston—successfully too—using Faneuil Hall and the United States soldiers to effect it. Then she repealed the Missouri Compromise. By this outrage, even the pulpit was stirred. Then came the outrages in Kansas—and then the worst outrage in Congress, the triumph of *central* ruffianism. A wound was inflicted upon Sumner,* probably incurable; but the wound to Massachusetts was *certainly* incurable.

Now, who thinks or cares for these things? Not the Republican party, certainly. The moss has grown over them, and would speedily render them illegible if *we* did not annually scrape it off, and keep the testimony open to public view.

Wilson and Banks would like a Southern candidate better than even Fremont, if he would run better. The Republican party really has no issue—never has had an issue with the South. Even the Whigs said the annexation of Texas was virtually a dissolution of the Union. But since then, all the successive outrages have not brought the Republican party to echo that statement. What a mockery to the memory of John Quincy Adams to submit successively to these increasing outrages. . . .

How much must be piled on the already enormous mountain of outrage inflicted on us by the South before the Republicans will see that Disunion is needful?

The letters of these men at the Worcester Convention† are so much subterfuge and evasion. What *can* reconcile them to disunion, if the recent atrocities of the Slave Power fail to do it? These last outrages, instead of quickening the sensibilities of the North, have acted like a paralytic stroke, deadening and benumbing them.

Let the Republicans come here and tell us *how long* they would have us wait.

Lucy Stone wished to give some of her experience among the leading members of the Republican party. One said in his speeches in that party—'We are not concerned in acting for the negroes'; among the mountains of Pennsylvania another said he had to forswear all sympathy with slaves, or he should not have got a vote; towards Wisconsin, one said, discussing with a slave-

---

* After making an antislavery speech U.S. Senator Charles Sumner of Massachusetts had been caned in the Senate, May, 1856, by Representative Preston Brooks of South Carolina.—T.N.

† The Worcester Disunion Convention met January 15, 1857, "to consider the practicability, probability, and expediency of a separation between the free and slave States." Henry Wilson, Republican senator from Massachusetts sent a letter calling "such movements . . . crimes against liberty."—T.N.

holder—'I am a Republican, and don't care a damm for the niggers'; Horace Greeley says he has no objection to vote for a slaveholder—and so with all the leaders of that party—and the party itself does not propose a single measure for the slave. They wish for the overthrow of Southern despotism, because its whip is stretched over *them;* but they do not know the might of moral power, and they trust for success to a compromising policy that constantly defeats its own ends. The position of the *party* and of its *leaders* deserves the severest criticism: but I believe the great body of *voters* in the party, and of sympathizers with it, to be far more deluded than dishonest, or even selfish; and I am sure that great numbers of noble young men, who have hitherto heard nothing nearer anti-slavery than Republican stump speeches, might now profitably hear the higher truths of our platform.

WENDELL PHILLIPS agreed most heartily with the concluding remark of Lucy Stone. We must work through public opinion, and this public opinion will of course find its way through its customary civil and religious channels. Of course, we desire political action against slavery. But we must criticise the shortcomings of such political action, and of those who are *nearest* to us, namely, the Republicans. Men see with their theories, not with their eyes, and our business is to correct those theories. I want to consolidate in Massachusetts an unflinching and intelligent *purpose* against slavery.

If a negro kills his master to-night, write his name by the side of Warren; say that he is a William Tell in disguise, or a John Hancock in eclipse. I want to accustom Massachusetts to the idea of insurrection; to the idea that every slave has a right to seize his liberty on the spot. This is making liberty practical.

The Boston *Transcript* writes an eulogistic obituary of [Preston—T.N.] Brooks—the chaplain at Washington is to preach a sermon at his funeral—and the President, the Cabinet, and both Houses of Congress, will be in attendance to do honor to the memory of that assassin. Shall these acts pass without censure? Shall Massachusetts fail to point out the great truth of the essential barbarity of slavery over those eulogized remains? By no means. How hard soever may be this duty, the nation is to be educated, and thoroughly impregnated with anti-slavery convictions. I want to teach the right moral doctrine to-day; to educate the conscience of Massachusetts in such a manner that the young soldiery of Boston may be ashamed to darken State street with their presence when another Anthony Burns is taken away.* (Applause.) When Lord Brougham stood before the House of Lords, he said that he knew no one there but the Queen. Now, I want the Abolitionist to say, 'I know no one but the slave.' (Applause.)

Mr. Wilson's letter says disunion is a crime against liberty. We need to teach such a man that *justice* and *liberty* are the most valuable of all human possessions, to which everything else is to be sacrificed. The Abolitionist must say—I know no interest here but that of the slave, and his interest I shall seek, even if the country goes to pieces.

So far, the North has been uniformly defeated. Look at Sumner, and say if free speech has been secured on the floor of Congress. The Republicans should seek the abolition of slavery in the States themselves, and refuse to vote a dollar of appropriations until that is done.

I should like to frighten Henry Wilson with the sight of a State committing this 'crime against liberty.'

I do not agree in the severe censure against Sumner for not writing to the Worcester Convention. In his last letter (of acceptance), there is no mention of the Union, and we are to judge by his silence here as well as there.

If the United States Court shall reverse Judge Shaw's decision in the Med case,† we want a Chief Justice like him of Wisconsin to restore it, and men with souls strong enough to take the responsibility of defending it.

FRIDAY

. . . H. C. WRIGHT said—The supremacy of man over his incidents is the stand-point from which I view the American Constitution and Union, and all governmental, and religious institutions. Institutions for men, not men for institutions. This

---

* A slave who had been returned to his master from Boston in 1854.—T.N.

† Judge Lemuel Shaw, Chief Justice of the Massachusetts Supreme Court from 1830 to 1860, made a decision in 1836 that a slave taken voluntarily by his master into a free state was thereby made free.—T.N.

sentiment underlies all my efforts against slavery, war, and other social wrongs. Man is never to be sacrificed in his physical, intellectual, social, or spiritual nature, to preserve an institution. The man should never be merged in the citizen, the individual in the organization; but the organization, whether political or religious, should be merged in the individual, and the authority of all governments be in subjection to the authority of each individual soul. How can any man, who respects the nature he bears, sustain an institution, in Church or State, that requires the sacrifice of human life or liberty? . . . The American Union was formed ostensibly to protect life and liberty; to sustain and perpetuate that Union, about one million of human beings have been slain, and four millions are now held and used as chattels.

Christendom has been surfeited with eulogies on the Bible, the Constitution, and the Union. From Sabbath to Sabbath, from the pulpits of the land, the shout is raised, 'The Holy Bible!' 'The Holy Scriptures!' 'The Word of God!'—but what pulpit pleads for the holiness and sanctity of the man, woman and child? Human beings are hung, shot and enslaved to vindicate the sanctity of the Bible. So millions must be blotted from the record of humanity, and herded with beasts, to sustain the authority of the Constitution and to perpetuate the Union. Down with every book, every Constitution, down with the Union, down with all governments and churches, that cannot exist without killing or enslaving men.

Twenty-three years have I warred against slavery, and tried to stir up all around me, slaves and enslavers, to insurrection, and rebellion against the Slave Power. I have sought to array the public mind in an open and determined hostility to the slaveholders. In this effort, *Man,* and not the Bible, nor the Constitution, nor the Union, has been my client. I would rescue man from the auction-block, without one moment's thought for the existence or welfare of any being or power that would hold him there. As a slaveholder, no law or institution, no man or being in the universe, can have the least claim to our respect. To all books, constitutions, governments, churches, and beings, that sanction slavery, I have only this to say, 'Get behind me, Satan! thou art an offence to me.' To us, as Abolitionists, slaveholders, as such, have no rights; outlawed by humanity, they are to be exterminated, as slaveholders, from the face of the earth. We can make no truce with them. Our only warfare against them is for *death* or *victory*. Republicans, Democrats, Know-Nothings, and all, shout, 'Great is the Constitution—it shall be held sacred!' Why not say, 'Great is man—he must and shall be held sacred'? They talk about the 'glorious Union;' but not a word about the glory of life and liberty.

We, as Abolitionists, must have our hearts renewed; we must be baptized with the Holy Ghost—i. e., with reverence for man, rather than for institutions. We need give ourselves no concern about the interests and glory of God; God will take care of himself. Man, in the person of the imbruted slave, is our client—the *only* client of the Anti-Slavery enterprise. Our business is to vindicate the sanctity and glory of man, as insulted and outraged in the slave. Let us look after our brother, who needs our help, and who can be benefitted by our love and reverence. What we do to and for humanity, outraged in the slave, we do to and for God. We owe no love, no reverence, no duties to God, aside from those we owe to man. I cannot love and reverence any being who has no love and respect for human nature. Whoever or whatever enslaves and desecrates our common humanity, in my person, or in the person of any man, woman or child, is an object of abhorrence in my soul.

I wish to call attention to the present excitement at the South respecting slave insurrections. I believe that resistance to tyrants is obedience to God. Every slaveholder is a tyrant. Resistance to him is the right and duty of the slave. Our right and duty, as Abolitionists is to arouse every slave to a bold, determined, open resistance to the authority and power of his enslavers. We owe it as a duty to ourselves and to humanity, to excite every slave to *rebellion* against his master. A rebel against slavery! An insurrectionist against slaveholders! A traitor to a slaveholding government! An infidel to a slaveholding religion! An atheist to a slaveholding God! These are titles of which we may well be proud. To render myself worthy of them have I toiled for twenty-five years; and I shall toil until death, and to all eternity.

But how shall we manifest our spirit of rebellion against slavery? How *actualize* our resistance to tyrants, our insurrection against slaveholders, our *treason* against the Union and Government that would turn man into a beast? Every man must actualize his resistance and rebellion—his treason—by such means as he thinks right and most efficient. Would you deem it right—a duty—to kill the man who would enslave you? Then, you being judge, it is your right and duty to kill the man who would enslave your brother. Franklin Pierce* would deem it a duty to shoot the man who would enslave his wife and child; then, he being witness, it is the right and duty of each and every slave in the nation to shoot Franklin Pierce when he would enslave them.

Each man must be true to himself. It is all he can do—to act up to his highest light—to be true to his own conviction of duty. Is it right for the slave to actualize his resistance to his master by arms and blood? The slave knows no higher law than violence to protect himself and his family against slaveholders.—Let him be true to himself—to his *present self*—ever looking and striving for a higher and nobler self. Henry Wilson, Charles Sumner, J. R. Giddings and William Seward, believe that *armed* resistance to slaveholders is obedience to God. They would deem it their duty to kill the man that would attempt to enslave them. Why do they not proclaim in Congress the right and duty of the slave to kill their masters who enslave them?

I believe life, as well as liberty, is sacred. No power in the universe can have the right to kill or enslave a human being. It is not possible to protect life by killing men, any more than you can protect truth by telling lies. Human life, as well as liberty, can never be violated, in defence, or as a penalty, without a violation of inalienable rights. But almost the entire community hold, that life may be rightfully taken in defence of liberty. Church and State proclaim the duty of armed resistance against slaveholders. But they would confine this to the white man. The moment we talk of *armed* resistance and insurrection by fire and sword on the part of the slave, they shrink with horror before the idea. They exalt the white man as a hero and a saint, who strikes dead the man who would enslave him; but let some Nat Turner strike the dagger to the heart of his enslaver, and the whole nation is horrified, and hastens to crush him. The right and duty of

---

* Franklin Pierce was President of the United States from 1853 to 1856.—T.N.

the slave to actualize his resistance by pouring out the heart's blood of the slaveholders, is an idea which the advocates of violence and blood must meet.

Henry Ward Beecher and his coadjutors consider Sharp's rifles the most efficient and *only* gospel salvation for Kansas. Why not preach Sharp's rifles as the only gospel of salvation to Virginia and Alabama? They say the only efficient gospel to the free State men and Border Ruffians is Sharp's rifle, and they raise funds to furnish them with this religion. Why do they not raise money to send the same gospel to the slaves of Kentucky and Maryland, and teach them how to read and practice that gospel? If these are the best means of grace for Kansas, much more so for Louisiana. Every slaveholder is a Border Ruffian, and every man who, by swearing allegiance to the Union, pledges himself to put down slave insurrections—is a Border Ruffian, whose salvation, according to this doctrine, is to be secured by the torch and sabre, the rifle and revolver. We have appealed, for twenty-five years, to the conscience and reason of the slaveholder. The last few months have demonstrated the efficiency of appealing to their fears. It is a fact of great significance to the South, that the Northern press and pulpit have expressed no sympathy with slaveholders in the recent slave insurrections. This shows progress.

The slaves of George Washington had as good a right to cut their master's throat as he had to throw his cannon balls and bombshells from Dorchester Heights upon the British in Boston harbor. It is the right and duty of the slaves of Senators Mason and Toombs to kill their masters as really as it was of our fathers to kill their oppressors at Bunker Hill and Yorktown. I do not believe it was, or is, the right or duty of either. But slaveholders in this nation think that *armed* rebellion against oppressors is obedience to God. They being witnesses, it is the right and duty of every slave to obtain his freedom, by killing those who enslave him, if need be. It is the right and duty of the people of the North, themselves being witnesses, to incite the slaves to insurrection, and to furnish them with arms and ammunition to carry out their purpose. . . . Every man at the North who would fight with deadly weapons to defend his own liberty, should, on his own principle, encourage and assist the slave to resist, by arms, those who enslave them.

Mr. Buffum—Shall this Society encourage a resort to force by slaves? As I understand the original platform, the Declaration of Sentiments, of this Society, everything of this sort is discouraged. [Mr. B. here read an extract from the 'Declaration,' and proceeded:]*

Such were the principles declared by the first publications of this Society. If the founders of it made a mistake, let us say so. I hold Mr. Wright to consistency with his own principles. I have heard him ridicule Henry Ward Beecher for his inconsistencies, and I wish him to avoid the same error. His language conveys the impression of encouragement to violence, whether that can be critically extracted from it or not.

Situated as the slaves are in this country, I think it a fatal error, as a matter of policy, to encourage such violence, where the resources of violence are so entirely against them.

I would rather see people inconsistent in wickedness than consistent. . . .

. . . If Brigham Young believes it is his duty to practice polygamy, is he a bad man if he does not practice it?

H. C. Wright—Certainly. His sense of right and duty is utterly perverted, in regard to marriage, as was that of Abraham, Jacob, David and Solomon; yet, believing that God, as he conceives of him, enjoins polygamy, he sins against the highest conviction of his own soul, (not against Nature,) if he does not practice it. I believe in an unchangeable God, and an unchangeable rule of right in regard to marriage, which pronounces polygamy, sanctioned or unsanctioned by human laws, unnatural and monstrous. That man is a traitor to his own soul, who disobeys his own convictions of right.

But there is not a living man who believes that God, as he understands him, enjoins slavery. If he says he does, he utters what he knows to be false. I judge him by applying his doctrine to himself. He would shoot me, should I attempt to enslave him, even by the command of what I called God. He could not pos-

* Probably the following: "Our principles forbid the doing of evil that good might come, and lead us to reject, and entreat the oppressed to reject, the use of all carnal weapons for deliverance from bondage, relying solely upon those which are spiritual, and mighty through God to the pulling down of nations."—T.N.

sibly think that God required me to enslave him. He is a self-convicted liar when he says God requires him to enslave me. We should be willing that others should treat us as we treat them.

If I believed *armed* insurrection against oppressors to be right, in any sense, I would go up and down the non-slave States and organize an armed aggression from the North against the South, to free the slaves. Every slaveholder in Congress and in the nation, *he, not I, being witness,* ought to be shot, and any slave, or friend of liberty, has a right to shoot him. He would consider any man an outlaw, a pirate, who should attempt to enslave him. He is a *self-convicted* outlaw, or pirate, when he enslaves another; and, on his own principle, any man, woman or child has a right to shoot him down, wherever he can be found.

Mr. PILLSBURY. On the ideas of our friend Wright we all seem, at the North, to be border ruffians. No man objects to sympathy with Hungary against Austrians, though the Hungarians fight. What the border ruffians are to the Free State men in Kansas, and what Russia was to Hungary, that every supporter of this Union is to the slave. Every slave lives in a state of war with his master, the slave the victim. But every consideration of right prompts us to wish in this contest that the slave should be successful.

But when the Republicans are questioned where their sympathies are, they deny, Henry Wilson denies, that they are with the slaves. When those men dare to say in Congress of the slaves, what they have always said of the Hungarians, the slaves will have a better chance of regaining their liberty.

(Mr. PHILLIPS. If that principle is to be taken logically, how are we to avoid the conclusions of Mr. Buffum? How do you call upon us to sympathize with the slaves, in doing what must be injurious?)

I do not agree with the statement of Mr. Wright, that, violence never did any good. I am not a Non-Resistant. The only difficulty I find, is this: We *are* in a state of war to begin with, and I join with Henry C. Wright in calling for sympathy on the right side, on the side of the slave.

If the slave's exodus must be through the Red Sea, let it come that way. I do not incite to insurrection, nor provide the means to carry it on; but I demand that we feel, speak and act with the oppressed, and against the oppressor.

Without the North to hold down the victim, the South could not plunder him as she has done.

(Mr. MAY. Every one, doubtless, comes here meaning to contribute to the cause. The Committee on Finance will now proceed to collect.)

Our principles as a society have not been violated. We do not advise or incite to insurrection. The slave does not need it. We incite to a love of freedom, and leave the slave to choose his own means to attain it.

The slaves have as good a right, and infinitely more reason than our fathers had to assert their freedom by violence.

ABBY K. FOSTER. We need to speak specially about funds. It is important not to forget or neglect this subject. It was well said at the Festival, by Oliver Johnson and others—'Whether the cause owes much or little to our labors, we owe everything to the cause.'

Let us not be slack in *paying*, at least, a part of this great debt. Our agents meet with contempt, scorn and malignity in the course of their labors. The snows and cold winds are warmth and comfort, compared with the hearts they meet; and, while they are suffering thus, and get so much less than the slaves, (whipped and burned to death on suspicion,) can we do better than contribute largely—give hundreds where we once gave dollars, while we sit comfortably at home and read the reports of their labors.

How sad that Mr. Wasson sees so justly the reality of a war in Kansas, and not in Carolina; is willing to wait twenty-five years for the latter, when he demands immediate action in the former.

WENDELL PHILLIPS. This question of finance is the allotted, and most important business of this time. We must have means to push this moral question. Many have given fifty dollars for Sharp's rifles, and only five or ten for these higher objects which we present. The politicians have had their harvest; the coming three years are ours by right, and we must now test the honesty of those who have made professions of sympathy with the slave.

We can create a public opinion in Massachusetts in the right direction if we have the money. We wish to send out into Massachusetts and New England, the same voices which we have heard here to-day. If you wish to convert Henry Wilson, send Henry C. Wright to lecture after him, and follow with an appeal for the slave, every appeal which he makes for himself and his party.

The question of Kansas is not to be settled on the soil of Kansas, but at Washington. The most powerful influence you can bring to bear on Kansas, must go from the Northern States through Washington.

EDWIN THOMPSON. Most of the money given to this cause, is given by those of least means. I wish the history of the hardest, and most self-denying workers in the Anti-Slavery cause, could be written. Why should not men of property give the means of sending out such men as Parker Pillsbury, who have the most efficacious talent, but not the means of subsistence, while their time and labor are given to the cause?

Mr. MAY mentioned donations of fifty and twenty dollars from young men of small means, as good examples.

Mr. GARRISON. If this were a Kansas meeting, Sharp's rifles would be popular. It alters the case, when the persons to be aided are blacks. Suggest, for a moment, the idea of arming the slaves, and the whole North will be filled with horror. It is all hypocrisy, a destitution of humanity.

But our work is not carried on by Sharp's rifles. We wish to send the living speaker to carry truth to the hearts of men. Those who give here, give for this purpose, not for Sharp's rifles. It is our purpose to deal by moral instrumentalities.

Our declaration of sentiments precludes no signer from the right of self-defence. We merely lay down the ideas upon which, as an Anti-Slavery Society, we propose to act. But was it wrong in Paul to ask the Jews—'Ye who are under the law, do you not hear the law?' We have a perfect right to hold men to their own avowed principles, and judge them by their conformity or nonconformity to what they admit to be the standard of right.

WENDELL PHILLIPS. I go for Mr. Wright's resolutions. I do not think them inconsistent with the declaration of sentiments. They do not *countenance or aid* the slaves to insurrection. We are not a non-resistant society—and have taken no ground on that matter. We claim for the slave his extremest rights. He is in a state of war, and has a claim to the property he has earned, and to the liberty which is his inalienable right.

February 6, 1857

ANNUAL MEETING OF THE MASSACHUSETTS ANTI-SLAVERY SOCIETY

. . . . . .

Committee on Business—Wm. Lloyd Garrison, Wendell Phillips, Parker Pillsbury, Maria W. Chapman, Eliza Lee Follen, Abby Kelley Foster, Charles E. Hodges, Henry C. Wright.

. . . . . .

WENDELL PHILLIPS followed in a speech full of interest and instruction. His view of the policy of the in-coming administration, meekly seeking at first to conciliate the opposing sections of the Union, only at last to yield every point to slaveholding imperiousness and arrogance, was set forth with great keenness, and elicited much applause. He ridiculed the idea that there is any value for the North in the existing Union, or that anybody here really cared for it, save the selfish, pensioned men that live upon its pay. He showed what a curse, what a tyrannical power the Union is to the Northern States; illustrating his position most forcibly in the case of Margaret Garner and the State of Ohio. Liberty and Slavery cannot live together; the sooner we come to that conclusion, the better. We want to see the day when we may walk Boston streets without being compelled to hang the head with shame as we remember the mournful processions of Thomas Simms and Anthony Burns, and not feel utterly self-condemned as we think of the early martyrs in the contest for American liberty.

The Resolutions which had been before the Society during its meetings, and fully discussed, were unanimously adopted.

The Society then adjourned, *sine die.*

March 13, 1857

SLAVE INSURRECTIONS

EARLVILLE, La Salle, Co. Ill.,
Feb. 24, 1857

DEAR MR. GARRISON:

I am glad to see many of the leading Abolitionists coming fully up to the sticking-point of endorsing, by speech and resolution, the efforts of the slave to gain his liberty by the same means that his oppressors use to keep him in bondage.

Admitting the Non-Resistant idea to be true,—and, as Parker Pillsbury says, 'I fear it is,'—I see not why the non-resistant Abolitionist cannot sympathize with and even encourage slave insurrections. The existing relation of slave and slaveholder is one of intrinsic war, which results in the greatest injustice to the slave, and an appalling sacrifice of human life, all on one side! Let the case be partially reversed. The slave, by a successful rebellion, regains his liberty, justice is restored, and human life is sacrificed on the *other* side. Now, supposing that those who believe in non-resistance had it entirely in their power to decide whether the former or latter policy shall prevail, which would be more consistent with non-resistance? A man's *duty* is the same, be his *influence* great or small. If ADIN BALLOU had an influence sufficiently powerful to produce the change supposed, his duty would remain the same; and would it be to preserve the present relation of slave and slaveholder, at the price of the slave's life, or would it be to restore the slave to freedom at the price, if need be, of the life of the master? Clearly, the conclusion is, that if there is a reasonable prospect that the slaves of the South can gain their liberty by insurrection, non-resistants could aid them in doing so, for the reason that it is better to *save life,* and *do justice,* than *to destroy life* that *injustice may be done.*

Now, my non-resistant friend, if I have made out a clear case for your conscience, give a hearty God-speed to the next slave rebellion, and help it all you can. That brave old man and true, JOSHUA R. GIDDINGS, has lately declared, in the very ears of the slaveholders at Washington, that he would assist the slave in his efforts to be free. The *theory* of emancipation has been pretty well discussed. Twenty-five years of anti-slavery debate ought to have resulted at least in a programme of action—to have prepared the way for some practical steps toward bringing about the desired object. Certainly, we are not going to continue the discussion twenty-five years longer without testing our theory by some practical experiments! I would suggest that the time has come to hit the Slave Power whenever and wherever it seems to hurt the most, provided the blows do not recoil upon ourselves. The only questions necessary to ask are, Is it wrong? and, Do the slaveholders like it? If the answer is No, then pay on; the more they dislike it, the more they should take. Nothing scares the slaveholders like insurrection. The mere report of the secret intention of half-a-dozen slaves to rise turns every slaveholder south of Mason and Dixon's line pale as death—no matter what his natural complexion may be. The bloody ghost of insurrection haunts the Slave Power perpetually with visions of a terrible retribution at the hands of those it has so long crushed and degraded. While it yet trembles with the fright caused by the late rumors, let Abolitionists not fail to seize the moment to encourage the slave by a timely expression of sympathy in his behalf, and to remind the slaveholder that this sympathy is fast hardening into something more substantial—that peradventure it may take the form of lead and steel. Would this be equivalent to revolution? The justification is, that revolution is the only hope of the slave; consequently, the quicker it comes, the better.

The events of the last few years, and especially the late Presidential election, are very satisfactory evidences that liberty can never be established in the United States, except by a radical change in the organic structure of the existing government. . . .

. . . While we have not strength to meet this issue in the ordinary way, owing to the advantageous entrenchment of our enemies, we have strength to *revolutionize*. We can count on the assistance of at least three million slaves in the enemy's country, who would join the standard of revolution, three-fifths of whose strength would be against us in a political contest. Change the *interests* of the Northern allies of slavery, and you would change their *principles*, and thereafter they would trouble us no more than weathercocks trouble the wind; so that, if we did not gain their strength, the party of slavery would at least lose it.

But it is said we should have the United States Government to contend against. The United States Government is the people, and if the people are with us, the Government is with us. There is no power above the people, except a superstitious regard for the Constitution, and the moment the people will it, this great American Juggernaut will be broken in pieces, and an emancipated nation will be prepared to worship the true God. Revolution, peaceably if we can, but—*Revolution!*

Yours, for the slave, A. J. GROVER

Uncle Tom and an Anti-Tom Convention

Over and over again Garrison had to confront the contradictions in his position of nonviolence. The zeal and relief with which the Northern liberals seized on Uncle Tom's Cabin *as a document which might, in itself, melt the hearts of the slaveholders and inspire them into emancipating their noble slaves annoyed Garrison greatly. He felt that the book and the enthusiasm it aroused had a racist quality in it. His condemnation of it in a review reveals the underlying confusion of his own position.*

The Negroes around Garrison were all very militant. The "Uncle Tom" prototype was exposed in The Liberator *a year before Mrs. Stowe innocently made him a distasteful symbol of submission. Edmund Quincy, who had served several times as editor of* The Liberator *in Garrison's absence, wrote in 1851 that Josiah Henson, who became her model, "was a time-serving sycophant, unworthy to represent, and unfit to be trusted with the interests of his people." He was exposed again during the sharp conflict within the Negro community.*

The great Charles Lenox Remond, the Negro Abolitionist from Salem, Massachusetts, and for years the president of the Essex County Anti-Slavery Society, delivered the new position of the Garrisonians. It was militant and completely nonpacifist. Remond and Wendell Phillips were becoming more and more outspoken, their outright militancy unchecked by Garrison. Remond's anger against the Dred Scott Decision and Supreme Court Chief Justice Taney was shared by all of the Negroes. Robert Morris was the first Boston Negro to gain prominence as a member of the bar and led the first school boycott in Boston in the early 1850's.

March 26, 1852

Uncle Tom's Cabin; or, Life among the Lowly . . .

. . . We are curious to know whether Mrs. Stowe is a believer in the duty of non-resistance for the white man, under all possible outrage and peril, as well as for the black man; whether she is for self-defence on her own part, or that of her husband or friends or country, in case of malignant assault, or whether she impartially disarms all mankind in the name of Christ, be the danger or suffering what it may. . . . That all the slaves at the South ought, 'if smitten on the one cheek, to turn the other also' . . . 'be obedient to their masters,' wait for a peaceful deliver-

ance, and abstain from all insurrectionary movements—is every
where taken for granted, because the VICTIMS ARE BLACK. *They*
cannot be animated by a Christian spirit, and yet return blow for
blow, or conspire for the destruction of their oppressors. *They*
are required by the Bible to put away all wrath, to submit to
every conceivable outrage without resistance, to suffer with
Christ if they would reign with him. None of *their* advocates may
seek to inspire *them* to imitate the example of the Greeks, the
Poles, the Hungarians, our Revolutionary sires; for such teaching would evince a most unchristian and blood-thirsty disposition.
For *them* there is no hope of heaven, unless *they* give the most
literal interpretations to the non-resisting injunctions contained
in the Sermon on the Mount, touching the treatment of enemies.
. . . Nothing can be plainer than that such conduct is obligatory
upon *them;* and when, through the operations of divine grace,
they are enabled to manifest a spirit like this, it is acknowledged
to be worthy of great commendation, as in the case of 'Uncle
Tom.'

But, for those whose skin is of a different complexion, the case
is materially altered. When they are spit upon and buffeted,
outraged and oppressed, talk not then of a non-resisting Savior—
it is fanaticism! Talk not of overcoming evil with good—it is
madness! Talk not of peacefully submitting to chains and stripes
—it is base servility! Talk not of servants being obedient to their
masters—let the blood of the tyrants flow! How is this to be
explained or reconciled? Is there one law of submission and non-
resistance for the black man, and another law of rebellion and
conflict for the white man? When it is the whites that are trodden
in the dust, does Christ justify them in taking up arms to vindicate their rights? And when it is the blacks that are thus treated,
does Christ require them to be patient, harmless, long-suffering,
and forgiving? And are there two Christs? . . .

August 13, 1858

ANNIVERSARY OF BRITISH WEST INDIA EMANCIPATION

Convention of the Colored Citizens of Massachusetts

. . . The State Mass Convention commenced its session at the City Hall at 11 o'clock in the forenoon.* The hall was crowded, and a feeling of deep interest seemed to pervade the meeting.

. . . a stirring address was made by Charles L. Remond. . . . He wanted, on this occasion, something more than display, something more than music, something more than prayers, if any of those should be offered. What he wanted was, to see a position taken—a defiant position towards every living man that stood against them; towards legislatures, and congresses, and supreme courts—never forgetting Judge Taney. Mr. Remond expressed his fervent conviction that the colored people would gain nothing by twaddling and temporizing. They were strong enough to defy American slavery. For his part, he was very sorry that so many colored people had suffered themselves to be led by white men— considerate white men, indeed, but white men, after all. He wanted to see black men stand up for and by themselves. He had heard of a white Young America—he wanted to see a black Young America, also; and he wanted to see the two Young Americans marching together, boldly and bravely. Mr. Remond then announced that he was prepared to spit upon the decision of Judge Taney, and said that though Judge Taney was an old story, he could never say all he wanted to upon the subject. On this occasion, however, he would vary his declaration of contempt for that individual, by including every other man, and every institution that joined in the work of making him no free man. He had heard Father Henson's name called. He didn't believe Father Henson could understand our position. He believed Massachusetts black men were ahead of Canadian black men. He wouldn't hear of such a thing as liberty in Canada; he must have liberty in America, for he would be satisfied with nothing qualified. . . .

* Held Aug. 2, 1858, in New Bedford, Mass.—T.N.

. . . Rev. Josiah Henson, of Canada, 'Uncle Tom,' took the platform. He considered the question of slavery as one of life and death. The colored people were all of the same condition and class. They were as one man. He was a Canadian now. Canada was the freest spot he knew in the world. He was a peace man in heart, but a fighting man in brain. But who were we going to fight? who would pay the expenses? He thanked God he ever put foot on British soil. There were some mean men there, and some mean men here. He hoped something would be done besides *talk*. Usually at these Conventions men get mad, and swear they will not attend another. . . . He said that he came to the convention for the purpose of seeing if some measures could not be adopted for improving the condition of the colored man. We are glad to hear of the excellent success of the emancipation movement in the West Indies, but we want to see if we cannot do something here. He referred to Mr. Remond's remark that he meant to fight against the Dred Scott decision; also to his remark, implying that Canadian freedom did not amount to much. For his part, he (Father Henson) held up both hands for Canada. It was the only place he had found where there was any freedom. He thought a good run was better than a bad stand! He was glad the colored people of New England were so much better off than those of Canada, if they were.

He seemed, however, to entertain some doubt on that point. Father Henson said he should not have spoken now, but some people had requested him to come forward, so that the people might see him. And now, said he, how do you like the looks? Don't you think I am a very clever fellow? He closed by saying that he would give way, and would speak again by and by.

Lewis Hayden made some objections to the phraseology of the resolutions.

C. L. Remond said that not a few minds are bewildered by the discussions on this subject. He wanted no long resolutions, but a short one, saying that we *defy* the Dred Scott decision. It makes no difference what Mr. Hayden and Mr. Morris think of the decision; we know that the Court has trampled upon all our dearest rights and aspirations. In reply to Mr. Henson, he repeated that what he said was not in joke, but in earnest. He had been well treated in Canada, he preferred to live here in the United States, and to fight the battles of freedom here. He threw back the taunt of Father Henson, that he had been 'gassing.' There are colored schools and colored churches in Canada, and he had known colored men to be denied admission to the hotels there.

He objected to drawing the attention of the colored men away from the United States to Canada, or Liberia, or Jamaica. We must resolve to remain here, in defiance of Judge Taney. Mr. Henson says we must make 'the best of things.' It is this making the best of things which keeps our brethren in servitude, and keeps us under the yoke of prejudice. We must resist. When Lucy Stone Blackwell refused to pay her taxes in New Jersey, she did more for the enfranchisement of woman than she could have done by all her speeches. When our rights are conceded to us, a more manly set of men than we are cannot be found. If there is a man who is not willing to do his duty, let him go to Canada. He supposed there would be cowards, and time-servers, and apologists among colored men as among whites, and he felt contempt for them as for whites. As for Judge Taney, he would admit that he was a richer, more accomplished, perhaps a taller man than himself, but he had no more right to freedom.

Robert Morris, Esq. of Boston, was the next speaker. He complimented Mr. Remond, very highly, and then proceeded to discuss the Dred Scott decision. He thought the decision powerless in Massachusetts, for the courts would not respect it. There was no necessity for our going away. It was a serious mistake to go away. No young man has any right to go off, and leave us to fight the battle alone. There is work enough here, and by and by the contest will come. Slavery is not to be abolished by peaceable means. It is not to be prayed away, nor will the slaves run away. It will be abolished by the strong arm. . . .

Mr. Morris said he hoped that we should not only trample upon the Dred Scott decision, but also upon the Fugitive Slave Bill. In this connection, he gave a graphic description of the noble conduct of a colored woman who assisted in the rescue of Shadrack.

Mr. Morris then came out with great strength on the school

question. 'When we wanted our children to go to the Public Schools in Boston,' he said, 'they offered them schools, and white teachers; but no, we wouldn't have them. Then they offered to give us colored teachers; no, we wouldn't stand that either. Then the School Committee said—'Well, if you won't be satisfied either way, you shall have them as we choose.' So we decided on a desperate step, but it turned out to be a successful one. We went round to every parent in the city, and had all the children removed from the Caste Schools; we made all our people take their children away. And in six months we had it all our own way—and that's the way we always should act. Let us be bold, and they'll have to yield to us. Let us be bold, if any man flies from slavery, and comes among us. When he's reached us, we'll say, he's gone far enough. If any man comes here to New Bedford, and they try to take him away, you telegraph to us in Boston, and we'll come down three hundred strong, and stay with you; and we won't go until he's safe. If he goes back to the South, we'll go with him. And if any man runs away, and comes to Boston, we'll send to you, if necessary, and you may come up to us three hundred strong, if you can—come men, and women too.' . . .

EVENING SESSION

. . . Dr. J. B. Smith did not consider the colored people as enjoying equal privileges with the whites in Massachusetts. . . . Some think Massachusetts has made great progress. He could not see it. So long as she is silent, we can have but little confidence in what she will do for us in our hour of peril. Judge Taney calculated somewhat correctly the state of public sentiment. No State has yet spoken against the Dred Scott decision. He demanded to be upon an equality with the whites. He had the same manhood and the same rights as they. He didn't believe the whites thought the colored men inferior. He had no respect for the Supreme Court that would so infamously take from him his rights. It is a great misfortune that the colored man is so submissive. He is too religious in the wrong sense. His fears are played upon. He is taught to look forward to the new Jerusalem, as an asylum from all his woes. He wanted a part of that new Jerusalem here. Better that every colored man in the nation were struck down dead, than to live another year as he is now. The fear of hell was taught us. We were told that God, in His own time, would work out deliverance. God's time to do right was *now*. No doubt it was intended to re-open the African slave trade. He did not much regret it. Equalize the numbers of whites and blacks in the country, and it would be 'hands off.'

C. L. Remond regretted that he was obliged to ask for rights which every pale-faced vagabond from across the water could almost at once enjoy. He did not go so far as Uncle Tom, and kiss the hand that smote him. He didn't believe in such a Christianity. He didn't object to the 'decision,' and the slave bill, any more than to the treatment of the colored race in Iowa and Kansas. The exodus for the colored men of this country is over the Constitution and through the Union. He referred to parties, and asked what either of them had done for freedom. The free soil and republican parties had, alike, been false. We must depend upon our own self-reliance. If we recommend to the slaves in South Carolina to rise in rebellion, it would work greater things than we imagine. If some black Archimedes does not soon arise with his lever, then will there spring up some black William Wallace with his claymore, for the freedom of the colored race. He boldly proclaimed himself a traitor to the government and the Union, so long as his rights were denied him for no fault of his. Our government would disgrace the Algerines and Hottentots. Were there a thunderbolt of God which he could invoke to bring destruction upon this nation, he would gladly do it. . . .

Robert Morris spoke of the progress of the colored people in this State. Formerly they were all slaves; now they are free, and can vote. He believed in voting. He should stump his district, and thought he might be elected to the Legislature. He advised the colored people to stand together and vote together. Let them demand a member of the school committee, and then a representative. Let the children, black and white, be educated together, and prejudice is conquered. Children never have any feeling against the colored people until taught it by their parents. Intelligence will be the great regulator. He would have the plantations at the South made uninhabitable through fear of the uprising of the slaves. . . .

TUESDAY

. . . Mr. Nell, of the Business Committee, then commenced the reading of Resolutions. The following two were adopted without discussion:—

Resolved, That we heartily endorse the petition to be addressed to the Massachusetts Legislature by the Massachusetts Anti-Slavery Society, for the enacting that no person who has been held as a slave shall be delivered up by any officer or court, State or Federal, within this Commonwealth, to any one claiming him on the ground that he owes 'service or labor' to such claimant by the laws of one of the slave States of this Union.

Resolved, That in due appreciation of the glorious fact, that in the good old Bay State there now exists no proscription of our children from the public schools, we would urge all parents and guardians to use their every influence to secure the punctual attendance at school of the children in their localities.

. . . The following resolution was next submitted:—

Resolved: That though some colored Americans have been induced, from various promptings, to increase their fortunes by leaving their homes for other climes, the majority are now, as ever, determined to remain in the United States, until, at least, the last fetter falls from the last American slave.

Mr. Henson, of Canada, opposed the resolution. He did not think this Convention had a right to dictate what action colored people in other States should adopt. Massachusetts sometimes went so far as to set law and gospel at defiance.

Mr. Nell said that the resolution did not question the right of a man to emigrate if he chose, but simply advised in the matter. He wished to put his foot upon the colonization scheme.

Mr. Blain spoke against emigration. We were born here, and here let us stay.

Mr. Isaiah C. Ray also spoke against it. He said, when the fugitive slave bill was passed, he told the colored people to send a fugitive to his house, and he would protect him. Let the colored people in the U. States remain where they belong.

The resolution was adopted.

Mr. Remond moved that a committee of five be appointed to prepare an address suggesting to the slaves at the South to create an insurrection. He said he knew his resolution was in one sense revolutionary, and in another, treasonable, but so he meant it. He doubted whether it would be carried. But he didn't want to see people shake their heads, as he did see them on the platform, and turn pale, but to rise and talk. He wanted to see the half-way fellows take themselves away, and leave the field to men who would encourage their brethren at the South to rise with bowie-knife and revolver and musket.

Father Henson doubted whether the time had come for the people of Massachusetts to take any such step. As for turning pale, he never turned pale in his life. [Father Henson is a very black man.] He didn't want to fight any more than he believed Remond did. He believed that if the shooting time came, Remond would be found out of the question. As he didn't want to see three or four thousand men hung before their time, he should oppose any such action, head, neck and shoulders. If such a proposition were carried out, everything would be lost. Remond might talk, and then run away, but what would become of the poor fellows that must stand? And then the resolution was ridiculous for another reason. How could documents be circulated among the negroes at the South? Catch the masters permitting that, and you catch a weasel asleep. However, they had nothing to fight with at the South—no weapons, no education. 'When I fight,' said Father H., 'I want to whip somebody.'

Mr. Troy, of Windsor, Canada, wanted to see the slaves free, for he had relatives who were the property of Senator Hunter, of Virginia; but he knew no such step as was now proposed could help them at all. He hoped the Convention would vote the thing down.

Capt. Henry Johnson concurred with the last two speakers. It was easy to talk, but another thing to act. He was opposed to insurrection. In his opinion, those who were the loudest in their professions, were the first to run. The passage of the resolution would do no good. It would injure the cause. If we were equal in numbers, then there might be some reason in the proposition. If an insurrection occurred, he wouldn't fight.

Mr. Remond expressed himself as quite indifferent whether his motion was carried or not. He was in collusion with no one, and he cared nothing if no one supported him. It had been intimated that he would skulk in time of danger. The men who said so, judged of him by themselves. Some had said that the address could not be circulated at the South; in that case, its adoption could certainly do no harm. Others had said, many lives would be lost if an insurrection should come about. He had counted the cost. If he had one hundred relations at the South, he would rather see them die to-day, than to live in bondage. He would rather stand over their graves, than feel that any pale-faced scoundrel might violate his mother or his sister at pleasure. He only regretted that he had not a spear with which he could transfix all the slaveholders at once. To the devil with the slaveholders! Give him liberty, or give him death. The insurrection could be accomplished as quick as thought, and the glorious result would be instantaneously attained.

A vote was taken, and the motion was lost. This was by far the most spirited discussion of the Convention. . . .

Parker vs. Garrison

Theodore Parker, considered by many the greatest American preacher, had been involved physically in three rescues, or attempted rescues, of fugitive slaves. He had no qualms about resisting the South with force and arms and was to act as one of the "secret six" who helped John Brown prepare for Harper's Ferry. He and Garrison were close personal friends and his Transcendentalist theology was the only one that Garrison ever accepted. However, when he took after the slaveholders with the cleaver of his mighty rhetoric, Garrison's profound and innate pacifism could not resist an anguished moment of protest.

June 11, 1858

SPEECH OF REV. THEODORE PARKER

At the New England Anti-Slavery Convention,
Wednesday Morning, May 26, 1858
[CONCLUDED]

. . . I hate war, but injustice worse than war. Had I lived in the sixteenth century, I would have entreated the Pope; and when he would not be supplicated with words, I would have persuaded him with the battle-axe. In the 17th century, I would have argued, and quoted Magna Charta, customs, statutes; and when the Tyrant would not yield, I would have shown him, what Cromwell also taught, that kings, too, had a joint in their necks, and the People could find it. In the 18th century, I would have petitioned, and remonstrated, and cast 'myself at the foot of the throne,' as our fathers did; but when spurned from that throne, I would have done as they did, cast my pewter spoons and platters into bullets, sold my last load of hay to buy a musket, beaten my ploughshare into a sword, and said 'Liberty first, ploughing afterwards.' So, in the 19th century, sad as it is, I think we must come at last to that same issue. . . .

June 4, 1858

THE NEW ENGLAND ANTI-SLAVERY CONVENTION

. . . Mr. GARRISON— . . . When the Anti-Slavery cause was launched, it was baptized in the spirit of peace. We proclaimed to the country and the world, that the weapons of our warfare were not carnal, but spiritual, and we believed them to be mighty through God to the pulling down even of the stronghold of slavery; and for several years, great moral power accompanied our cause wherever presented. Alas! in the course of the fearful developments of the Slave Power, and its continued aggressions on the rights of the people of the North, in my judgment a sad change has come over the spirit of anti-slavery men, generally speaking. We are growing more and more warlike, more and more disposed to repudiate the principles of peace, more and more disposed to talk about 'finding a joint in the neck of the tyrant,' and breaking that neck, 'cleaving tyrants down from the crown to the groin,' with the sword which is carnal, and so inflaming one another with the spirit of violence, and for a bloody work. Just in proportion as this spirit prevails, I feel that our moral power is departing, and will depart. I say this not so much as an Abolitionist as a man. I believe in the spirit of peace, and in sole and absolute reliance on truth, and the application of it to the hearts and consciences of the people. I do not believe that the weapons of liberty ever have been, or ever can be, the weapons of despotism. I know that those of despotism are the sword, the revolver, the cannon, the bomb-shell; and, therefore, the weapons to which tyrants cling, and upon which they depend, are not the weapons for me, as a friend of liberty. I will not trust the war-spirit any where in the universe of God, because the experience of six thousand years proves it not to be at all reliable in such a struggle as ours. . . .

Then I think we are more and more disposed to run into politics; so that if we have gone back, or are standing still, as my friend Mr. Foster seems inclined to believe, I think he has a good deal to answer for on that ground, for he is for setting aside our old method, and considers our work now to be the organization of a new political party, as our great instrumentality for abolishing slavery. Now, I feel sure, that just so far as this mania for politics shall grow upon us, we shall be less and less potent in the moral field. Our work is with the conscience . . .

I pray you, Abolitionists, still to adhere to that truth. Do not get impatient; do not become exasperated; do not attempt any new political organization; do not make yourselves familiar with the idea that blood must flow. Perhaps blood will flow—God knows, I do not; but it shall not flow through any counsel of mine. Much as I detest the oppression exercised by the Southern slaveholder, he is a man, sacred before me. He is a man, not to be harmed by my hand, nor with my consent. He is a man, who is grievously and wickedly trampling upon the rights of his fellow-man; but, all I have to do with him is to rebuke his sin, to call him to repentance, to leave him without excuse for his tyranny. He is a sinner before God—a great sinner; yet, while I will not cease reprobating his horrible injustice, I will let him see that in my heart there is no desire to do him harm,—that I wish to bless him here, and bless him everlastingly,—and that I have no other weapon to wield against him but the simple truth of God, which is the great instrument for the overthrow of all iniquity, and the salvation of the world. (Loud applause.)

Stephen S. Foster Dissents

Stephen S. Foster was one of the greatest of the Garrisonians. He had stood by Garrison in the worst of times. James Russell Lowell wrote of him that he "studied mineralogy, not with soft book upon the knee, but learned the properties of stones by contact sharp of flesh and bones. And made the experimentum crucis, *with his own body's vital juices." In short, he was the most jailed, pelted, and roughed-up Abolitionist of them all. Now he and his wife, Abby Kelley Foster, the first great woman Abolitionist, were growing old. Everyone remarked at the 1858 New England Anti-Slavery Convention on the heart-rending tiredness and roughness of Abby's voice when she made the appeal for funds, remembering her as a fresh-faced Quaker girl entering the movement twenty toil-worn years before. They were all getting so old and tired that Foster could not bear to have Garrison attack them as he did, and he lashed out at him as brutally as his enemies had in the old days. He called upon Garrison to admit that consistency "requires the abolitionist who believes in the propriety and necessity of using violence against the invader of his own rights, to use it also in behalf of the slave."*

June 25, 1858

WHITHER ARE WE DRIFTING?

Dear Garrison:

The official report of the recent New England A. S. Convention contains the substance of a speech, delivered by you on that occasion, which I deem essentially at variance with the true spirit and genius of Anti-Slavery, erroneous in some of its important statements, unjust to myself, and injurious to our common cause. I was desirous of replying to it on the occasion of its delivery, but finding no convenient opportunity, I now ask the privilege of reviewing it through your columns.

The speech commences by dissenting from the 'sombre view of the condition of the Anti-Slavery cause' which it attributes to me on that occasion.

I wish to say here that it was of our *Society,* and not of the cause, that I presented so *'sombre a view.'* The distinction is a very important one, and I was careful to make it apparent; so much so that, while I represented the *cause* as having made great progress, during the last eight years, I said that our *Society* had actually declined in numbers, and had made little or no advancement in the amount of its annual collections, the circulation of its papers, or the numerical strength of the agents in its employ. In this view of our prospects I may be in error; but, if not, if it be once conceded that our Society does not, in some degree, keep pace with the progress of the cause, the conclusion seems to me inevitable that there is something wrong in our policy. If our 'method' fully met the wants of the cause, in proportion as the community became enlightened and interested in it, they would give us their countenance and support. But, so far as my observation has gone, such has not been the result. We have not succeeded in securing the support of the converts we have made; but all our labors have gone to swell the ranks of a party whose highest aim is to stop the further extension of slavery. Why is this? If our position is the only true one, ought we not to be making converts to it? And if we cannot make them now, when can we ever hope to do it? Will the future afford us any greater facilities than the present? Or can we reasonably hope to accomplish to-morrow, by the same means, what is beyond our power of accomplishment to-day?

But, granting my view of the prospects of our Society is correct, you proceed to assign 'two reasons for it—to your mind, potent reasons.'

It is to these reasons that I wish more especially to direct your attention; as they seem to me to have been presented on the spur of the occasion, without much reflection, and by no means entitled to the importance you attach to them, even if they are not entirely without foundation.

The first of these reasons is a 'sad change' which you think has 'come over the spirit of Anti-Slavery men touching the spirit of peace.' You say, 'When the Anti-Slavery cause was launched, it was baptized in the spirit of peace. We proclaimed to the country and the world, that the weapons of our warfare were not carnal, but spiritual,' &c. 'But now we are growing more and more warlike, more and more disposed to repudiate the principles of peace.' This, it seems to me, is, from first to last, an entire misapprehension of all the facts in the case. The Anti-Slavery cause, if I understand its history, was launched by persons, nearly all of whom were believers in the propriety and necessity of armed resistance to tyranny and injustice, and the very men who stood god-fathers at the altar of its baptism were, virtually, girt about with the sword. Were not even you, at that time, a supporter of this blood-stained government? In those early days of which you speak, we were in the constant use of the sword, in the hands of an armed police, for the protection of our own persons and property. It was only in the slave's behalf that we abjured its use. The slaveholder was the only tyrant whose life and person were sacred in our eyes. In this regard, a 'change' has come over us; but to me it is any thing but 'sad.' We are beginning, at last, to comprehend the breadth of our principles, and to contemplate a faithful and impartial application of them. We are beginning to feel that the slave is indeed a man; that he has rights as sacred as our own; and therefore that he is entitled, at our hands, to the same kind and the same measure of protection that we ask for ourselves. Do you regret this change? Do you wish to see men who will 'cleave tyrants down from the crown to the groin,' in defence of their own liberty, and who feel that they are in the way of duty in so doing, fold their arms, and merely *remonstrate,* while chains are being placed upon the limbs of their brother? For one, I freely confess I do not. I think it a great gain when we can make others consistent, and true to themselves, however widely their views of duty may differ from ours; and I should hail the day as one of glorious triumph when this now slaveholding nation should thus cleave down every persistent tyrant within its limits.

You say, 'I believe in the spirit of peace, and in the sole and absolute reliance on truth, and the application of it to the hearts and consciences of the people.' So do I. But the truth on which I more especially rely for the overthrow of slavery is the divine command, 'All things whatsoever ye would that others should do to you, do ye even so to them.' Nor must it be forgotten that this truth, while it requires the slaveholder to release his grasp on the throat of his victim, also requires the abolitionist who believes in the propriety and necessity of using violence against the invader of his own rights, to use it also in behalf of the slave; and that it is only while acting thus consistently with his own principles that he can have any moral power over the conscience of the enslaver. Hence, these new evidences of our consistency, and of fidelity to our professions of regard for the slave as a man and a brother, instead of weakening our moral power, and crippling our growth, must, I think, have essentially enhanced both: and if, as a Society, we are standing still, or are on the decline, the cause must be found elsewhere than in a supposed increase of the war spirit in our ranks.

You tell us, in this connection, that you 'do not believe that the weapons of liberty ever can be the weapons of despotism'—by which I understand you to mean that the cause of liberty never can be advanced by the use of violence.

This statement surprises me, more especially as it is in direct conflict with your daily and most approved conduct; and I can only regard it as a hasty expression, uttered without thought, in the hurry of debate. Did you not introduce into this very Convention a resolution that 'a memorial to the next Legislature should be circulated in every city, town, and village, throughout the Commonwealth, asking that body to make a decree, that henceforth every fugitive from slavery, on coming into this State, be free against all claimants and pursuers'? Now, you know very well that such a decree, issued by such a body, could not possibly be of any use, unless it was understood that it would be enforced, if need be, at the point of the bayonet. You have reason to suppose that, if issued in compliance with your petition, it would be so enforced. Indeed, you, in effect, ask that it may be so enforced; and, of course, you believe that its enforcement would be beneficial to the cause of freedom; otherwise, you would not ask abolitionists to spend their time in circulating the memorial. How then can you believe that the weapons of despotism never have been, and never can be, the weapons of liberty? The truth is, the sword is like alcoholic drinks, sometimes useful, but generally hurtful, and always *dangerous;* and hence the sooner it shall be banished from the earth, the better. But, if we cannot succeed in inspiring our countrymen with confidence in spiritual weapons, let us, at least, insist that they shall use their carnal ones in the cause of liberty and justice, and not in the cause of oppression.

Your second reason for the decline of our Society is an increasing tendency among us to political action. . . .

You say, 'I pray you, Abolitionists, do not attempt any new political organization.' You know very well that if a genuine anti-slavery political party is ever to be formed, it must be done by Abolitionists, as pro-slavery men will never organize an anti-slavery party. Hence, in counselling Abolitionists not to organize a *new* party, you place before them the inevitable alternative of acting with one of the existing parties, or not acting politically at all. The Society, I believe, to be, mainly, with you on this point, as the *'loud applause'* which followed the conclusion of your speech would indicate to all who were present to witness it. Hence, it is obvious that the Society is, at present, opposed to all political action, except in connection with existing parties; and these it is constantly, though not always consistently, denouncing as pro-slavery. But the people with whom, and on whom we are to operate, are, with scarcely an exception, politicians. They have no faith in Non-Resistance as an efficient means of protection against wrong and outrage, and cannot, therefore, accept it as the proper instrumentality for the overthrow of this giant evil. We have, therefore, driven them to the necessity, if they act with us, of either accepting an instrumentality in which they have no confidence, or of submitting to our constant rebukes for their pro-slavery political connections—a position which men of spirit and sense are not like to accept.

Here, then, I apprehend, and not in any talk about 'finding a joint in the neck of the tyrant,' and breaking that neck, nor in any unusual tendency to 'run into political action,' is to be found the chief cause of our present embarrassment. We have placed ourselves in a position, where, from the very nature of the case, growth is impossible. While the cause is steadily advancing, through the various influences which are operating upon it, prominent among which is the madness of the Slave Power, we, as a Society, are stationary, or on the decline. Nor has the expedient to which we have had recourse, of placing upon our platform, by special invitation, popular speakers whom our policy has driven into fellowship with a pro-slavery political party, been of any avail. On the contrary, it has, in my judgment, only served to aggravate the evil; since those speakers have, undoubtedly, on each occasion, by the combined force of their eloquence and their example, carried with them some of our members to the ranks of the party with which they stand identified, besides confirming many of those who have never acted with us, in their hostile position.

Here, then, is precisely where we part. You are in favor, if I understand you, of a platform where moral resistance to slavery alone shall be taught and enforced, with the single exception of petitioning our pro-slavery legislatures for action in behalf of the slave. I am for one on which all honest Abolitionists can stand, shoulder to shoulder against a common foe; leaving each to select his own weapons, whether peaceful or warlike, conservative or revolutionary; and I would welcome alike him with the ballot, and him with the sword of the spirit, bidding both work in loving fellowship for the same great and glorious end. The Society *was* with me. It *is* with you.

My present aim is to bring it back to 'our old method'; to restore the 'ancient landmarks'; to bring together, and unite in one solid phalanx, the scattered factions of Freedom's contending host.

The experience of the last half-dozen years does not, I think, attest the wisdom of your policy. Let mine be tried but half that length of time, and if it shall leave our ranks with their present diminished numbers, and our treasury with its scanty dimes, I will abandon it, and frankly confess my mistake.

S. S. FOSTER

REMARK. This is a long letter in reply to a few words uttered by us at the N. E. Anti-Slavery Convention with reference to the tone and tendency of a long, and, as it seemed to us, a somewhat lugubrious speech made by our friend Mr. Foster; and though it presents many points for close criticism, we forbear to make a single comment upon it, as we utterly despair stating the positions entertained by him in a manner satisfactory to himself, and as we cannot afford space for columns in reply to what we express in a few sentences. For such a controversy, we have no taste. Our readers will make their own comments.—*Ed. Lib.*

Adin Ballou vs. Garrison

At the opposite pole from Parker, Garrison had to contend with Adin Ballou. The quiet but intense animosity which grew between Ballou and Garrison reveals clearly the determination of the latter to keep his consciousness open to fresh effusions of light. Ballou was to the end the doctrinaire Christian pacifist and demonstrated how closely this attitude locks its practitioners into a dogma. When Garrison originated his program of "No Union with Slaveholders," Ballou suspected that it was revolutionary, "a movement which can go through only under the resolution, 'PEACEFULLY IF WE CAN, FORCIBLY IF WE MUST.'"

In November, 1859, Ballou attacked Garrison, saying that petitions for dissolution served "red revolution." Garrison's reply was mild at this time, saying there was scope for an honest difference of opinion within the movement. But some years later, in July, 1863, he blasted Ballou, saying, at one of Ballou's "sacred services," that there was no divine authority for the Sabbath, to set it apart mere superstition and pernicious, that prayers and so-called worship was essentially pharisaical, that it was untruthful and superstitious to call the Bible a holy book, that authority to determine what is right or wrong in religion was vested absolutely in the individual. "That Jesus Christ was not to be regarded as an infallible and perfect religious teacher. That it is wholly from human nature that we must settle all ethical questions. That NON-RESISTANCE is in no way necessarily connected with or dependent upon, the teaching, example or official authority of Jesus Christ. That although Non-Resistance holds human life in all cases inviolable, yet it is perfectly consistent for those professing it to petition, advise and strenuously urge a pro-war government to abolish slavery solely by the war power."

November 4, 1859

ADIN BALLOU IN REPLY
TO J. MILLER McKIM

[From the Practical Christian]

. . . It is plain, then, that the original platform of the American Anti-Slavery Society was common ground for the most scrupulous Non-Resistants, along with political and legal governmentalists operating in a 'Constitutional way.' But everything bloody, insurrectionary, revolutionary, was precluded. Has there been any change? We shall see.

At the Annual Meeting of the Society in New York, May, 1844, the doctrine of 'NO UNION WITH SLAVEHOLDERS' was inserted as a new plank in the platform. . . .

. . . Almost from that day to this, the leaders and active mass of the Society have been earnestly agitating for a *Dissolution of the Union by States;* that is, for the non-slaveholding States as such to dissolve their governmental Union with the slaveholding States. This would be right and honorable enough, per se, if there were anti-slavery virtue enough in the co-governing people to do it governmentally. But it is a *revolutionary* movement with which our religious principles will allow us to have nothing to do. It is for agitators, politicians, legislators, revolutionaries and warriors to execute. It is a movement which can go through only under the resolution, 'PEACEFULLY IF WE CAN, FORCIBLY IF WE MUST.' We were once asked to appear before a Committee of the Massachusetts Legislature in behalf of the Dissolution petitioners; but we could not do so. Nor could we sign any petition of the kind, however carefully framed. Such petitions mean red revolution, and can hardly succeed without it. This has become a prominent object of the Society, either directly or indirectly, and many of the lesser issues have a close connection with it. Of course, the revolutionary and pro-war genius is in the ascendant on the platform. How could it be otherwise?

. . . And it is lamentably true that this Society is converting these same *peace* men into *war* men more effectively than any other. Its *end* is so good, its appeals are so stirring, its advocates are so eloquent, that the Non-Resistants can hardly help going in for a little bloodshed, for the sake of the poor slave, human rights and liberty. It seems almost a duty to do evil that good may come in such a case! . . .

. . . The last Annual Report of the American Anti-Slavery Society, for the years ending May 1, 1857, and May 1, 1858, refers to the *Massachusetts Disunion Convention*, held at Worcester, Jan. 15, 1857, and says, p. 91:—

'As was to have been expected, the Convention was made up mostly of those who, acting with the American Anti-Slavery Society or its auxiliaries, were alrcady com-

mitted to the measure it was summoned to discuss; but
with these came a few others, willing—in the words of
one of them—to enroll themselves "among those who go
for the Abolition of Slavery at the price of dissolution,
if need be" . . .'

Among the Resolutions was the following:—

> '*Resolved,* That the sooner the separation takes place,
> the more peaceful it will be; but that peace or war is
> *a secondary consideration,* in view of our present perils.
> Slavery must be conquered, "peaceably if we can, forcibly
> if we must." '

At a meeting of the *Massachusetts Anti-Slavery Society* near
the end of the same month, Henry C. Wright said:—

> 'I shall say a word on the dissolution of the Union
> and the formation of a Northern Republic; and also on
> the right and duty of insurrection of slaves against their
> masters. These have been the topics of our past meet-
> ings, and they are topics which need to be kept before
> the people. How can a priest or political leader fill this
> function properly? Let State, county, and town meetings
> be called, and issue addresses to slaves, inculcating the
> right of insurrection—the right to gain their liberty by
> such means as shall seem best to them.
> 'I wish to form a new Union on the principle, "No union
> with slaveholders." The people are ready for it—they are
> only waiting for leaders; and I hope they will soon *cease*
> to wait for them. The people have got to begin, and the
> leaders will follow.'

Mr. Wright offered the following resolution:—

> '*Resolved,* That we recognize the right and duty of in-
> surrection on the part of slaves, against the authority and
> power of those who enslave them; and we deem it our
> privilege to embrace every opportunity to assist and in-
> cite slaves to rebellion.'

. . . We were not present at that meeting, but noticed this
proceeding, and protested against it in an editorial article headed,
Are Non-Resistants for Murder?
Passing over many sayings and doings of the same sort, we

come to those of the last Annual Meeting of the Massachusetts Anti-Slavery Society, January, 1859, in Boston. Parker Pillsbury said :—

> 'Whoever expects to see slavery extinguished but in a Red Sea of blood, knows little of the philosophy of human experience and of human needs; and whoever believes in the use of the sword, and is not preparing himself for its use, is not up to the exigencies of this hour; and the young men who are not training themselves in the art of war, are probably only prolonging a strife that must end at last, either in complete submission to the Slave Power, or in scenes of blood at the very mention of which we well might tremble.'

Wendell Phillips said :—

> 'I like, therefore, these speeches about insurrection; for it seems to me that when the air is full of them, it is because the volcano and the earthquake are at work. That is why we smell the gas. The chinks are opening; the lava is breaking out. Now, not only the South and Southwest, not only valiant old Ossawatomie Brown, but the vanguard of thinkers, doubters, and apprehenders, all over the country, have been talking for the last five years of insurrection. It is not only in our meetings, but if you watch the papers, or look anywhere, you will see it; just as fifteen years ago, Northern men began to talk about disunion in a whisper, and now it has been talked about until it may almost be said to be capable of cool calculation.'

. . . Many similar sentiments were expressed by different speakers. Mr. Garrison, and Mr. Holden of Lynn, declared their non-sympathy with such resorts to violence, but nine-tenths of the audience were ready to applaud them.

Theodore Parker . . . has repeatedly uttered his approval of bloodshed and war in behalf of the slave and the good cause of liberty. He has been rapturously applauded on such occasions by the multitude present, but we have heard no one utter a word of dissent. . . .

Once more: In the *Liberator* of Sept. 23, 1859, Henry C. Wright gives an account of the great Anniversary Meeting of the Western Anti-Slavery Society, held at Alliance, O., Sept. 4. He says:—

'All the resolutions will come to you in due time. Be assured that this Convention is a glorious testimony against slavery, and in favor of freedom in Ohio, showing conclusively that the people are ready, to a great extent, for revolution in favor of freedom: ready to dissolve the union with slaveholders, and form a union with the slaves.

'A UNION WITH SLAVES! Yes, that is what the people of the North will shortly demand. Let every movement towards such a Union—a Union between the North and the Slave—pledging itself to take sides with the slave in all his efforts, whether by flight or insurrection, to free himself from the hell and horrors of American slavery, as sustained and administered by American Christians and republicans.'

If these facts and proofs do not make out our case, it must fail. . . . though they are only samples of the mass which must remain unadduced for want of time and space. . . .

Garrison Calls for Success to Insurrections

The accursed question Garrison had been avoiding all these years—should man nobly dare to be free regardless of the means?—finally came up for judgment in the context of an irrevocable act. John Brown attacked Harper's Ferry October 16-17, 1859, with a band of blacks and whites together. Blood was spilled on both sides; Brown was immediately doomed to a martyr's death. By now, speakers calling for slave insurrections, or justifying them, had become commonplace on the platform of the American Anti-Slavery Society. Wendell Phillips, Thomas Wentworth Higginson, Richard J. Hinton and the militant Negroes William Wells Brown, Frederick Douglass, Charles Lenox Remond, and Henry Garnet made no bones about it, yet Garrison, and most of these others, were completely overwhelmed by shock and surprise at Brown's act of supreme defiance and sacrifice. Garrison is most often quoted on Brown as having called the Raid "a misguided, wild and apparently insane" effort; as having said that his views were in opposition to it, although (the usual disclaimer) all those who glory in revolutionary ancestors should not deny the slaves the right to follow their example. But almost immediately the outpouring of antislavery pride and sympathy for the act of John Brown convinced Garrison that Brown "in firing his gun, he has merely told us what time of day it is. It is high noon, thank God." From October 28 on, The Liberator fully supported the prophet of blood and war, and the following excerpt from Garrison's speech on the evening of Brown's execution shows how he finally answered the accursed question: "Success to every slave insurrection at the South, and in every slave country."

December 16, 1859

SPEECH OF WM. LLOYD GARRISON

At the Meeting in Tremont Temple, Dec. 2d, relating to the Execution of John Brown

. . . For thirty years I have been endeavoring to effect, by peaceful, moral and religious instrumentalities, the abolition of American slavery; and, if possible, I hate slavery thirty times more than I did when I began, and I am thirty times more, if possible, an abolitionist of the most uncompromising character. (Loud applause.) . . .

A word or two in regard to the characteristics of John Brown. He was of the old Puritan stock—a Cromwellian who 'believed in God,' and at the same time 'in keeping his powder dry.' He believed in 'the sword of the Lord and of Gideon,' and acted accordingly. Herein I differed widely from him. But, certainly, he was no 'infidel'—oh, no! How it would have added to the fiendish malignity of the New York *Observer*, if John Brown had only been an 'infidel,' evangelically speaking! But being exactly of the *Observer* pattern of theology, that fact has been a very hard pill to swallow; yet, so bent upon sustaining slavery in our land is that wicked journal, that it is pre-eminently ferocious in its spirit toward John Brown, and has been loudly clamorous for his execution, notwithstanding his religious faith.

As it respects his object at Harper's Ferry, it has been truly stated here by those who have preceded me, and by John Brown himself, whose declarations to the court have been read. The man who brands him as a traitor is a calumniator. (Applause.) The man who says that his object was to promote murder, or insurrection, or rebellion, is, in the language of the apostle, 'a liar, and the truth is not in him.' (Loud applause.) John Brown meant to effect, if possible, a peaceful exodus from Virginia; and had not his large humanity overpowered his judgment in regard to his prisoners, he would in all probability have succeeded, and not a drop of blood would have been shed. But it is asked, 'Did he not have stored up a large supply of Sharp's rifles and spears? What did they mean?' Nothing offensive, nothing aggressive. Only this:—he designed getting as many slaves as he could to join him, and then putting into their hands those instruments for self-defence. But, mark you! self-defence, not in standing their ground, but on their retreat to the mountains; on their flight to Canada; not with any design or wish to shed the blood or harm the hair of a single slaveholder in the State of Virginia, if a conflict could be avoided. Remember that he had the whole town in his possession for thirty-six hours; and if he had been the man so basely represented in certain quarters, he might have consummated any thing in the way of violence and blood. But, all the while, he was counselling the strictest self-defence, and forbearance to the utmost, even when he had his enemies completely in his power.

As to his trial, I affirm that it was an awful mockery, before heaven and earth! He was not tried in a court of JUSTICE. Mark how they crowded the counts together in one indictment—MURDER, TREASON, and INSURRECTION! Of what was John Brown convicted? Who knows? Perhaps some of the jury convicted him of treason; others of murder; and others, again, of insurrection. Who can tell? There was no trial on any specific point. John Brown has been judicially assassinated. It was the trial of the lamb by the wolf—nothing less. . . .

Was John Brown justified in his attempt? Yes, if Washington was in his; if Warren and Hancock were in theirs. If men are justified in striking a blow for freedom, when the question is one of a threepenny tax on tea, then, I say, they are a thousand times more justified, when it is to save fathers, mothers, wives and children from the slave-coffle and the auction-block, and to restore to them their God-given rights. (Loud applause.) Was John Brown justified in interfering in behalf of the slave population of Virginia, to secure their freedom and independence? Yes, if LaFayette was justified in interfering to help our revolutionary fathers. If Kosciusko, if Pulaski, if Steuben, if De Kalb, if all who joined them from abroad were justified in that act, then John Brown was incomparably more so. If you believe in the right of assisting men to fight for freedom who are of your own color—(God knows nothing of color or complexion—human rights know nothing of these distinctions)—then you must cover, not only with a mantle of charity, but with the admiration of your hearts, the effort of John Brown at Harper's Ferry.

I am trying him by the American standard; and I hesitate not to say, with all deliberation, that those who are attempting to decry him are dangerous members of the community; they are those in whom the love of liberty has died out; they are the lineal descendants of the tories of the Revolution, only a great deal worse. (Applause.) If the spirit of '76 prevailed to-day, as it did at that period, it would make the soil of the Commonwealth too hot to hold them. (Loud applause.) See the consistency, the vigilance, the determination of the South in support of her slave system! She moves and acts as by one impulse. Every man on her soil who is suspected of cherishing the principles of liberty is tabooed, persecuted, and brutally outraged, especially if he be from the North. She makes clean work of it, and is consistent. On the other hand, how is it at the North? Presses which are venomously pro-slavery in spirit, and wholly Southern in their design, are every where allowed; presses which insult the good name and fame of the old Commonwealth, dishonor her illustrious dead, and contemn her glorious memories, for the purpose of 'crushing out' the spirit of freedom, and making absolute the sway of a ferocious slave oligarchy—and this they do with impunity. Now I say that if the North should, in defence of her free institutions, imitate the example of the South in support of slavery, there would be a speedy and thorough cleaning out of our cities and towns, of those who are desecrating the ground upon which they stand. (Loud applause.) And it would be a more hopeful state of things than it is now; for this toleration is not the result of principle, but the lack of it— it is not a noble forbearance, but a loss of vital regard for the cause of liberty.

A word upon the subject of Peace. I am a non-resistant—a believer in the inviolability of human life, under all circumstances; I, therefore, in the name of God, disarm John Brown, and every slave at the South. But I do not stop there; if I did, I should be a monster. I also disarm, in the name of God, every slaveholder and tyrant in the world. (Loud applause.) For wherever that principle is adopted, all fetters must instantly melt, and there can be no oppressed, and no oppressor, in the nature of things. How many agree with me in regard to the doctrine of the inviolability of human life? How many non-resistants are there here to-night? (A single voice—'I.') There is one! (Laughter.) Well, then, you who are otherwise are not the men to point the finger at John Brown, and cry 'traitor' —judging you by your own standard. (Applause.) Nevertheless, I am a non-resistant and I not only desire, but have labored unremittingly to effect, the peaceful abolition of slavery, by an appeal to the reason and conscience of the slaveholder; yet, as a peace man—an 'ultra' peace man—I am prepared to say, 'Success to every slave insurrection at the South, and in every slave country.' (Enthusiastic applause.) And I do not see how I compromise or stain my peace profession in making that declaration. Whenever there is a contest between the oppressed and the oppressor,—the weapons being equal between the parties,—God knows my heart must be with the oppressed, and always against the oppressor. Therefore, whenever commenced, I cannot but wish success to all slave insurrections. (Loud applause.) I thank God when men who believe in the right and duty of wielding carnal weapons are so far advanced that they will take those weapons out of the scale of despotism, and throw them into the scale of freedom. It is an indication of progress, and a positive moral growth; it is one way to get up to the sublime platform of non-resistance; and it is God's method of dealing retribution upon the head of the tyrant. Rather than see men wear their chains in a cowardly and servile spirit, I would, as an advocate of peace, much rather see them breaking the head of the tyrant with their chains. Give me, as a non-resistant, Bunker Hill, and Lexington, and Concord, rather than the cowardice and servility of a Southern slave plantation. . . .

Reply to the *Practical Christian*

Garrison's position on John Brown completely estranged him from the doctrinaire pacifists and New Testament Fundamentalists. Adin Ballou kept sniping; at him in his paper the Practical Christian. *Garrison reluctantly issued a counterblast which confirmed for all time that he had abandoned pure pacifism and nonresistance.*

January 13, 1860

'THE PRACTICAL CHRISTIAN'

The last two or three numbers of this excellent paper have been largely occupied with articles from the pen of its editor, Adin Ballou, severely condemnatory of the course of John Brown, and of all who have expressed any sympathy with him—articles that seem to us to be somewhat lacking in magnanimity, in tenderness of spirit, and in a philosophical view of events, but rather characterized by haste and heat; by a tone which would not be indulged in, we think, with reference to Moses, or Joshua, or Washington; and by a process of reasoning which is to us far from being conclusive or satisfactory. We have very great respect for the intellectual clearness and moral insight of our Hopedale coadjutor, and for many years past have seldom found occasion to dissent from his convictions in any direction; but we cannot view the Harper's Ferry event as he does—arbitrarily and invidiously, as it appears to us—and therefore must be true to our own convictions. We fully appreciate his anxiety to keep the non-resistance standard erect, and hope never to be left consciously to violate our peace principles; but there is scope for an honest difference of opinion as to what is such a violation, without any heat or dogmatism. We are not tenacious of defending the extract made in the *Practical Christian* from our speech at the Tremont Temple; but, thanking our bro. Ballou for inserting it, we are content to leave it to the good sense and the fair judgment of all who may read it, in connection with the criticisms appended to it in that paper. What we then said, we said deliberately; nor do we feel called upon to alter one word, by a fresh examination of the subject. Our language was, that, as an 'ultra' peace man, we were prepared to say, whenever commenced,—'Success to every slave insurrection at the South, and in every slave country!' Our bro. Ballou, on the contrary, says he 'wishes them no success, but the speediest failure'! In such a conflict, then, he hopes the oppressor will succeed against the oppressed; that the wrong side will triumph over the right; that the fetters may be more strongly riveted rather than broken; and that U.S. marines and Virginia troops may overcome the Virginia slaves in every encounter! Had he lived in 'the times that tried men's souls,' he would have wished that the mother country might vanquish the American colonies, and that Cornwallis might be the victor at Yorktown, instead of Washington! And so of every other struggle for liberty with the sword since the world began! But it is not possible that he means this; yet, if he does not, he has made a false issue with us, and is using words to no purpose. 'We deplore,' he says, 'that this case of John Brown should have been turned so effectively against Christian non-resistance, and made so seductive an argument for bloody resistance, insurrectionism, and revolution.' We have no such fear, and come to no such conclusion. Where freedom reigns, though obtained by the sword, we expect a growth of the peace principle, which is utterly impossible where slavery holds undisputed mastery. Is there no such thing as progress toward the highest Christian position?

Phillips on Brown

Wendell Phillips was now the true embodiment of the American Anti-Slavery Society, as John Brown embodied the American Abolitionist. Untrammeled by Garrison's prior restraints on his militancy, Phillips became the leading and most prophetical voice of radicalism in the country.

December 23, 1859

WENDELL PHILLIPS ON THE PURITAN PRINCIPLE AND JOHN BROWN

• • • • •

What has John Brown done for us? The world doubted, over the horrid word 'insurrection,' whether the victim had a right to arrest the course of his master, and even at any expense of blood, to vindicate his rights; and Brown said to his neighbors in the old school-house at North Elba, sitting among the snow,—where nothing grows but men—wheat freezes,—'I can go South and show the world that he has a right to rise, and can rise.' He went, girded about by his household, carrying his sons with him. Proof of a life devoted to an idea! Not a single, spasmodic act of greatness, coming out with no back-ground, but the flowering of sixty years. The proof of it, that every thing around him grouped itself harmoniously, like the planets around the central sun. He went down to Virginia, took possession of a town, and held it. He says—'You thought this was strength; I demonstrate it is weakness. You thought this was civil society; I show you it is a den of pirates.' Then he turned around in his sublimity, with his Puritan devotional heart, and said to the millions, 'Learn!' And God lifted a million hearts to his gibbet, as the Roman cross lifted a million hearts to it, in that divine sacrifice of two thousand years ago. To-day, more than a statesman could have taught in seventy years, one act of a week has taught

these eighteen millions of people. That is the Puritan principle. . . .

=====

☞ It is utterly impossible for us to chronicle in our columns
a hundredth part of what is transpiring on the all-exciting question of slavery in the country. To do this, we need to publish
a daily *Liberator,* of twice its present size. We have on hand
the proceedings of scores of commemorative meetings held in
different parts of the country on the day of the execution of John
Brown, all of which we should be glad to publish if it were practicable. No such popular demonstration of sympathy and exalted
appreciation has been witnessed at the North since the death
of George Washington. Well may the South tremble! . . .

John Brown Was Right

*John A. Andrew, a Boston lawyer, became involved with John Brown,
gave him twenty-five dollars when Brown was on the way to Harper's
Ferry, and was called before the Mason Committee, a forerunner of the
House Un-American Activities Committee, set up to "inquire into the
late invasion and seizure of the public property at Harper's Ferry." He
was roughly handled there but upon returning to Massachusetts found
that he was considered the strongest candidate the Republican Party had
for the office of Governor of the State. The opposition press made great
hue and cry over this statement he made about Brown: "Whether the
enterprise of John Brown and his associates in Virginia was wise or
foolish, right or wrong; I only know that, whether the enterprise itself
was the one or the other, John Brown himself is right."*

*Garrison came powerfully to Andrew's defense, involving himself at
long last in active political campaigning. Andrew won easily, although
a vote for him was clearly for John Brown and abolition. He became
perhaps the greatest of war governors. Garrison's endorsement of him
was that "John Brown was right."*

September 7, 1860

. . . *John Brown was right*, because he faithfully 'remembered
those in bonds as bound with them,' and did for them what he
would have had them do for him in like circumstances.

John Brown was right, because he abhorred the practice of
reducing to chains and slavery those whom God created 'but a
little lower than the angels.'

John Brown was right, because he denied the validity of unrighteous and tyrannical enactments, and maintained the supremacy and binding obligation of the 'Higher Law.'

John Brown was right in all that he did—in his spirit and object, in his measures and warlike instruments, in taking the
Arsenal and capturing Col. Washington, in killing 'Mr. Beckham,
the Mayor, and Mr. Boerly, the grocer'—if Washington and
Hancock and Warren were right—if Putnam, and Prescott, and
the soldiers under them, on Bunker Hill, were right—if the Revolutionary struggle was right—if Wallace, and Tell, and Wrinkel-
reid, and Leonidas were right, in resisting tyranny unto blood!

Only John Brown was before them all, and nobler than any of them, inasmuch as he gave his life to free others of a different race from a horrible bondage, with a spirit more than patriotic, because deeply religious and profoundly reverent toward God.

The *Courier* is politically foolish and morally demented in supposing that any party capital is to be made in the old Bay State, or out of it, in stabbing the memory and insulting the grave of John Brown, whom Christendom has already apotheosised as one of the bravest and noblest of those who have fallen martyrs to a great idea. It may rant and rave, give its sympathies to the traffickers in human flesh, and advocate the right to hunt slaves on Massachusetts soil, but it cannot stop the march of Freedom.

Phillips on Lincoln's Election

Wendell Phillips was a remarkably astute judge of political tides, and although he later turned against Lincoln, and Garrison, when Lincoln ran for a second term, he did not separate Lincoln's victory at the polls from the pro-Brown sentiment engulfing the North.

November 16, 1860

WENDELL PHILLIPS UPON THE PRESIDENTIAL ELECTION

LADIES AND GENTLEMEN: If the telegraph speaks truth, for the first time in our history, the *slave* has chosen a President of the United States. (Cheers.) We have passed the Rubicon, for Mr. Lincoln rules to-day as much as he will after the 4th of March. It is the moral effect of this victory, not anything which his administration can or will probably do, that gives value to this success. Not an Abolitionist, hardly an anti-slavery man, Mr. Lincoln consents to represent an anti-slavery idea. A pawn on the political chessboard, his value is in his position; with fair effort, we may soon change him for Knight, Bishop or Queen, and sweep the board. (Applause.) This position he owes to no merit of his own, but to lives that have roused the nation's conscience, and deeds that have ploughed deep into its heart. Our childish eyes gazed with wonder at Maelzel's chess player, and the pulse almost stopped when, with the pulling of wires and creaking of wheels, he moved a pawn and said, 'Check!' Our wiser fathers saw a man in the box. There was a great noise at Chicago, much pulling of wires and creaking of wheels, then forth steps Abraham Lincoln. But John Brown was behind the curtain, and the cannon of March 4th will only echo the rifles at Harper's Ferry. Last year, we stood looking sadly at that gibbet against the Virginia sky. One turn of the kaleidoscope— it is Lincoln in the balcony of the Capitol, and a million of hearts beating welcome below. (Cheers.) . . .

Valedictory

Garrison was acutely aware that the South was arming and plotting disunion to take place if Lincoln were elected. He felt all efforts to save the Union were idiotic and that secession would mean that the "covenant with death and agreement with hell" would be forever shattered. This is all he had ever asked for. Even more than Phillips, he made the connection between Brown, Lincoln, secession, and civil war, and so, from the election of Lincoln on, he advised Abolitionists to "stand still and see the salvation of God" rather than maintain their habitual position of dissent.

He admitted the war constantly presented paradoxical and complex features impossible to justify on a day-to-day basis, but he pointed out to his pacifist critics that they had always warned the people that unless the slaves were set free, a terrible woe would come to the nation: now that it had come, why waste time deploring the blood and pain justly earned by the guilt of racism? He defended the government "because, as between the combatants . . . there is nothing but violence, robbery, confiscation, perfidy, lynch law, usurpation and a most diabolical purpose on the side of the secessionists. . . . The war must go on to its consummation and among the salutary lessons it will teach will be the impossibility of oppressing the poor and the needy, or consenting thereto, by entering into a 'covenant with death' without desolating judgments following in its train."

Garrison had uttered from time to time severe criticisms of Lincoln's vacillating toward the Negro, writing in December, 1861, in a private letter, that Lincoln "had not a drop of anti-slavery blood in his veins," but he felt, in spite of the government's timidity, "one cheering fact overrides all these considerations, that our free North is absolutely unendurable to the slaveholding South: that we have so far advanced in our love of liberty, and sympathy for the oppressed as a people, that it is not possible any longer for the traffickers in slaves to walk with us." He understood it was more important to realize what the South could not do than what the North did not do, and that the war would not end with slavery still in existence unless there was a total Southern victory.

He had a private interview in 1864 with Lincoln and was satisfied that the President would amplify the Emancipation Proclamation with a constitutional amendment to settle the slavery question forever. His wife had a paralytic stroke and his own weariness at trying to keep up The Liberator, now that its prime purpose had been answered, was almost unendurable. Phillips and many others wanted to carry on the movement as if nothing had been settled. Garrison did not want to and there was a sad split here. He decided to give up the paper and the terrible *financial responsibility it involved: he often had to leave his sick wife and go on lecture tours to pay the paper bill. In concrete terms, he, and he alone, had "met the payroll," no matter how many well-meaning supporters came forward in times of crisis with a last-minute contribution. It was now, after all, only one of thousands of Abolitionist papers; every Northern city and village, almost, had one because of the triumph of his original idea. "Nothing is more clear in my own mind," he said, "than that this is the fitting time to dissolve our organization, and to mingle with the millions of our countrymen in one common effort to establish justice and liberty throughout the land."*

This did not mean giving up his vast contribution to independent journalism. He maintained his role as the nation's foremost denunciatory prophet in spite of the long hours he had to spend at his paralytic wife's bedside in addition to attending to his own precarious health. He was now a contributor to the New York Independent, *where he had sixty thousand readers instead of twenty-five hundred. He was still implacably opposed to the unquenched spirit of slavery, his final great incandescent anger being aroused over the Tilden-Hayes deal, which withdrew the occupying federal troops from the still racist, Negro-beating, Negro-exploiting, Negro-lynching South. This withdrawal caused, in turn, a mass exodus of Negroes, whose militancy and advance would make them special targets of the racists returned to power with the lifting of the federal pressures upon them. In the Boston* Traveller *of April 24, 1879, a month before his death, was his last published utterance.*

After pointing out that the Negroes in flight were the only "industrious unoffending, law-abiding and loyal portion of the population in that quarter," he rises to a peak of prophecy which makes his words needed today as never before:

What of the four millions of colored people in the entire South? . . . The American Government is but a mockery and deserves to be overthrown, if they are to be left without protection, as sheep in the midst of wolves. If the nation, having decreed their emancipation, and invested them under the Constitution with all the rights of citizenship, can neither devise nor find a way to vindicate their manhood, then its acts have been farcical, and the local usurpation of a contemptible body of aristocratic factionists is more than a match for the loyalty and strength of the American people; and it is the latter who are as effectually 'bulldozed' and ruled by the 'shotgun' policy as the colored people themselves.

It is clear, therefore, that the battle of liberty and equal rights is to be fought all over again, not in the party sense in the ordinary use of that term, but by the uprising and consolidating of a loyal, freedom-loving North. . . . Let the edict go forth, trumpet-tongued, that there shall be a speedy end put to this bloody misrule; that no disorganizing Southern theory of State rights shall defiantly dominate the Federal Government to the subversion of the Constitution; that the millions of loyal colored citizens at the South, now under ban and virtually disenfranchised, shall be put in the safe enjoyment of their rights—shall freely vote and be fairly represented—just where they are located. . . .

December 29, 1865

VALEDICTORY

The Last Number of the Liberator

"The last! the last! the last!
O, by that little word
How many thoughts are stirred—
That sister of THE PAST!"

The present number of the *Liberator* is the completion of its thirty-fifth volume, and the termination of its existence.

Commencing my editorial career when only twenty years of age, I have followed it continuously till I have attained my sixtieth year—first, in connection with *The Free Press,* in Newburyport, in the spring of 1826; next, with *The National Philanthropist,* in Boston, in 1827; next, with *The Journal of the Times,* in Bennington, Vt., in 1828-9; next, with *The Genius of Universal Emancipation,* in Baltimore, in 1829-30; and, finally, with the *Liberator,* in Boston, from the 1st of January, 1831, to the 1st of January, 1866;—at the start, probably the youngest member of the editorial fraternity in the land, now, perhaps, the oldest, not in years, but in continuous service,—unless Mr. Bryant, of the New York *Evening Post,* be an exception.

Whether I shall again be connected with the press, in a similar capacity, is quite problematical; but, at my period of life, I feel no prompting to start a new journal at my own risk, and with the certainty of struggling against wind and tide, as I have done in the past.

I began the publication of the *Liberator* without a subscriber, and I end it—it gives me unalloyed satisfaction to say—without a farthing as the pecuniary result of the patronage extended to it during thirty-five years of unremitted labors.

From the immense change wrought in the national feeling and sentiment on the subject of slavery, the *Liberator* derived no advantage at any time in regard to its circulation. The original "disturber of the peace," nothing was left undone at the beginning, and up to the hour of the late rebellion, by Southern slaveholding villany on the one hand, and Northern pro-slavery malice on the other, to represent it as too vile a sheet to be countenanced by any claiming to be Christian or patriotic; and it always required rare moral courage or singular personal independence to be among its patrons. Never had a journal to look such opposition in the face—never was one so constantly belied and caricatured. If it had advocated all the crimes forbidden by the moral law of God and the statutes of the State, instead of vindicating the sacred claims of oppressed and bleeding humanity, it could not have been more vehemently denounced or more indignantly repudiated. To this day—such is the force of prejudice—there are multitudes who cannot be induced to read a single number of it, even on the score of curiosity, though their views on the slavery question are now precisely those which it has uniformly advocated. Yet no journal has been conducted with such fairness and impartiality; none has granted such freedom in its columns to its opponents; none has so scrupulously and uniformly presented all sides of every question discussed in its pages; none has so readily and exhaustively published, without note or comment, what its enemies have said to its disparagement, and the vilification of its editor; none has vindicated primitive Christianity, in its spirit and purpose—"the higher law," in its supremacy over nations and governments as well as individual conscience—the Golden Rule, in its binding obligation upon all classes—the Declaration of Independence, with its self-evident truths—the rights of human nature, without distinction of race, complexion or sex—more earnestly or more uncompromisingly; none has exerted a higher moral or more broadly reformatory influence upon those who have given it a careful perusal; and none has gone beyond it in asserting the Fatherhood of God and the brotherhood of man. All this may be claimed for it without egotism or presumption. It has ever been "a terror to evil-doers, and a praise to them that do well." It has excited the fierce hostility of all that is vile and demoniacal in the land, and won the affection and regard of the purest and noblest of the age. To me it has been unspeakably cheering, and the richest compensation for whatever of peril, suffering and defamation I have been called to encounter, that one uniform testimony has been borne, by those who have had its weekly perusal, as to the elevating and quickening influence of the *Liberator* upon their character and lives; and the deep grief they are expressing in view of its discontinuance is overwhelmingly affecting to my feelings. Many of these date their subscription from the commencement of the paper, and they have allowed nothing in its columns to pass without a rigid scrutiny. They speak, therefore, experimentally, and "testify of that which they have seen and do know." Let them be assured that my regret in the separation which is to take place between us, in consequence of the discontinuance of the *Liberator*, is at least as poignant as their own; and let them feel, as I do, comforted by the thought that it relates only to the weekly method of communicating with each other, and not to the principles we have espoused in the past, or the hopes and aims we cherish as to the future.

Although the *Liberator* was designed to be, and has ever been, mainly devoted to the abolition of slavery, yet it has been instrumental in aiding the cause of reform in many of its most important aspects.

I have never consulted either the subscription list of the paper or public sentiment in printing, or omitting to print, any article touching any matter whatever. Personally, I have never asked any one to become a subscriber, nor any one to contribute to its support, nor presented its claims for a better circulation in any lecture or speech, or at any one of the multitudinous anti-slavery gatherings in the land. Had I done so, no doubt its subscription list might have been much enlarged.

In this connection, I must be permitted to express my surprise that I am gravely informed, in various quarters, that this is no time to retire from public labor; that though the chains of the captive have been broken, he is yet to be vindicated in regard to the full possession of equal civil and political rights; that the freedmen in every part of the South are subjected to many insults and outrages; that the old slaveholding spirit is showing itself in every available form; that there is imminent danger that, in the hurry of reconstruction and readmission to the Union, the late rebel States will be left free to work any amount of mischief; that there is manifestly a severe struggle yet to come with the Southern "powers of darkness," which will require the utmost vigilance and the most determined efforts on the part of the friends of impartial liberty—&c., &c., &c. Surely, it is not meant by all this that I am therefore bound to continue the publication of the *Liberator*; for that is a matter for me to determine, and no one else. As I commenced its publication without asking leave of any one, so I claim to be competent to decide when it may fitly close its career.

Again—it cannot be meant, by this presentation of the existing state of things at the South, either to impeach my intelligence, or to impute to me a lack of interest in behalf of that race, for the liberation and elevation of which I have labored so many years! If, when they had no friends, and no hope of earthly redemption, I did not hesitate to make their cause my own, is it to be supposed that, with their yokes broken, and their friends and advocates multiplied indefinitely, I can be any the less disposed to stand by them to the last—to insist on the full measure of justice and equity being meted out to them—to retain in my breast a lively and permanent interest in all that relates to their present condition and future welfare?

I shall sound no trumpet and make no parade as to what I shall do for the future. After having gone through with such a struggle as has never been paralleled in duration in the life of any reformer, and for nearly forty years been the target at which all poisonous and deadly missiles have been hurled, and having seen our great national iniquity blotted out, and freedom "proclaimed throughout all the land to all the inhabitants thereof," and a thousand presses and pulpits supporting the claims of the colored population to fair treatment where not one could be found to do this in the early days of the anti-slavery conflict, I might—it seems to me—be permitted to take a little repose in my advanced years, if I desired to do so. But, as yet, I have neither asked nor wished to be relieved of any burdens or labors connected with the good old cause. I see a mighty work of enlightenment and regeneration yet to be accomplished at the South, and many cruel wrongs done to the freedmen which are yet to be redressed; and I neither counsel others to turn away from the field of conflict, under the delusion that no more remains to be done, nor contemplate such a course in my own case.

The object for which the *Liberator* was commenced—the extermination of chattel slavery—having been gloriously consummated, it seems to me specially appropriate to let its existence cover the historic period of the great struggle; leaving what remains to be done to complete the work of emancipation to other instrumentalities, (of which I hope to avail myself,) under new auspices, with more abundant means, and with millions instead of hundreds for allies.

Most happy am I to be no longer in conflict with the mass of my fellow-countrymen on the subject of slavery. For no man of any refinement or sensibility can be indifferent to the approbation of his fellow-men, if it be rightly earned. But to obtain it by going with the multitude to do evil—by pandering to despotic power or a corrupt public sentiment—is self-degradation and personal dishonor:

> "For more true joy Marcellus exiled feels,
> Than Caesar with a senate at his heels."

Better to be always in a minority of one with God—branded as madman, incendiary, fanatic, heretic, infidel—frowned upon by "the powers that be," and mobbed by the populace—or consigned ignominiously to the gallows, like him whose "soul is marching on," though his "body lies mouldering in the grave," or burnt to ashes at the stake like Wickliffe, or nailed to the cross like him who "gave himself for the world,"—in defence of the RIGHT, than like Herod, having the shouts of a multitude, crying, "It is the voice of a god, and not of a man!"

Farewell, tried and faithful patrons! Farewell, generous benefactors, without whose voluntary but essential pecuniary contributions the *Liberator* must have long since been discontinued! Farewell, noble men and women who have wrought so long and so successfully, under God, to break every yoke! Hail, ye ransomed millions! Hail, year of jubilee! With a grateful heart and a fresh baptism of the soul, my last invocation shall be—

> "Spirit of Freedom. On—
>   On! pause not in thy flight

Till every clime is won
  To worship in thy light:
Speed on thy glorious way,
  And wake the sleeping lands!
Millions are watching for the ray,
  And lift to thee their hands.
Still 'Onward!' be thy cry—
  Thy banner on the blast;
And, like a tempest, as thou rushest by,
  Despots shall shrink aghast.
On! till thy name is known
  Throughout the peopled earth;
On! till thou reign'st alone,
  Man's heritage by birth;
On! till from every vale, and where the mountains rise,
The beacon lights of Liberty shall kindle to the skies!"

                       WM. LLOYD GARRISON.

BOSTON, DECEMBER 29, 1865.

Index